Turbo Pascal

version 3.0

Reference Manual

TABLE OF CONTENTS

LIST OF FIGURES

LIST OF TABLES

INTRODUCTION

This book is a reference manual for the TURBO Pascal system as implemented for the PC-DOS, MS-DOS, CP/M-86, and CP/M-80 operating systems. Although making thorough use of examples, it is not meant as a Pascal tutorial or textbook, and at least a basic knowledge of Pascal is assumed.

A TURBO Pascal Tutorial, however, is also available from Borland. Please see page 3 for ordering information.

The Pascal Language

Pascal is a general-purpose, high level programming language originally designed by Professor Niklaus Wirth of the Technical University of Zurich, Switzerland and named in honor of Blaise Pascal, the famous French Seventeenth Century philosopher and mathematician.

Professor Wirth's definition of the Pascal language, published in 1971, was intended to aid the teaching of a systematic approach to computer programing, specifically introducing *structured programming*. Pascal has since been used to program almost any task on almost any computer and it is today established as one of the foremost high-level languages; whether the application is education, hobby, or professional programming.

TURBO Pascal

TURBO Pascal is designed to meet the requirements of all categories of users: it offers the student a friendly interactive environment which greatly aids the learning process; and in the hands of a programmer it becomes an extremely effective development tool providing both compilation and execution times second to none.

TURBO Pascal closely follows the definition of Standard Pascal as defined by K. Jensen and N. Wirth in the *Pascal User Manual and Report*. The few and minor differences are described in Appendix D. In addition to the standard, a number of extensions are provided, such as:

Absolute address variables
Bit/byte manipulation
Direct access to CPU memory and data ports
Dynamic strings
Free ordering of sections within declaration part
Full support of operating system facilities
In-line machine code generation
Include files
Logical operations on integers
Overlay system
Program chaining with common variables
Random access data files
Structured constants
Type conversion functions

IBM PC and compatibles only:

Colors
Graphics
Turtlegraphics
Windows
Sound

Furthermore, many extra standard procedures and functions are included to increase the versatility of TURBO Pascal.

Structure of This Manual

As this manual describes slightly different TURBO Pascal implementations, namely PC-DOS, MS-DOS, CP/M-86, and CP/M-80, the reader should keep the following structure in mind:

1: Chapter 1 describes the installation and use of TURBO Pascal, the built-in editor, etc. This information applies to all implementations.

2: The main body of the manual, chapters 2 through 18, describe the common parts of TURBO Pascal, i.e. those parts of the language which are identical in all three versions. These include Standard Pascal and many extensions. As long as you use the language as described in these chapters, your programs will be fully portable between implementations.

3: Chapters 19, 20, 21, and 22 describe items which have not been covered in previous chapters because they differ among implementations, for example special features, requirements, and limitations of each implementation. In particular, you should notice that chapter 19 explains all the IBM PC extensions such as colors, graphics, sound, windows, etc. To avoid confusion, you need only read the chapter(s) pertaining to your implementation.

Parts of chapters 20, 21, and 22 deal with technicalities such as internal data formats, interrupts, direct memory and port accesses, in-line assembly code, user written I/O drivers, etc. **It is assumed that the reader has previous knowledge of such matters, and no attempt is made to teach these things.** Remember that these chapters are implementation dependent, so programs using techniques described there are no longer directly portable between implementations.

In fact, you need not bother with these chapters at all if your aim is to write plain Pascal code, or if portability between the different TURBO implementations is important to you.

4: Chapter 23 describes TURBO-BCD. This is a special version of TURBO Pascal for PC-DOS, MS-DOS, and CP/M-86 which uses binary coded decimal (BCD) arithmetic for higher precision in real operations; especially useful for business applications.

5: Chapter 24 describes the special 16-bit TURBO-87 which uses the optional 8087 co-processor for added speed and extended range in *Real* arithmetic.

6: The appendices are common to all implementations and contain summaries of language elements, syntax diagrams, error messages, details on installation procedures, an alphabetical subject Index, etc.

7: Appendix N contains answers to a number of the most common questions—please read it if you have any problems.

TURBO Pascal equipped with either BCD or 8087 options is available for an additional fee at better dealers nationwide. Call (800) 556-2283 for the dealer nearest you. To order by credit card, call (800) 255-8008, in California call (800) 742-1133.

Typography

The body of this manual is printed in normal typeface. Special characters are used for the following special purposes:

```
Typewriter
```
Typewriter-characters are used to illustrate program examples and screen output. Screen images are furthermore shown in rectangular fields of thin lines.

Italics

Italics are used in general to emphasize sections of the text. In particular, pre-defined standard identifiers and elements in syntax descriptions (see below) are printed in italics. The meaning of the use of italics thus depends on the context.

Boldface

Boldface is used to mark reserved words; and also to highlight particularly important passages in the text.

Syntax Descriptions

The entire syntax of the Pascal language expressed as *Backus-Naur Forms* is collected in in Appendix I which also describes the typography and special symbols used in these forms.

Where appropriate syntax descriptions are also used more specifically to show the syntax of single language elements as in the following syntax description of the function *Concat:*

Concat (*St1* , *St2* { , *StN* })

Reserved words are printed in **boldface**, identifiers use mixed upper and lower case, and elements explained in the text are printed in *italics*.

The text will explain that *St1, St2*, and *StN* must be string expressions. The syntax description shows that the word *Concat* must be followed by two or more string expressions, separated by commas and enclosed in parentheses. In other words, the following examples are legal (assuming that *Name* is a string variable):

```
Concat('TURBO',' Pascal')
Concat('TU','RBO',' Pascal')
Concat('T','U','R','B','O',Name)
```

Notes:

Chapter 1
USING THE TURBO SYSTEM

This chapter describes the installation and use of the TURBO Pascal system, specifically the built-in editor.

.COM and .CMD files

Files with the extension .COM mark the executable program files in CP/M-80 and PC-DOS / MS-DOS. In CP/M-86 these will instead be marked .CMD. Thus, whenever .COM-files are mentioned in the following, it should be understood as .CMD if your operating system is CP/M-86.

BEFORE USE

Before using the TURBO Pascal you should, for your own protection, make a work-copy of the distribution diskette and store the original safely away. Remember that the User's License allows you to make as many copies as you need **for your own personal use** and for **backup purposes** only. Use a file-copy program to make the copy, and make sure that all files are successfully transferred.

IMPORTANT NOTE !!!

TURBO Pascal provides a number of compiler directives to control special runtime facilities such as index checking, recursion, etc. PLEASE NOTICE that the default settings of these directives will optimize execution speed and minimize code size. Thus, a number of runtime facilities (such as index checking and recursion) are deselected until explicitly selected by the programmer. All compiler directives and their default values are described in Appendix C. (De-selecting recursion applies to CP/M-80 only; in 16-bit versions recursion is always possible.)

Files On The Distribution Disk

The distribution disk contains the following files:

TURBO.COM

The TURBO Pascal program: compiler, editor, and all. When you enter the command TURBO on your terminal, this file will load, and TURBO will be up and running.

TURBO.OVR

Overlay file for TURBO.COM (CP/M-80 version only). Needs only be present on the run-time disk if you want to execute .COM files from TURBO.

TURBO.MSG

Text file containing error messages. Needs not be present on your run-time disk if you will accept the system without explanatory compile-time error messages. Errors will in that case just print out an error number, and the manual can be consulted to find the explanation. In any case, as the system will automatically point out the error, you may find it an advantage to use TURBO without these error messages; it not only saves space on the disk, but more importantly, it gives you approx. 1.5 Kbytes extra memory for programs. This message file may be edited if you wish to translate error messages into another language as described in Appendix H.

TINST.COM

Installation program. Just type TINST at your terminal, and the program takes you through a completely menu-driven installation procedure. This and the following files need not be present on your run-time disk.

TINST.DTA

Terminal installation data (not present on IBM PC versions).

TINST.MSG

Messages for the installation program. Even this file may be translated into any language desired.

.PAS files

Sample Pascal programs.

GRAPH.P

IBM PC versions only. Contains the **external** declarations necessary to use the extended graphics and turtlegraphics routines contained in GRAPH.BIN. Only necessary on the run-time disk if you want to do turtlegraphics.

GRAPH.BIN

IBM PC versions only. This file contains the extended graphics and turtlegraphics machine language routines. Only necessary on the run-time disk if you want to do extended or turtle graphics.

READ.ME

If present, this file contains the latest corrections or suggestions on the use of the system.

Only *TURBO.COM* **must** be on your run-time disk. A fully operative TURBO Pascal thus requires only **30 K** of disk space (37 K for 16-bit systems). *TURBO.OVR* is required only if you want to be able to execute programs from the TURBO menu. *TURBO.MSG* is needed only if you want on-line compile-time error messages. The *TINST* files are used only for the installation procedure, and the GRAPH files are needed only when you want to do extended graphics or turtlegraphics. The example .PAS files, of course, may be included on the run-time disk if so desired, but they are not necessary.

Starting TURBO Pascal

When you have a copy of the system on your work-disk, enter the command

TURBO

at your terminal. The system will log on with the following message:

```
TURBO Pascal system         Version N.NNX
                                   [System]

Copyright (C) 1983,1984 by BORLAND Inc

No terminal selected

Include error messages (Y/N)? ■
```

Figure 1-1: Log-on Message

N.NNX specifies your release number and *[System]* indicates the operating environment (operating system and CPU), for example CP/M-86 on IBM PC . The second-last line tells you which screen is installed. At the moment none - but more about that later.

If you enter a **Y** in response to the error message question, the error message file will be read into memory (if it is on the disk), briefly displaying the message Loading TURBO.MSG. You may instead answer **N** and save about 1.5 Kbytes of memory. Then the TURBO main menu will appear:

```
Logged drive: A

Work file:
Main file:

Edit      Compile  Run   Save
Dir       Quit  compiler Options

Text:      0 bytes
Free: 62903 bytes
```

Figure 1-2: Main Menu

The menu shows you the commands available, each of which will be described in following sections. Each command is executed by entering the associated capital letter (highlighted after terminal installation if your terminal has that feature). Don't press < RETURN > ; the command executes immediately. The values above for Logged drive and memory use are for the sake of example only; the values shown will be the actual values for your computer.

IBM PC users who are satisfied with the 'Default display mode' can use TURBO as it comes and may skip the following and go to page 14. If you're an non-IBM PC user, you may use TURBO without installation if you don't plan to use the built-in editor - but assuming that you do, type **Q** now to leave TURBO for a minute to perform the installation.

Installation

Type TINST to start the installation program. All *TINST* files and the *TURBO.COM* file must be on the logged drive. This menu will appear:

```
                TURBO Pascal installation menu.
           Choose installation item from the following:

   [S]creen installation  |  [C]ommand installation  |  [Q]uit

                      Enter S, C, or Q:
```

Figure 1-3: Installation Main Menu

IBM PC Screen Installation

When you hit **S** to perform Screen installation, a menu will appear which lets you select the screen mode you want the TURBO environment to use (see Appendix L for details). When you have made your choice, the main menu re-appears, and you may now continue with the **Command** installation described on pages 350 pp, or you may terminate the installation at this point by entering **Q** for Quit.

Non-IBM PC Screen Installation

Now hit **S** to select Screen installation. A menu containing the names of the mostly used terminals will appear, and you may choose the one that suits you by entering the appropriate number. If your terminal is not on the menu, nor compatible with any of these (note that a lot of terminals are compatible with ADM-3A), then you must perform the installation yourself. This is quite straightforward, but you will need to consult the manual that came with your terminal to answer the questions asked by the installation menu. See Appendix L for details.

When you have chosen a terminal, you are asked if you want to modify it before installation. This can be used if you have for example an ADM-3A compatible terminal with some additional features. Choose the ADM-3A and add the required commands to activate the special features. If you answer **Yes**, you will be taken through a series of questions as described in Appendix L.

Normally, you will answer **No** to this question, which means that you are satisfied with the pre-defined terminal installation. Now you will be asked the operating frequency of your microprocessor. Enter the appropriate value (2, 4, 6 or 8, most probably 4).

After that, the main menu re-appears, and you may now continue with the **C**ommand installation described in the next section or you may terminate the installation at this point by entering **Q** for Quit.

Installation of Editing Commands

The built-in editor responds to a number of commands which are used to move the cursor around on the screen, delete and insert text, move text etc. Each of these functions may be activated by either a primary or a secondary command. The secondary commands are installed by Borland and comply with the 'standard' set by *WordStar*. The primary commands are un-defined for most systems, and using the installation program, they may easily be defined to suit your taste or your keyboard. IBM PC systems are supplied with the arrows and dedicated function keys installed as primary commands as described in chapter 19.

Please turn to appendix L for a full description of the editor command installation.

The Menu

After installation, you once again activate TURBO Pascal by typing the command TURBO. Your screen should now clear and display the menu, this time with the command letters highlighted. If not, check your installation data.

```
Logged drive: A

Work file:
Main file:

Edit       Compile  Run    Save
Dir        Quit  compiler Options

Text:        0 bytes
Free: 62903 bytes

> ■
```

Figure 1-4: Main Menu

By the way, whenever highlighting is mentioned here, it is assuming that your screen has different video attributes to show text in different intensities, inverse, underline or some other way. If not, just disregard any mention of highlighting.

This menu shows you the commands available to you while working with TURBO Pascal. A command is activated by pressing the associated upper case (highlighted) letter. Don't press <RETURN>, the command is executed immediately. The menu may very well disappear from the screen when working with the system; it is easily restored by entering an 'illegal command', i.e. any key that does not activate a command. <RETURN> or <SPACE> will do perfectly.

The following sections describe each command in detail.

Logged Drive Selection

The **L** command is used to change the currently logged drive. When you press **L**, this prompt:

`New drive:` ■

invites you to enter a new drive name, that is, a letter from A through P, optionally followed by a colon and terminated with < RETURN >. If you don't want to change the current value, just hit < RETURN >. The **L** command performs a disk-reset, even when you don't change the drive, and should therefore be used whenever you change disks to avoid a fatal disk write error.

The new drive is not immediately shown on the menu, as it is not automatically updated. Hit for example < SPACE > to display a fresh menu which will show the new logged drive.

Work File Selection

The **W** command is used to select a work file which is the file to be used to Edit, Compile, Run, eXecute, and Save. The **W** command will issue this command:

`Work file name:` ■

and you may respond with any legal file name: a name of one through eight characters, an optional period, and an optional file type of no more than three characters:

`FILENAME.TYP`

If you enter a file name without period and file type, the file type *PAS* is automatically assumed and appended to the name. You may explicitly specify a file name with no file type by entering a period after the name, but omitting the type.

Examples:
```
PROGRAM       becomes PROGRAM.PAS
PROGRAM.      is not changed
PROGRAM.FIL   is not changed
```

File types .BAK, .CHN, and .COM/.CMD should be avoided, as TURBO uses these names for special purposes.

When the Work file has been specified, the file is read from disk, if present. If the file does not already exist, the message `New File` is issued. If you have edited another file which you have not saved, the message:

`Workfile X:FILENAME.TYP not saved. Save (Y/N)?` ∎

warns you that you are about to load a new file into memory and overwrite the one you have just worked on. Answer **Y** to save or **N** to skip.

The new work file name will show on the menu the next time it is updated, like when you hit < SPACE > .

Main File Selection

The **M** command may be used to define a main file when working with programs which use the compiler directive $I to include a file. The Main file should be the file which which contains the include directives. You can then define the Work file to be different from the Main file, and thus edit different include files while leaving the name of the Main file unchanged.

When a compilation is started, and the Work file is different from the Main file, the current Work file is automatically saved , and the Main file is loaded into memory. If an error is found during compilation, the file containing the error (whether it is the Main file or an include file) automatically becomes the Work file which may then be edited. When the error has been corrected and compilation is started again, the corrected Work file is automatically saved, and the Main file is re-loaded.

The Main file name is specified as described for the Work file name in the previous section.

Edit Command

The **E** command is used to invoke the built-in editor and edit the file defined as the Work file. If no Work file is specified, you are first asked to specify one. The menu disappears, and the editor is activated. More about the use of the editor on pages 19 pp.

While you may use the TURBO system to compile and run programs without installing a terminal, the use of the editor requires that your terminal be installed. See page 12.

Compile Command

The **C** command is used to activate the compiler. If no Main file is specified, the Work file will be compiled, otherwise the Main file will be compiled. In the latter case, if the Work file has been edited, you will be asked whether or not to save it before the Main file is loaded and compiled. The compilation may be interrupted at any moment by pressing a key.

The compilation may result either in a program residing in memory, in a .COM file, or in a .CHN file. The choice is made on the compiler **O**ptions menu described on pages 190 (PC/MS-DOS systems), 227 (CP/M-86), and 259 (CP/M-80). The default is to have the program residing in memory.

Run Command

The **R** command is used to activate a program residing in memory or, if the **C**-switch on the compiler **O**ptions menu is active, a TURBO object code file (.COM or .CMD file). If a compiled program is already in memory, it will be activated. If not, a compilation will automatically take place as described above.

Save Command

The **S** command is used to save the current Work file on disk. The old version of this file, if any, will be renamed to .BAK, and the new version will be saved.

Directory Command

The **D** command gives you a directory listing and information about remaining space on the logged drive. When hitting **D**, you are prompted thus:

```
Dir mask: ■
```

You may enter a drive designator or a drive designator followed by a file name or a mask containing the usual wildcards * and ?. Or you may just hit < RETURN > to get a full directory listing.

Quit Command

The **Q**uit command is used to leave the TURBO system. If the Work file has been edited since it was loaded, you are asked whether you want to save it before quitting.

compiler Options

The **O** command selects a menu on which you may view and change some default values of the compiler. It also provides a helpful function to find run-time errors in programs compiled into object code files.

As these options vary between implementations, further discussion is deferred to chapters 20, 21, and 22.

The TURBO Editor

The built-in editor is a full-screen editor specifically designed for the creation of program source text. If you are familiar with MicroPro's *WordStar*, you need but little instruction in the use of the TURBO editor, as all editor commands are exactly like the ones you know from *WordStar*. There are a few minor differences, and the TURBO editor has a few extensions; these are discussed on page 34. You may install your own commands 'on top' of the *WordStar* commands, as described on page 13; and IBM PC systems come with arrows and dedicated function keys already installed. The *WordStar* commmands, however, may still be used.

Using the TURBO editor is simple as can be: when you have defined a Work file and hit **E**, the menu disappears, and the editor is activated. If the Work file exists on the logged drive, it is loaded and the first page of text is displayed. If it is a new file, the screen is blank apart from the *status line* at the top.

You leave the editor and return to the menu by pressing **Ctrl-K-D**; more about that later.

Text is entered on the keyboard just as if you were using a typewriter. To terminate a line, press the < RETURN > key (or CR or ENTER or whatever it is called on your keyboard). When you have entered enough lines to fill the screen, the top line will scroll off the screen, but don't worry, it is not lost, and you may page back and forth in your text with the editing commands described later.

Let us first take a look at the meaning of the *status line* at the top of the screen.

The Status Line

The top line on the screen is the status line containing the following information:

```
Line n    Col n    Insert    Indent    X:FILENAME.TYP
```

Figure 1-5: Editor Status Line

Line n

> Shows the number of the line containing the cursor counted from the start of the file.

Col n

> Shows the number of the column containing the cursor counted from the left of the line.

Insert

> Indicates that characters entered on the keyboard will be inserted at the cursor position. Existing text to the right of the cursor will move to the right as you write new text. Using the *insert mode on/off* command (**Ctrl-V** by default) will instead display the text **Overwrite**. Text entered on the keyboard will then overwrite characters under the cursor instead of inserting them.

Indent

> Indicates that auto-indent is in effect. It may be switched off by the *auto-indent on/off* command (**Ctrl-Q-I** by default).

X:FILENAME.TYP

> The drive, name, and type of the file being edited.

Editing Commands

As mentioned before, you use the editor almost as a typewriter, but as this is a computerized text editor it offers you a number of editing facilities which make text manipulation, and in this case specifically program writing, much easier than on paper.

The TURBO editor accepts a total of 45 editing commands to move the cursor around, page through the text, find and replace text strings, etc, etc. These commands can be grouped into the following four categories:

Cursor movement commands,
Insert and delete commands,
Block commands, and
Miscellaneous commands

Each of these groups contain logically related commands which will be described separately in following sections. The following table provides an overview of the commands available:

```
CURSOR MOVEMENT COMMANDS:
   Character left              To top of screen
   Character right             To top of file
   Word left                   To top of file
   Word right                  To end of file
   Line up                     To left on line
   Line down                   To right on line
   Scroll up                   To beginning of block
   Scroll down                 To end of block
   Page up                     To last cursor position
   Page down

INSERT & DELETE COMMANDS:
   Insert mode on/off          Delete right word
   Insert line                 Delete character under cursor
   Delete line                 Delete left character
   Delete to end of line

BLOCK COMMANDS:                MISC. EDITING COMMANDS:
   Mark block begin            End edit
   Mark block end              Tab
   Mark single word            Auto tab on/off
   Copy block                  Restore line
   Move block                  Find
   Delete block                Find & replace
   Read block from disk        Repeat last find
   Write block to disk         Control character prefix
   Hide/display block
```

Table 1-1: Editing Command Overview

In a case like this, the best way of learning is by doing; so start TURBO, specify one of the demo Pascal programs as your **W**ork file, and enter **E** to start Editing. Then use the commands as you read on.

Hang on, even if you find it a bit hard in the beginning. It is not just by chance we have chosen to make the TURBO editor *WordStar* compatible - the logic of these commands, once learned, quickly become so much a part of you that the editor virtually turns into an extension of your mind. Take it from one who has written megabytes worth of text with that editor.

Each of the following descriptions consists of a heading defining the command, followed by the default keystrokes used to activate the command, with room in between to note which keys to use on your terminal, if you use other keys. If you have arrow keys and dedicated word processing keys (insert, delete, etc.), it might be convenient to use these. Please refer to pages 13 pp for installation details.

The following descriptions of the commands assume the use of the default *WordStar* compatible keystrokes.

A Note on Control Characters

All commands are issued using control characters. A control character is a special character generated by your keyboard when you hold down the < CONTROL > (or < CTRL >) key on your keyboard and press any key from A through Z (well, even the [, \,], ^, and _ keys generate control characters for that matter).

The < CONTROL > key works like the < SHIFT > key: if you hold down the < SHIFT > key and press A, you will get a capital A; if you hold down the < CONTROL > key and press A, you will get a Control-A (Ctrl-A for short).

Before You Start: How To Get Out

The command which takes you out of the editor is described on page 30, but you may find it useful to know already now that the **Ctrl-K-D** command exits the editor and returns you to the menu environment. This command does not automatically save the file; that must be done with the **S**ave command from the menu.

Basic Movement Commands

The most basic thing to learn about an editor is how to move the cursor around on the screen. The TURBO editor uses a special group of control characters to do that, namely the control characters **A**, **S**, **D**, **F**, **E**, **R**, **X**, and **C**.

Why these? Because they are conveniently located close to the control key, so that your left little finger can rest on that while you use the middle and index fingers to activate the commands. Furthermore, the characters are arranged in such a way on the keyboard as to logically indicate their use. Let's examine the basic movements: cursor up, down, left, and right:

```
         E
     S   D
         X
```

These four characters are placed so that it is logical to assume that **Ctrl-E** moves the cursor up, **Ctrl-X** down, **Ctrl-S** to the left, and **Ctrl-D** to the right. And that is exactly what they do. Try to move the cursor around on the screen with these four commands. If your keyboard has repeating keys, you may just hold down the control key and one of these four keys, and the cursor will move rapidly across the screen.

Now let us look at some extensions of those movements:

```
         E   R
     A   S   D   F
         X   C
```

The location of the **Ctrl-R** next to the **Ctrl-E** suggests that **Ctrl-R** moves the cursor up, and so it does, only not one line at a time but a whole page. Similarly, **Ctrl-C** moves the cursor down one page at a time.

Likewise with **Ctrl-A** and **Ctrl-F**: **Ctrl-A** moves to the left like **Ctrl-S**, but a whole word at a time, and **Ctrl-F** moves one word to the right.

The two last basic movement commands do not move the cursor but scrolls the entire screen upwards or downwards in the file:

```
     W   E   R
     A   S   D   F
     Z   X   C
```

Ctrl-W scrolls upwards in the file (the lines on the screen move down), and **Ctrl-Z** scrolls downwards in the file (the lines on the screen move up).

Character left   **Ctrl-S**
Moves the cursor one character to the left non-destructively, without affecting the character there. <BACKSPACE> may be installed to have the same effect. This command does not work across line breaks; when the cursor reaches the left edge of the screen, it stops.

Character right   **Ctrl-D**
Moves the cursor one character to the right non-destructively, without affecting the character there. This command does not work across line breaks, i.e. when the cursor reaches the right end of the screen, the text starts scrolling horizontally until the cursor reaches the extreme right of the line, in column 128, where it stops.

Word left   **Ctrl-A**
Moves the cursor to the beginning of the word to the left. A word is defined as a sequence of characters delimited by one of the following characters: Ispacel < > , ; . ( ) [ ] ^ ' * + − / $. This command works across line breaks.

Word right   **Ctrl-F**
Moves the cursor to the beginning of the word to the right. See the definition of a word above. This command works across line breaks.

Line up   **Ctrl-E**
Moves the cursor to the line above. If the cursor is on the top line, the screen scrolls down one line.

Line down   **Ctrl-X**
Moves the cursor to the line below. If the cursor is on the second-last line, the screen scrolls up one line.

Scroll up   **Ctrl-W**
Scrolls 'up' towards the beginning of the file, one line at a time (the entire screen scrolls down). The cursor remains on its line until it reaches the bottom of the screen.

Scroll down   **Ctrl-Z**
Scrolls 'down' towards the end of the file, one line at a time (the entire screen scrolls up). The cursor remains on its line until it reaches the top of the screen.

Page up   **Ctrl-R**
   Moves the cursor one page up with an overlap of one line; the cursor
   moves one screenful less one line backwards in the text.

Page down   **Ctrl-C**
   Moves the cursor one page down with an overlap of one line; the cursor
   moves one screenful less one line forwards in the text.

Extended Movement Commands

   The commands discussed above will let you move freely around in your
   program text, and they are easy to learn and understand. Try to use
   them all for a while and see how natural they feel.

   Once you master them, you will probably sometimes want to move more
   rapidly. The TURBO editor provides six commands to move rapidly to
   the extreme ends of lines, to the beginning and end of the text, and to
   the last cursor position.

   These commands require **two** characters to be entered: first a **Ctrl-Q**
   and then one of the following control characters: **S, D, E, X, R,** and **C**.
   They repeat the pattern from before:

$$
\begin{array}{cc}
\text{E} & \text{R} \\
\text{S} \quad \text{D} & \\
\text{X} & \text{C} \\
\end{array}
$$

   Ctrl-Q-S moves the cursor to the extreme left of the line, and **Ctrl-Q-D**
   moves it to the extreme right of the line. **Ctrl-Q-E** moves the cursor to
   the top of the screen, **Ctrl-Q-X** moves it to the bottom of the screen.
   Ctrl-Q-R moves the cursor all the way 'up' to the start of the file, **Ctrl-
   Q-C** moves it all the way 'down' to the end of the file.

To left on line   **Ctrl-Q-S**
   Moves the cursor all the way to the left edge of the screen, to column
   one.

To right on line   **Ctrl-Q-D**
   Moves the cursor to the end of the line to the position following the last
   printable character on the line. Trailing blanks are always removed from
   all lines to preserve space.

To top of screen   **Ctrl-Q-E**
    Moves the cursor to the top of the screen.

To bottom of screen   **Ctrl-Q-X**
    Moves the cursor to the bottom of the screen.

To top of file   **Ctrl-Q-R**
    Moves to the first character of the text.

To end of file   **Ctrl-Q-C**
    Moves to the last character of the text.

Finally the **Ctrl-Q** prefix with a **B**, **K**, or **P** control character allows you to jump far within the file:

To beginning of block   **Ctrl-Q-B**
    Moves the cursor to the the position of the *block begin* marker set with **Ctrl-K-B** (hence the Q-B). The command works even if the block is not displayed (see *hide/display block* later), or the *block end* marker is not set.

To end of block   **Ctrl-Q-K**
    Moves the cursor to the position of the *block end* marker set with **Ctrl-K-K** (hence the Q-K). The command works even if the block is not displayed (see *hide/display block* later), or the *block begin* marker is not set.

To last cursor position   **Ctrl-Q-P**
    Moves to the last **P**osition of the cursor. This command is particularly useful to move back to the last position after a **S**ave operation or after a find or find/replace operation.

Insert and Delete Commands

These commands let you insert and delete characters, words, and lines. They can be divided into three groups: one command which controls the text entry mode (insert or overwrite), a number of simple commands, and one extended command.

Notice that the TURBO editor provides a 'regret' facility which lets you 'undo' changes *as long as you have not left the line*. This command (**Ctrl-Q-L**) is described on page 31.

Insert mode on/off   **Ctrl-V**

When you enter text, you may choose between two entry modes: *Insert* and *Overwrite*. Insert mode is the default value when the editor is invoked, and it lets you insert new text into an existing text. The existing text to the right of the cursor simply moves to the right while you enter the new text.

Overwrite mode may be chosen if you wish to replace old text with new text. Characters entered then replace existing characters under the cursor.

You switch between these modes with the *insert mode on/off* command **Ctrl-V**, and the current mode is displayed in the status line at the top of the screen.

Delete left character   **< DEL >**

Moves one character to the left and deletes the character there. Any characters to the right of the cursor move one position to the left. The < BACKSPACE > key which normally backspaces non-destructively like **Ctrl-S** may be installed to perform this function if it is more conveniently located on your keyboard, or if your keyboard lacks a < DELETE > key (sometimes labeled < DEL >, < RUBOUT >, or < RUB >). This command works across line breaks, and can be used to remove line breaks.

Delete character under cursor   **Ctrl-G**

Deletes the character under the cursor and moves any characters to the right of the cursor one position to the left. This command does not work across line breaks.

Delete right word   **Ctrl-T**

Deletes the word to the right of the cursor. A word is defined as a sequence of characters delimited by one of the following characters: |space| < > , ; . ( ) [ ] ^ ' " + − / $. This command works across line breaks, and may be used to remove line breaks.

Insert line   **Ctrl-N**

Inserts a line break at the cursor position. The cursor does not move.

Delete line   **Ctrl-Y**

Deletes the line containing the cursor and moves any lines below one line up. The cursor moves to the left edge of the screen. No provision exists to restore a deleted line, so take care!

Delete to end of line   **Ctrl-Q-Y**
Deletes all text from the cursor position to the end of the line.

Block Commands

All block commands are extended commands (two characters each in the standard command definition), and you may ignore them at first if you feel a bit dazzled at this point. Later on, when you feel the need to move, delete, or copy whole chunks of text, you should return to this section.

For the persevering, we'll go on and discuss the use of *blocks*.

A block of text is simply any amount of text, from a single character to several pages of text. A block is marked by placing a *Begin block* marker at the first character and an *End block* marker at the last character of the desired portion of the text. Thus marked, the block may be copied, moved, deleted, and written to a file. A command is available to read an external file into the text as a block, and a special command conveniently marks a single word as a block.

Mark block begin   **Ctrl-K-B**
This command marks the beginning of a block. The marker itself is not visible on the screen, and the block only becomes visibly marked when the *End block* marker is set, and then only if the screen is installed to show some sort of highlighting. But even if the block is not visibly marked, it is internally marked and may be manipulated.

Mark block end   **Ctrl-K-K**
This command marks the end of a block. As above, the marker itself is not visible on the screen, and the block only becomes visibly marked when the *Begin block* marker is also set.

Mark single word   **Ctrl-K-T**
This command marks a single word as a block, and thus replaces the *Begin block* - *End block* sequence which is a bit clumsy when marking just one word. If the cursor is placed within a word, then this word will be marked; if not then the word to the left of the cursor will be marked. A word is defined as a sequence of characters delimited by one of the following characters: |space| < > , ; . ( ) [ ] ^ ' * + − / $.

Hide/display block   **Ctrl-K-H**

This command causes the visual marking of a block (dim text) to be alternately switched off and on. Block manipulation commands (copy, move, delete, and write to a file) work only when the block is displayed. Block related cursor movements (jump to beginning/end of block) work whether the block is hidden or displayed.

Copy block   **Ctrl-K-C**

This command places a copy of a previously marked block starting at the cursor position. The original block is left unchanged, and the markers are placed around the new copy of the block If no block is marked, the command performs no operation, and no error message is issued.

Move block   **Ctrl-K-V**

This command moves a previously marked block from its original position to the cursor position. The block disappears from its original position and the markers remain around the block at its new position. If no block is marked, the command performs no operation, and no error message is issued.

Delete block   **Ctrl-K-Y**

This command deletes the previously marked block. No provision exists to restore a deleted block, so be careful!

Read block from disk   **Ctrl-K-R**

This command is used to read a file into the current text at the cursor position, exactly as if it was a block that was moved or copied. The block read in is marked as a block. When this command is issued, you are prompted for the name of the file to read. The file specified may be any legal filename. If no file type is specified, .PAS is automatically assumed. A file without type is specified as a name followed by a period.

Write block to disk   **Ctrl-K-W**
This command is used to write a previously marked block to a file. The block is left unchanged, and the markers remain in place. When this command is issued, you are prompted for the name of the file to write to. If the file specified already exists, a warning is issued before the existing file is overwritten. If no block is marked, the command performs no operation, and no error message is issued.The file specified may be any legal filename. If no file type is specified, .PAS is automatically assumed. A file without type is specified as a name followed by a period. Avoid the use of file types .BAK, .CHN, and .COM/.CMD, as they are used for special purposes by the TURBO system.

Miscellaneous Editing Commands

This section collects a number of commands which do not logically fall into any of the above categories. They are nonetheless important, especially this first one:

End edit   **Ctrl-K-D**
This command ends the edit and returns to the main menu. The editing has been performed entirely in memory, and any associated disk file is not affected. Saving the edited file on disk is done explicitly with the **S**ave command from the main menu or automatically in connection with a compilation or definition of a new Work file.

Tab   **TAB/Ctrl-I**
There are no fixed tab positions in the TURBO editor. Instead, tab positions are automatically set to the beginning of each word on the line immediately above the cursor. This provides a very convenient automatic tabbing feature especially useful in program editing where you often want to line up columns of related items, like variable declarations and such. Remember that Pascal allows you to write extremely beautiful source texts - do it, not for the sake of the purists, but more importantly to keep the program easy to understand, especially when you return to make changes after some time.

Auto indent on/off   **Ctrl-Q-I**

The auto indent feature provides automatic indenting of successive lines. When active, the indent of the current line is repeated on each following line, that is, when you hit < RETURN >, the cursor does not return to column one but to the starting column of the line you just terminated. When you want to change the indent, use any of the cursor right or left commands to select the new column. When auto indent is active, the message **Indent** is displayed in the status line, and when passive the message is removed. Auto indent is active by default.

Restore line   **Ctrl-Q-L**

This command lets you regret changes made to a line *as long as you have not left the line*. The line is simply restored to its original contents regardless of what changes you have made. But only as long as you remain on the line; the moment you leave it, changes are there to stay. For this reason, the *Delete line* (**Ctrl-Y**) command can regrettably only be regretted, not restored. Some days you may find yourself continuously falling asleep on the Ctrl-Y key, with vast consequences. A good long break usually helps.

Find   **Ctrl-Q-F**

The Find command lets you search for any string of up to 30 characters. When you enter this command, the status line is cleared, and you are prompted for a search string. Enter the string you are looking for and terminate with < RETURN >. The search string may contain any characters, also control characters. Control characters are entered into the search string with the **Ctrl-P** prefix. Example: enter a **Ctrl-A** by holding down the Control key while pressing first P, then A. You may thus include a line break in a search string by specifying **Ctrl-M Ctrl-J**. Notice that **Ctrl-A** has a special meaning: it matches any character and may be used as a wildcard in search strings.

Search strings may be edited with the *Character Left, Character Right, Word Left,* and *Word Right* commands. *Word Right* recalls the previous search string which may then be edited. The search operation may be aborted with the Abort command (**Ctrl-U**).

When the search string is specified, you are asked for search options. The following options are available:

B   Search backwards. Search from the current cursor position towards the
        beginning of the text.
G   Global search. Search the entire text, irrespective of the current cursor
        position.
n   n = any number. Find the n'th occurrence of the search string, counted
        from the current cursor position.
U   Ignore upper/lower case. Regard upper and lower case alphabeticals as
        equal.
W   Search for whole words only. Skip matching patterns which are embed-
        ded in other words.

Examples:
W   search for whole words only. The search string 'term' will only match
     the word 'term', not for example the word 'terminal'.
BU   search backwards and ignore upper/lower case. 'Block' will match both
     'blockhead' and 'BLOCKADE', etc.
125 Find the 125th occurrence of the search string.

Terminate the list of options (if any) with < RETURN > , and the search
starts. If the text contains a target matching the search string, the cursor is positioned at the end of the target. The search operation may be
repeated by the *Repeat last find* command (**Ctrl-L**).

Find and replace   **Ctrl-Q-A**
The Find and Replace command lets you search for any string of up to
30 characters and replace it with any other string of up to 30 characters.
When you enter this command, the status line is cleared, and you are
prompted for a search string. Enter the string you are looking for and
terminate with < RETURN > . The search string may contain any characters, also control characters. Control characters are entered into the
search string with the **Ctrl-P** prefix. Example: enter a **Ctrl-A** by holding
down the Control key while pressing first P, then A. You may thus include a line break in a search string by specifying **Ctrl-M Ctrl-J**. Notice
that **Ctrl-A** has a special meaning: it matches any character and may be
used as a wildcard in search strings.

Search strings may be edited with the *Character Left, Character Right,*
Word Left, and *Word Right* commands. *Word Right* recalls the previous
search string which may then be edited. The search operation may be
aborted with the Abort command (**Ctrl-U**).

When the search string is specified, you are asked to enter the string to replace the search string. Enter up to 30 characters; control character entry and editing is performed as above, but **Ctrl-A** has no special meaning in the replace string. If you just press < RETURN >, the target will be replaced with nothing, in effect deleted.

Finally you are prompted for options. The search and replace options are:

B Search and replace backwards. Search and replace from the current cursor position towards the *beginning* of the text.
G Global search and replace. Search and replace in the entire text, irrespective of the current cursor position.
n n = any number. Find and replace *n* occurrences of the search string, counted from the current cursor position.
N Replace without asking. Do not stop and ask *Replace (Y/N)* for each occurrences of the search string.
U Ignore upper/lower case. Regard upper and lower case alphabeticals as equal.
W Search and replace whole words only. Skip matching patterns which are embedded in other words.

Examples:
N10 Find the next ten occurrences of the search string and replace without asking.
GW Find and replace whole words in the entire text. Ignore upper/lower case.

Terminate the list of options (if any) with < RETURN >, and the search and replace starts. Depending on the options specified, the string may be found. When found (and if the **N** option is not specified), the cursor is positioned at the end of the target, and you are asked the question: Replace (Y/N)? on the prompt line at the top of the screen. You may abort the search and replace operation at this point with the Abort command (**Ctrl-U**). The search and replace operation may be repeated by the *Repeat last find* command (**Ctrl-L**).

Repeat last find   **Ctrl-L**
This command repeats the latest *Find* or *Find and replace* operation exactly as if all information had been re-entered.

Control character prefix   **Ctrl-P**

> The TURBO editor allows you to enter control characters into the file by prefixing the desired control character with a **Ctrl-P**, that is, first press **Ctrl-P**, then press the desired control character. Control characters will appear as low-lighted capital letters on the screen (or inverse, depending on your terminal).

Abort operation   **Ctrl-U**

> The **Ctrl-U** command lets you abort any command in process whenever it pauses for input, like when Search and Replace asks *Replace Y/N?*, or during entry of a search string or a file name (block Read and Write).

The TURBO editor vs. WordStar

Someone used to *WordStar* will notice that a few TURBO commands work slightly different, and although TURBO contains only a subset of *WordStar's* commands, a number of special features not found in *WordStar* have been added to enhance the editing of program source code. These differences are discussed in the following.

Cursor Movement

The cursor movement controls **Ctrl-S, D, E,** and **X** move freely around on the screen and do not jump to column one on empty lines. This does not mean that the screen is full of blanks; on the contrary, all trailing blanks are automatically deleted. This way of moving the cursor is especially useful for example when matching indented **begin - end** pairs.

Ctrl-S and **Ctrl-D** do not work across line breaks. To move from one line to another you must use **Ctrl-E, Ctrl-X, Ctrl-A,** or **Ctrl-F.**

Mark Single Word

Ctrl-K-T is used to mark a single word as a block which is more convenient than the two-step process of marking the beginning and the end of the word separately.

End Edit

The **Ctrl-K**-D command ends editing and returns you to the menu. As editing in TURBO is done entirely in memory, this command does not change the file on disk (as it does in WordStar). Updating the disk file must be done explicitly with the **S**ave command from the main menu or automatically in connection with a compilation or definition of a new Work file. TURBO's **Ctrl-K-D** does not resemble WordStar's **Ctrl-K-Q** (quit edit) command either, as the changed text is not abandoned; it is left in memory ready to be **C**ompiled or **S**aved.

Line Restore

The **Ctrl-Q-L** command restores a line to its contents before edit *as long as the cursor has not left the line.*

Tabulator

No fixed tab settings are provided. Instead, the automatic tab feature sets tabs to the start of each word on the line immediately above the cursor.

Auto Indentation

The **Ctrl-Q-I** command switches the auto indent feature on and off.

Notes:

Chapter 2
BASIC LANGUAGE ELEMENTS

Basic Symbols

The basic vocabulary of TURBO Pascal consists of basic symbols divided into letters, digits, and special symbols:

Letters
    A to Z, a to z, and _ (underscore)
Digits
    0 1 2 3 4 5 6 7 8 9
Special symbols
    + − * / = ^ < > ( ) [ ] { } . , : ; ' # $

No distinction is made between upper and lower case letters. Certain operators and delimiters are formed using two special symbols:

Assignment operator: : =
Relational operators: <>   <=   >=
Subrange delimiter: . .
Brackets: (. and .) may be used instead of [and]
Comments: (* and *) may be used instead of { and }

Reserved Words

Reserved words are integral parts of TURBO Pascal. They cannot be redefined and must therefore not be used as user defined identifiers.

* absolute	* external	nil	* shl
and	file	not	* shr
array	forward	* overlay	* string
begin	for	of	then
case	function	or	type
const	goto	packed	to
div	* inline	procedure	until
do	if	program	var
downto	in	record	while
else	label	repeat	with
end	mod	set	* xor

Throughout this manual, reserved words are written in **boldface**. The asterisks indicate reserved words not defined in standard Pascal.

Standard Identifiers

TURBO Pascal defines a number standard identifiers of predefined types, constants, variables, procedures, and functions. Any of these identifiers may be redefined but it will mean the loss of the facility offered by that particular identifier and may lead to confusion. The following standard identifiers are therefore best left to their special purposes:

Addr	Delay	Length	Release
ArcTan	Delete	Ln	Rename
Assign	EOF	Lo	Reset
Aux	EOLN	LowVideo	Rewrite
AuxInPtr	Erase	Lst	Round
AuxOutPtr	Execute	LstOutPtr	Seek
BlockRead	Exit	Mark	Sin
BlockWrite	Exp	MaxInt	SizeOf
Boolean	False	Mem	SeekEof
BufLen	FilePos	MemAvail	SeekEoln
Byte	FileSize	Move	Sqr
Chain	FillChar	New	Sqrt
Char	Flush	NormVideo	Str
Chr	Frac	Odd	Succ
Close	GetMem	Ord	Swap
ClrEOL	GotoXY	Output	Text
ClrScr	Halt	Pi	Trm
Con	HeapPtr	Port	True
ConInPtr	Hi	Pos	Trunc
ConOutPtr	IOresult	Pred	UpCase
Concat	Input	Ptr	Usr
ConstPtr	InsLine	Random	UsrInPtr
Copy	Insert	Randomize	UsrOutPtr
Cos	Int	Read	Val
CrtExit	Integer	ReadLn	Write
CrtInit	Kbd	Real	WriteLn
DelLine	KeyPressed		

Each TURBO Pascal implementation further contains a number of dedicated standard identifiers which are listed in chapters 20, 21, and 22.

Throughout this manual, all identifiers, including standard identifiers, are written in a combination of upper and lower case letters (see page 43). In the text (as opposed to program examples), they are furthermore printed in *italics*.

Delimiters

Language elements must be separated by at least one of the following delimiters: a blank, an end of line, or a comment.

Program Lines

The maximum length of a program line is 127 characters; any character beyond the 127th is ignored by the compiler. For this reason the TURBO editor allows only 127 characters on a line, but source code prepared with other editors may use longer lines. If such a text is read into the TURBO editor, line breaks will be automatically inserted, and a warning is issued.

Notes:

Chapter 3
STANDARD SCALAR TYPES

A data type defines the set of values a variable may assume. Every variable in a program must be associated with one and only one data type. Although data types in TURBO Pascal can be quite sophisticated, they are all built from simple (unstructured) types.

A simple type may either be defined by the programmer (it is then called a *declared scalar type*), or be one of the *standard scalar types*: **integer**, **real**, **boolean**, **char**, or **byte**. The following is a description of these five standard scalar types.

Integer

Integers are whole numbers; in TURBO Pascal they are limited to a range of − 32768 through 32767. Integers occupy two bytes in memory.

Overflow of integer arithmetic operations is not detected. Notice in particular that partial results in integer expressions must be kept within the integer range. For instance, the expression 1000 * 100 / 50 will not yield 2000, as the multiplication causes an overflow.

Byte

The type *Byte* is a subrange of the type *Integer*, of the range 0..255. Bytes are therefore compatible with integers. Whenever a *Byte* value is expected, an *Integer* value may be specified instead and vice versa, **except** when passed as parameters. Furthermore, *Bytes* and *Integers* may be mixed in expressions and *Byte* variables may be assigned integer values. A variable of type *Byte* occupies one byte in memory.

Real

The range of **real** numbers is 1E − 38 through 1E + 38 with a mantissa of up to 11 significant digits. Reals occupy 6 bytes in memory.

Overflow during an arithmetic operation involving reals causes the program to halt, displaying an execution error. An underflow will cause a result of zero.

Although the type **real** is included here as a standard scalar type, the following differences between **reals** and other scalar types should be noticed:

1) The functions *Pred* and *Succ* cannot take real arguments.
2) Reals cannot be used in array indexing.
3) Reals cannot be used to define the base type of a set.
4) Reals cannot be used in controlling **for** and **case** statements.
5) Subranges of reals are not allowed.

Boolean

A boolean value can assume either of the logical truth values denoted by the standard identifiers *True* and *False*. These are defined such that *False* < *True*. A *Boolean* variable occupies one byte in memory.

Char

A *Char* value is one character in the ASCII character set. Characters are ordered according to their ASCII value, for example: 'A' < 'B'. The ordinal (ASCII) values of characters range from 0 to 255. A *Char* variable occupies one byte in memory.

Chapter 4
USER DEFINED LANGUAGE ELEMENTS

Identifiers

Identifiers are used to denote labels, constants, types, variables, procedures, and functions. An identifier consists of a letter or underscore followed by any combination of letters, digits, or underscores. An identifier is limited in length only by the line length of 127 characters, and all characters are significant.

Examples:
```
TURBO
square
persons_counted
BirthDate
3rdRoot          illegal, starts with a digit
Two Words        illegal, must not contain a space
```

As TURBO Pascal does not distinguish between upper and lower case letters, the use of mixed upper and lower case as in *BirthDate* has no functional meaning. It is nevertheless encouraged as it leads to more legible identifiers. *VeryLongIdentifier* is easier to read for the human reader than *VERYLONGIDENTIFIER*. This mixed mode will be used for all identifiers throughout this manual.

Numbers

Numbers are constants of integer type or of real type. Integer constants are whole numbers expressed in either decimal or hexadecimal notation. Hexadecimal constants are identified by being preceded by a dollarsign: $ABC is a hexadecimal constant. The decimal integer range is − 32768 through 32767 and the hexadecimal integer range is $0000 through $FFFF.

Examples:
```
1
12345
-1
$123
$ABC
$123G        illegal, G is not a legal hexadecimal digit
1.2345       illegal as an integer, contains a decimal parts
```

The range of *Real* numbers is 1E-38 through 1E + 38 with a mantissa of up to 11 significant digits. Exponential notation may be used, with the letter *E* preceding the scale factor meaning "times ten to the power of". An integer constant is allowed anywhere a real constant is allowed. Separators are not allowed within numbers.

Examples:
```
1.0
1234.5678
-0.012
1E6
2E-5
-1.2345678901E+12
1                      legal, but it is not a real, it is an integer
```

Strings

A string constant is a sequence of characters enclosed in single quotes:

```
'This is a string constant '
```

A single quote may be contained in a string by writing two successive single quotes. Strings containing only a single character are of the standard type *char*. A string is compatible with an **array of** *Char* of the same length. All string constants are compatible with all **string** types.

Examples:
```
'TURBO'
'You''ll see'
''''
';'
' '
```

As shown in example 2 and 3, a single quote within a string is written as two consecutive quotes. The four consecutive single quotes in example 3 thus constitute a string containing *one* quote.

The last example - the quotes enclosing no characters, denoting *the empty string* - is compatible only with **string** types.

Control Characters

TURBO Pascal also allows control characters to be embedded in strings. Two notations for control characters are supported.
1) The # symbol followed by an integer constant in the range 0..255 denotes a character of the corresponding ASCII value, and
2) the ^ symbol followed by a character, denotes the corresponding control character.

Examples:

```
#10      ASCII 10 decimal (Line Feed).
#$1B     ASCII 1B hex (Escape).
^G       Control-G (Bell).
^l       Control-L (Form Feed).
^[       Control-[ (Escape).
```

Sequences of control characters may be concatenated into strings by writing them *without separators* between the individual characters:

```
#13#10
#27^U#20
^G^G^G^G
```

The above strings contain two, three, and four characters, respectively. Control characters may also be mixed with text strings:

```
'Waiting for input! '^G^G^G' Please wake up'
#27'U '
'This is another line of text '^M^J
```

These three strings contain 37, 3, and 31 characters, respectively.

Comments

A comment may be inserted anywhere in the program where a delimiter is legal. It is delimited by the curly braces { and }, which may be replaced by the symbols (* and *).

Examples:
```
{This is a comment}
(* and so is this *)
```

Curly braces may not be nested within curly braces, and (* . . *) may not be nested within (* . . *). However, curly braces may nested within (* . . *) and vise versa, thus allowing entire sections of source code to be commented away, even if they contain comments.

Compiler Directives

A number of features of the TURBO Pascal compiler are controlled through compiler directives. A compiler directive is introduced as a comment with a special syntax which means that whenever a comment is allowed in a program, a compiler directive is also allowed.

A compiler directive consists of an opening brace immediately followed by a dollar-sign immediately followed by one compiler directive letter or a list of compiler directive letters separated by commas. The syntax of the directive or directive list depends upon the directive(s) selected. A full description of each of the compiler directives follow in the relevant sections; and a summary of compiler directives is located in Appendix C. File inclusion is discussed in chapter 17.

Examples:
```
{$I-}
{$I INCLUDE.FIL}
{$R-,B+,V-}
(*$X-*)
```

Notice that no spaces are allowed before or after the dollar-sign.

Chapter 5
PROGRAM HEADING AND PROGRAM BLOCK

A Pascal program consists of a program heading followed by a program block. The program block is further divided into a declaration part, in which all objects local to the program are defined, and a statement part, which specifies the actions to be executed upon these objects. Each is described in detail in the following.

Program Heading

In TURBO Pascal, the program heading is purely optional and of no significance to the program. If present, it gives the program a name, and optionally lists the parameters through which the program communicates with the environment. The list consists of a sequence of identifiers enclosed in parentheses and separated by commas.

Examples:
```
program Circles;
program Accountant(Input,Output);
program Writer(Input,Printer);
```

Declaration Part

The declaration part of a block declares all identifiers to be used within the statement part of that block (and possibly other blocks within it). The declaration part is divided into five different sections:

1) Label declaration part
2) Constant definition part
3) Type definition part
4) Variable declaration part
5) Procedure and function declaration part

Whereas standard Pascal specifies that each section may only occur zero or one time, and only in the above order, TURBO Pascal allows each of these sections to occur any number of times in any order in the declaration part.

Label Declaration Part

Any statement in a program may be prefixed with a **label**, enabling direct branching to that statement by a **goto** statement. A label consists of a label name followed by a colon. Before use, the label must be declared in a label declaration part. The reserved word **label** heads this part, and it is followed by a list of label identifiers separated by commas and terminated by a semi-colon.

Example:
```
label 10, error, 999, Quit;
```

Whereas standard Pascal limits labels to numbers of no more than 4 digits, TURBO Pascal allows both numbers and identifiers to be used as labels.

Constant Definition Part

The constant definition part introduces identifiers as synonyms for constant values. The reserved word **const** heads the constant definition part, and is followed by a list of constant assignments separated by semi-colons. Each constant assignment consists of an identifier followed by an equal sign and a constant. Constants are either strings or numbers as defined on pages 43 and 44.

Example:
```
const
  Limit = 255;
  Max = 1024;
  PassWord = 'SESAM';
  CursHome = ^['V';
```

The following constants are predefined in TURBO Pascal which may be referenced without previous definition:

Name:	Type and value:
Pi	Real (3.1415926536E+00).
False	Boolean (the truth value false).
True	Boolean (the truth value true).
Maxint	Integer (32767).

As described in chapter 13, a constant definition part may also define typed constants.

Type Definition Part

A data type in Pascal may be either directly described in the variable declaration part or referenced by a type identifier. Several standard type identifiers are provided, and the programmer may create his own types through the use of the type definition. The reserved word **type** heads the type definition part, and it is followed by one or more type assignments separated by semi-colons. Each type assignment consists of a type identifier followed by an equal sign and a type.

Example:
```
type
  Number = Integer;
  Day = (mon,tues,wed,thur,fri,sat,sun);
  List = array[1..10] of Real;
```

More examples of type definitions are found in subsequent sections.

Variable Declaration Part

Every variable occurring in a program must be declared before use. The declaration must textually precede any use of the variable so that the variable is 'known' to the compiler when it is used.

A variable declaration consists of the reserved word **var** followed by one or more identifier(s), separated by commas, each followed by a colon and a **type**. This creates a new variable of the specified type and associates it with the specified identifier.

The 'scope' of this identifier is the block in which it is defined, and any block within that block. Note, however, that any such block within another block may define *another* variable using the *same* identifier. This variable is said to be *local* to the block in which it is declared (and any blocks within *that block*), and the variable declared on the outer level (the *global* variable) becomes inaccessible.

Example:
```
var
  Result, Intermediate, SubTotal: Real;
  I, J, X, Y: Integer;
  Accepted, Valid: Boolean;
  Period: Day;
  Buffer: array[0..127] of Byte;
```

Procedure and Function Declaration Part

A procedure declaration serves to define a procedure within the current procedure or program (see page 131). A procedure is activated from a procedure statement (see page 56), and upon completion, program execution continues with the statement immediately following the calling statement.

A function declaration serves to define a program part which computes and returns a value (see page 137). A function is activated when its designator is met as part of an expression (see page 54).

Statement Part

The statement part is the last part of a block. It specifies the actions to be executed by the program. The statement part takes the form of a compound statement followed by a period or a semi-colon. A compound statement consists of the reserved word **begin**, followed by a list of statements separated by semicolons, terminated by the reserved word **end**.

Chapter 6
EXPRESSIONS

Expressions are algorithmic constructs specifying rules for the computation of values. They consist of operands: variables, constants, and function designators combined by means of operators as defined in the following.

This section describes how to form expressions from the standard scalar types *Integer*, *Real*, *Boolean*, and *Char*. Expressions containing declared scalar types, **string** types, and **set** types are described on pages 63, 67, and 86, respectively.

Operators

Operators fall into five categories, denoted by their order of precedence:

1) Unary minus (minus with one operand only).
2) **Not** operator.
3) Multiplying operators: *, /, **div**, **mod**, **and**, **shl**, and **shr**.
4) Adding operators: +, −, **or**, and **xor**.
5) Relational operators: =, < >, <, >, < =, > =, and **in**.

Sequences of operators of the same precedence are evaluated from left to right. Expressions within parentheses are evaluated first and independently of preceding or succeeding operators.

If both of the operands of the multiplying and adding operators are of type *Integer*, then the result is of type Integer. If one (or both) of the operands is of type *Real*, then the result is also of type *Real*.

Unary Minus

The unary minus denotes a negation of its operand which may be of *Real* or *Integer* types.

Not Operator

The **not** operator negates (inverses) the logical value of its Boolean operand:

```
not True      = False
not False     = True
```

TURBO Pascal also allows the **not** operator to be applied to an *Integer* operand, in which case bitwise negation takes place.

Examples:
```
not 0         = -1
not -15       = 14
not $2345     = $DCBA
```

Multiplying Operators

Operator	Operation	Operand type	Result type
*	multiplication	Real	Real
*	multiplication	Integer	Integer
*	multiplication	Real, Integer	Real
/	division	Real, Integer	Real
/	division	Integer	Real
/	division	Real	Real
div	Integer division	Integer	Integer
mod	modulus	Integer	Integer
and	arithmetic **and**	Integer	Integer
and	logical **and**	Boolean	Boolean
shl	shift left	Integer	Integer
shr	shift right	Integer	Integer

Examples:
```
12 * 34           = 408
123 / 4           = 30.75
123 div 4         = 30
12 mod 5          = 2
True and False    = False
12 and 22         = 4
2 shl 7           = 256
256 shr 7         = 2
```

Adding Operators

Operator	Operation	Operand type	Result type
+	addition	Real	Real
+	addition	Integer	Integer
+	addition	Real, Integer	Real
−	subtraction	Real	Real
−	subtraction	Integer	Integer
	subtraction	Real, Integer	Real
or	arithmetic **or**	Integer	Integer
or	logical **or**	Boolean	Boolean
xor	arithmetic **xor**	Integer	Integer
xor	logical **xor**	Boolean	Boolean

Examples:

```
123+456         = 579
456-123.0       = 333.0
True or False   = True
12 or 22        = 30
True xor False  = True
12 xor 22       = 26
```

Relational Operators

The relational operators work on all standard scalar types: *Real, Integer, Boolean, Char,* and *Byte*. Operands of type *Integer, Real,* and *Byte* may be mixed. The type of the result Is always Boolean, i.e. *True* or *False*.

```
=     equal to
<>    not equal to
>     greater than
<     less than
>=    greater than or equal to
<=    less than or equal to
```

Examples:

a = b	true if a is equal to b.
a <> b	true if a is not equal to b.
a > b	true if a is greater than b.
a < b	true if a is less than b.
a >= b	true if a is greater than or equal to b.
a <= b	true if a is less than or equal to b.

Function Designators

A function designator is a function identifier optionally followed by a parameter list, which is one or more variables or expressions separated by commas and enclosed in parentheses. The occurrence of a function designator causes the function with that name to be activated. If the function is not one of the pre-defined standard functions, it must be declared before activation.

Examples:
```
Round(PlotPos)
Writeln(Pi * (Sqr(R)))
(Max(X,Y) < 25) and (Z > Sqrt(X * Y))
Volume(Radius,Height)
```

Chapter 7
STATEMENTS

The statement part defines the action to be carried out by the program (or subprogram) as a sequence of *statements*; each specifying one part of the action. In this sense Pascal is a sequential programming language: statements are executed sequentially in time; never simultaneously. The statement part is enclosed by the reserved words **begin** and **end** and within it, statements are separated by semi-colons. Statements may be either *simple* or *structured*.

Simple Statements

Simple statements are statements which contain no other statements. These are the assignment statement, procedure statement, **goto** statement, and empty statement.

Assignment Statement

The most fundamental of all statements is the assignment statement. It is used to specify that a certain value is to be assigned to a certain variable. An assignment consists of a variable identifier followed by the assignment operator **: =** followed by an expression.

Assignment is possible to variables of any type (except files) as long as the variable (or the function) and the expression are of the same type. As an exception, if the variable is of type *Real*, the type of the expression may be *Integer*.

Examples:
```
Angle := Angle * Pi;
AccessOK := False;
Entry := Answer = PassWord;
SpherVol := 4 * Pi * R * R;
```

Procedure Statement

A procedure statement serves to activate a previously defined user-defined procedure or a pre-defined standard procedure. The statement consists of a procedure identifier, optionally followed by a parameter list, which is a list of variables or expressions separated by commas and enclosed in parentheses. When the procedure statement is encountered during program execution, control is transferred to the named procedure, and the value (or the address) of possible parameters are transferred to the procedure. When the procedure finishes, program execution continues from the statement following the procedure statement.

Examples:
```
Find(Name,Address);
Sort(Address);
UpperCase(Text);
UpdateCustFile(CustRecord);
```

Goto Statement

A **goto** statement consists of the reserved word **goto** followed by a label identifier. It serves to transfer further processing to that point in the program text which is marked by the label. The following rules should be observed when using **goto** statements:

1) Before use, labels must be declared. The declaration takes place in a label declaration in the declaration part of the block in which the label is used.
2) The scope of a label is the block in which it is declared. It is thus not possible to jump into or out of procedures and functions.

Empty Statement

An 'empty' statement is a statement which consists of no symbols, and which has no effect. It may occur whenever the syntax of Pascal requires a statement but no action is to take place.

Examples:
```
begin end.
while Answer <> '' do;
repeat until KeyPressed; {wait for any key to be hit}
```

Structured Statements

Structured statements are constructs composed of other statements which are to be executed in sequence (compound statements), conditionally (conditional statements), or repeatedly (repetitive statements). The discussion of the **with** statement is deferred to pages 81 pp.

Compound Statement

A compound statement is used if more than one statement is to be executed in a situation where the Pascal syntax allows only one statement to be specified. It consists of any number of statements separated by semi-colons and enclosed within the reserved words **begin** and **end**, and specifies that the component statements are to be executed in the sequence in which they are written.

Example:
```
if Small > Big then
begin
  Tmp := Small;
  Small := Big;
  Big := Tmp;
end;
```

Conditional Statements

A conditional statement selects for execution a single one of its component statements.

If Statement

The **if** statement specifies that a statement be executed only if a certain condition (Boolean expression) is true. If it is false, then either no statement or the statement following the reserved word **else** is to be executed. Notice that **else** must not be preceded by a semicolon.

The syntactic ambiguity arising from the construct:

if *expr1* **then**
  if *expr2* **then**
    stmt1
  else
    stmt2

is resolved by interpreting the construct as follows:

if *expr1* **then**
begin
  if *expr2* **then**
    stmt1
  else
    stmt2
end

The **else**-clause part belongs generally to the last **if** statement which has no **else** part.

Examples:
```
if Interest > 25 then
  Usury := True
else
  TakeLoan := OK;

if (Entry < 0) or (Entry > 100) then
begin
  Write('Range is 1 to 100, please re-enter: ');
  Read(Entry);
end;
```

Case Statement

The **case** statement consists of an expression (the selector) and a list of statements, each preceded by a case label of the same type as the selector. It specifies that the one statement be executed whose case label is equal to the current value of the selector. If none of the case labels contain the value of the selector, then either no statement is executed, or, optionally, the statements following the reserved word **else** are executed. The **else** clause is an expansion of standard Pascal.

A case label consists of any number of constants or subranges separated by commas followed by a colon. A subrange is written as two constants separated by the subrange delimiter '..'. The type of the constants must be the same as the type of the selector. The statement following the case label is executed if the value of the selector equals one of the constants or if it lies within one of the subranges.

Valid selector types are all simple types, i.e. all scalar types except real.

Examples:
```
case Operator of
  '+': Result := Answer + Result;
  '-': Result := Answer - Result;
  '*': Result := Answer * Result;
  '/': Result := Answer / Result;
end;

case Year of
  Min..1939: begin
               Time := PreWorldWar2;
               Writeln('The world at peace...');
             end;
  1946..Max: begin
               Time := PostWorldWar2
               Writeln('Building a new world.');
             end;
       else  begin
               Time := WorldWar2;
               Writeln('We are at war');
             end;
end;
```

Repetitive Statements

Repetitive statements specify that certain statements are to be executed repeatedly. If the number of repetitions is known before the repetitions are started, the **for** statement is the appropriate construct to express this situation. Otherwise the **while** or the **repeat** statement should be used.

For Statement

The **for** statement indicates that the component statement is to be repeatedly executed while a progression of values is assigned to a variable which is called the *control variable*. The progression can be ascending: **to** or descending: **downto** the *final value*.

The control variable, the *initial value*, and the *final value* must all be of the same type. Valid types are all simple types, i.e. all scalar types except real.

If the initial value is greater than the final value when using the **to** clause, or if the initial value is less than the final value when using the **downto** clause, the component statement is not executed at all.

Examples:
```
for I := 2 to 100 do if A[I] > Max then Max := A[I];

for I := 1 to NoOfLines do
begin
  Readln(Line);
  if Length(Line) < Limit then
    ShortLines := ShortLines + 1
  else
    LongLines := LongLines + 1
end;
```

Notice that the component statement of a **for** statement must *not* contain assignments to the control variable. If the repetition is to be terminated before the final value is reached, a **goto** statement must be used, although such constructs are not recommended - it is better programming practice use a **while** or a **repeat** statement instead.

Upon completion of a **for** statement, the *control variable* equals the *final value*, unless the loop was not executed at all, in which case no assignment is made to the control variable.

While statement

The expression controlling the repetition must be of type Boolean. The statement is repeatedly executed as long as *expression* is *True*. If its value is false at the beginning, the statement is not executed at all.

Examples:
```
while Size > 1 do Size := Sqrt(Size);

while ThisMonth do
begin
  ThisMonth := CurMonth = SampleMonth;
  Process;
  {process this sample by the Process procedure}
end;
```

Repeat Statement

The expression controlling the repetition must be of type Boolean. The sequence of statements between the reserved words **repeat** and **until** is executed repeatedly until the expression becomes true. As opposed to the **while** statement, the **repeat** statement is always executed at least once, as evaluation af the condition takes place at the end of the loop.

Example:
```
repeat
  Write(^M,'Delete this item? (Y/N)');
  Read(Answer);
until UpCase(Answer) in ['Y','N'];
```

Notes:

Chapter 8
SCALAR AND SUBRANGE TYPES

The basic data types of Pascal are the scalar types. Scalar types constitute a finite and linear ordered set of values. Although the standard type
Real is included as a scalar type, it does not conform to this definition.
Therefore, *Reals* may not always be used in the same context as other
scalar types.

Scalar Type

Apart from the standard scalar types (*Integer, Real, Boolean, Char*, and
Byte), Pascal supports user defined scalar types, also called declared
scalar types. The definition of a scalar type specifies, in order, all of its
possible values. The values of the new type will be represented by
identifiers, which will be the constants of the new type.

Examples:
```
type
  Operator = (Plus,Minus,Multi,Divide);
  Day      = (Mon,Tues,Wed,Thur,Fri,Sat,Sun);
  Month    = (Jan,Feb,Mar,Apr,May,Jun,Jul,Aug,Sep,Oct,Nov,Dec);
  Card     = (Club,Diamond,Heart,Spade);
```

Variables of the above type *Card* can assume one of four values, namely *Club*, *Diamond*, *Heart*, or *Spade*. You are already acquainted with the
standard scalar type Boolean which is defined as:

```
type
  Boolean = (False,True);
```

The relational operators $=$, $<>$, $>$, $<$, $>=$, and $<=$ can be applied to all scalar types, as long as both operands are of the same type
(reals and integers may be mixed). The ordering of the scalar type is
used as the basis of the comparison, i.e. the order in which the values
are introduced in the type definition. For the above type card, the following is true:

```
Club < Diamond < Heart < Spade
```

The following standard functions can be used with arguments of scalar type:

Succ(Diamond)	The successor of *Diamond* (Heart).
Pred(Diamond)	The predecessor of *Diamond* (Club).
Ord(Diamond)	The ordinal value of *Diamond* (1 [as the ordinal value of the first value of a scalar type is 0]).

The result type of *Succ* and *Pred* is the same as the argument type. The result type of *Ord* is *Integer*.

Subrange Type

A type may be defined as a subrange of another already defined scalar type. Such types are called subranges. The definition of a subrange simply specifies the least and the largest value in the subrange. The first constant specifies the lower bound and must not be greater than the second constant, the upper bound. A subrange of type *Real* is not allowed.

Examples:
```
type
  HemiSphere   = (North, South, East, West);
  World        = (East..West)
  CompassRange = 0..360;
  Upper        = 'A'..'Z';
  Lower        = 'a'..'z';
  Degree       = (Celc, Fahr, Ream, Kelv);
  Wine         = (Red, White, Rose, Sparkling);
```

The type *World* is a subrange of the scalar type *HemiSphere* (called the *associated scalar type*). The associated scalar type of *Compassrange* is *Integer*, and the associated scalar type of *Upper* and *Lower* is *Char*.

You already know the standard subrange type *Byte*, which is defined as:

```
type
  Byte = 0..255;
```

A subrange type retains all the properties of its associated scalar type, being restricted only in its range of values.

The use of defined scalar types and subrange types is strongly recommended as it greatly improves the readability of programs. Furthermore, run time checks may be included in the program code (see page 65) to verify the values assigned to defined scalar variables and subrange variables. Another advantage of defined types and subrange types is that they often save memory. TURBO Pascal allocates only one byte of memory for variables of a defined scalar type or a subrange type with a total number of elements less than 256. Similarly, integer subrange variables, where lower and upper bounds are both within the range 0 through 255, occupy only one byte of memory.

Type Conversion

The *Ord* function may be used to convert scalar types into values of type integer. Standard Pascal does not provide a way to reverse this process, i.e. a way of converting an integer into a scalar value.

In TURBO Pascal, a value of a scalar type may be converted into a value of another scalar type, with the same ordinal value, by means of the *Retype* facility. Retyping is achieved by using the type identifier of the desired type as a function designator followed by one parameter enclosed in parentheses. The parameter may be a value of any scalar type except *Real*. Assuming the type definitions on pages 63 and 64 , then:

```
Integer(Heart)  = 2
Month(10)       = Nov
HemiSphere(2)   = East
Upper(14)       = 'O'
Degree(3)       = Kelv
Char(78)        = 'N'
Integer('7')    = 55
```

Range Checking

The generation of code to perform run-time range checks on scalar and subrange variables is controlled with the **R** compiler directive. The default setting is { $R-}, i.e. no checking is performed. When an assignment is made to a scalar or a subrange variable while this directive is active (({ $R + }), assignment values are checked to be within range. It is recommended to use this setting as long as a program is not fully debugged.

Example:
```
program Rangecheck;
type
  Digit = 0..9;
Var
  Dig1,Dig2,Dig3: digit;
begin
  Dig1 := 5;              {valid}
  Dig2 := Dig1 + 3;      {valid as Dig1 + 3 < = 9}
  Dig3 := 47;            {invalid but causes no error}
  {$R+} Dig3 := 55;      {invalid and causes a run time error}
  {$R-} Dig3 := 167;     {invalid but causes no error}
end.
```

Chapter 9
STRING TYPE

TURBO Pascal offers the convenience of **string** types for processing of character strings, i.e. sequences of characters. String types are structured types, and are in many ways similar to **array** types (see chapter 10). There is, however, one major difference between these: the number of characters in a string (i.e. the *length* of the string) may vary dynamically between 0 and a specified upper limit, whereas the number of elements in an array is fixed.

String Type Definition

The definition of a string type must specify the maximum number of characters it can contain, i.e. the maximum length of strings of that type. The definition consists of the reserved word **string** followed by the maximum length enclosed in square brackets. The length is specified by an integer constant in the range 1 through 255. Notice that strings do not have a default length; the length must always be specified.

Example:
```
type
  FileName = string[14];
  ScreenLine = string[80];
```

String variables occupy the defined maximum length in memory plus one byte which contains the current length of the variable. The individual characters within a string are indexed from 1 through the length of the string.

String Expressions

Strings are manipulated by the use of *string expressions*. String expressions consist of string constants, string variables, function designators, and operators.

The plus-sign may be used to concatenate strings. The *Concat* function (see page 71) performs the same function, but the + operator is often more convenient. If the length of the result is greater than 255, a run-time error occurs.

Example:
```
'TURBO ' + 'Pascal'          = 'TURBO Pascal'
'123' + '.' + '456'          = '123.456'
'A ' + 'B' + ' C ' + 'D '    = 'A B C D '
```

The relational operators =, < >, >, <, > =, and < = are lower in precedence than the concatenation operator. When applied to string operands, the result is a Boolean value (*True* or *False*). When comparing two strings, single characters are compared from the left to the right according to their ASCII values. If the strings are of different length, but equal up to and including the last character of the shortest string, then the shortest string is considered the smaller. Strings are equal only if their lengths as well as their contents are identical.

Examples:
```
'A' < 'B'                                   is true
'A' > 'b'                                   is false
'2' < '12'                                  is false
'TURBO' = 'TURBO'                           is true
'TURBO ' = 'TURBO'                          is false
'Pascal Compiler' < 'Pascal compiler'       is true
```

String Assignment

The assignment operator is used to assign the value of a string expression to a string variable.

Example:
```
Age := 'fiftieth';
Line := 'Many happy returns on your ' +  Age + ' birthday
```

If the maximum length of a string variable is exceeded (by assigning too many characters to the variable), the exceeding characters are truncated. E.g., if the variable *Age* above was declared to be of type **string**[5], then after the assignment, the variable will only contain the five leftmost characters: 'fifth'.

String Procedures

The following standard string procedures are available in TURBO Pascal:

Delete

Syntax: Delete (*St* , *Pos* , *Num*);

Delete removes a substring containing *Num* characters from *St* starting at position *Pos*. *St* is a string variable and both *Pos* and *Num* are integer expressions. If *Pos* is greater than *Length* (*St*), no characters are removed. If an attempt is made to delete characters beyond the end of the string (i.e. *Pos* + *Num* exceeds the length of the string), only characters within the string are deleted. If *Pos* is outside the range 1..255, a run time error occurs.

If *St* has the value 'ABCDEFG' then:
```
Delete(St,2,4)    will give St the value 'AFG'.
Delete(St,2,10)  will give St the value 'A'.
```

Insert

Syntax: Insert (*Obj* , *Target* , *Pos*);

Insert inserts the string *Obj* into the string *Target* at the position *Pos*. *Obj* is a string expression, *Target* is a string variable, and *Pos* is an integer expression. If *Pos* is greater than Length(*Target*), then *obj* is concatenated to *Target*. If the result is longer than the maximum length of *Target*, then excess characters will be truncated and *Target* will only contain the leftmost characters. If *Pos* is outside the range 1..255, a run time error occurs.

If *St* has the value 'ABCDEFG' then: `Insert('XX',St,3)` will give *St* the value 'ABXXCDEFG'

Str

Syntax: Str (*Value* , *St*);

The *Str* procedure converts the numeric value of *Value* into a string and stores the result in *St*. *Value* is a write parameter of type integer or of type real, and *St* is a string variable. Write parameters are expressions with special formatting commands (see page 111).

If *I* has the value 1234 then: `Str(I:5,St)` gives *St* the value ' 1234'.

If *X* has the value 2.5E4 then: `Str(X:10:0,St)` gives *St* the value '   2500'.

8-bit systems only: a function using the *Str* procedure must **never** be called by an expression in a *Write* or *Writeln* statement.

Val

Syntax: Val (*St* , *Var* , *Code*);

Val converts the string expression *St* to an integer or a real value (depending on the type of *Var*) and stores this value in *Var*. *St* must be a string expressing a numeric value according to the rules applying to numeric constants (see page 43). Neither leading nor trailing spaces are allowed. *Var* must be an *Integer* or a *Real* variable and *Code* must be an integer variable. If no errors are detected, the variable *Code* is set to 0. Otherwise *Code* is set to the position of the first character in error, and the value of *Var* is undefined.

If *St* has the value '234' then:
`Val(St,I,Result)` gives *I* the value 234 and *Result* the value 0

If *St* has the value '12x' then:
`Val(St,I,Result)` gives *I* an undefined value and *Result* the value 3

If *St* has the value '2.5E4', and *X* is a *Real* variable, then:
`Val(St,X,Result)` gives *X* the value 2500 and *Result* the value 0

8-bit systems only: a function using the *Var* procedure must **never** be called by an expression in a *Write* or *Writeln* statement.

String Functions

The following standard string functions are available in TURBO Pascal:

Copy

Syntax: Copy (*St* , *Pos* , *Num*);

Copy returns a substring containing *Num* characters from *St* starting at position *Pos*. *St* is a string expression and both *Pos* and *Num* are integer expressions. If *Pos* exceeds the length of the string, the empty string is returned. If an attempt is made to get characters beyond the end of the string (i.e. *Pos* + *Num* exceeds the length of the string), only the characters within the string are returned. If *Pos* is outside the range 1..255, a run time error occurs.

If *St* has the value 'ABCDEFG' then:
Copy(St,3,2)   returns the value 'CD'
Copy(St,4,10)   returns the value 'DEFG'
Copy(St,4,2)   returns the value 'DE'

Concat

Syntax: Concat (*St1* , *St2* { , *StN* });

The *Concat* function returns is a string which is the concatenation of its arguments in the order in which they are specified. The arguments may be any number of string expressions separated by commas (*St1*, *St2* .. *StN*). If the length of the result is greater than 255, a run-time error occurs. As explained in page 68 , the + operator can be used to obtain the same result, often more conveniently. *Concat* is included only to maintain compatibility with other Pascal compilers.

If *St1* has the value 'TURBO' and *St2* the value 'is fastest' then:

Concat(Stl,' PASCAL ',St2)

returns the value 'TURBO PASCAL is fastest'

Length

Syntax: Length (*St*);

Returns the length of the string expression *St*, i.e. the number of characters in *St*. The type of the result is integer.

If *St* has the value '123456789' then:
`Length(St)` returns the value 9

Pos

Syntax: Pos (*Obj* , *Target*);

The *Pos* function scans the string *Target* to find the first occurrence of *Obj* within *Target*. *Obj* and *Target* are string expressions, and the type of the result is integer. The result is an integer denoting the position within *Target* of the first character of the matched pattern. The position of the first character in a string is 1. If the pattern is not found, *Pos* returns 0.

If *St* has the value 'ABCDEFG' then
`Pos('DE',St)` returns the value 4
`Pos('H',St)` returns the value 0

Strings and Characters

String types and the standard scalar type *Char* are compatible. Thus, whenever a string value is expected, a char value may be specified instead and vice versa. Furthermore, strings and characters may be mixed in expressions. When a character is assigned a string value, the length of the string must be exactly one; otherwise a run-time error occurs.

The characters of a string variable may be accessed individually through string indexing. This is achieved by appending an index expression of type integer, enclosed in square brackets, to the string variable.

Examples:
```
Buffer[5]
Line[Length(Line)-1]
Ord(Line[0])
```

As the first character of the string (at index 0) contains the length of the string, Length(String) is the same as Ord(String[0]). If assignment is made to the length indicator, it is the responsibility of the programmer to check that it is less than the maximum length of the string variable. When the range check compiler directive **R** is active (({ $R +)), code is generated which insures that the value of a string index expression does not exceed the maximum length of the string variable. It is, however, still possible to index a string beyond its current dynamic length. The characters thus read are random, and assignments beyond the current length will not affect the actual value of the string variable.

Notes:

Chapter 10
ARRAY TYPE

An array is a structured type consisting of a fixed number of components which are all of the same type, called the *component type* or the *base type*. Each component can be explicitly accessed by indices into the array. Indices are expressions of any scalar type placed in square brackets suffixed to the *array identifier*, and their type is called the *index type*.

Array Definition

The definition of an array consists of the the reserved word **array** followed by the index type, enclosed in square brackets, followed by the reserved word **of**, followed by the component type.

Examples:
```
type
   Day = (Mon,Tue,Wed,Thu,Fri,Sat,Sun)
Var
   WorkHour : array[1..8] of Integer;
   Week     : array[1..7] of Day;

type
   Players  = (Player1,Player2,Player3,Player4);
   Hand     = (One,Two,Pair,TwoPair,Three,Straight,
               Flush,FullHouse,Four,StraightFlush,RSF);
   LegalBid = 1..200;
   Bid      = array[Players] of LegalBid;
Var
   Player   : array[Players] of Hand;
   Pot      : Bid;
```

An array component is accessed by suffixing an index enclosed in square brackets to the array variable identifier:

```
Player[Player3] := FullHouse;
Pot[Player3] := 100;
Player[Player4] := Flush;
Pot[Player4] := 50;
```

As assignment is allowed between any two variables of identical type, entire arrays can be copied with a single assignment statement.

The R compiler directive controls the generation of code which will perform range checks on array index expressions at run-time. The default mode is passive, i.e. { $R-}, and the { $R + } setting causes all index expressions to be checked against the limits of their index type.

Multidimensional Arrays

The component type of an array may be any data type, i.e. the component type may be another array. Such a structure is called a *multidimensional array*.

Example:
```
type
   Card      = (Two,Three,Four,Five,Six,Seven,Eight,Nine,
                Ten,Knight,Queen,King,Ace);
   Suit      = (Hearts,Spade,Clubs,Diamonds);
   AllCards = array[Suit] of array[1..13] of Card;
Var
   Deck: AllCards;
```

A multi-dimensional array may be defined more conveniently by specifying the multiple indices thus:

```
type
   AllCards = array[Suit,1..13] of Card;
```

A similar abbreviation may be used when selecting an array component:

```
Deck[Hearts,10]
```
is equivalent to
```
Deck[Hearts][10]
```

It is, of course, possible to define multi-dimensional arrays in terms of previously defined array types.

Example:
```
type
  Pupils        = string[20];
  Class         = array[1..30] of Pupils;
  School        = array[1..100] of Class;
Var
  J,P,Vacant    : Integer
  ClassA,
  ClassB        : Class;
  NewTownSchool : School;
```

After these definitions, all of the following assignments are legal.

```
ClassA[J]:='Peter';
NewTownSchool[5][21]:='Peter Brown';
NewTownSchool[8,J]:=NewTownSchool[7,J];  (pupil no. J changed class)
ClassA[Vacant]:=ClassB[P];  (pupil no. P changes Class and number)
```

Character Arrays

Character arrays are arrays with one index and components of the standard scalar type *Char*. Character arrays may be thought of as *strings* with a constant length.

In TURBO Pascal, character arrays may participate in *string* expressions, in which case the array is converted into a string of the length of the array. Thus, arrays may be compared and manipulated in the same way as strings, and string constants may be assigned to character arrays, as long as they are of the same length. String variables and values computed from string expressions cannot be assigned to character arrays.

Predefined Arrays

TURBO Pascal offers two predefined arrays of type *Byte*, called *Mem* and *Port*, which are used to access CPU memory and data ports. These are discussed in chapters 20, 21, and 22.

Notes:

Chapter 11
RECORD TYPE

A **record** is a structure consisting of a fixed number of components, called *fields*. Fields may be of different type and each field is given a name, the *field identifier*, which is used to select it.

Record Definition

The definition of a record type consists of the reserved word **record** succeeded by a *field list* and terminated by the reserved word **end**. The field list is a sequence of *record sections* separated by semi-colons, each consisting of one or more identifiers separated by commas, followed by a colon and either a type *identifier* or a a a type *descriptor*. Each record section thus specifies the identifier and type of one or more fields.

Example:
```
type
  DaysOfMonth = 1..31;
  Date =        record
                  Day:    DaysOfMonth;
                  Month:  (Jan,Feb,Mar,Apr,May,Jun,
                           July,Aug,Sep,Oct,Nov,Dec);
                  Year:   1900..1999;
                end;
Var
  Birth: Date;
  WorkDay: array[1..5] of date;
```

Day, *Month*, and *Year* are field identifiers. A field identifier must be unique only within the record in which it is defined. A field is referenced by the variable identifier and the field identifier separated by a period.

Examples:

```
Birth.Month := Jun;
Birth.Year := 1950;
WorkDay[Current] := WorkDay[Current-1];
```

Note that, similar to array types, assignment is allowed between entire records of identical types. As record components may be of any type, constructs like the following record of records of records are possible:

```
type
  Name   = record
             FamilyName: string[32];
             ChristianNames: array[1..3] of string[16];
           end;
  Rate   = record
             NormalRate, OverTime,
             NightTime, Weekend: Integer
           end;
  Date   = record
             Day:    1..31;
             Month:  (Jan,Feb,Mar,Apr,May,Jun,
                      July,Aug,Sep,Oct,Nov,Dec);
             Year:   1900..1999;
           end;
  Person = record
             ID: Name;
             Time: Date;
           end;
  Wages  = record
             Individual: Person;
             Cost: Rate;
           end

  Var   Salary, Fee: Wages;
```

Assuming these definitions, the following assignments are legal:

```
Salary := Fee;
Salary.Cost.Overtime := 950;
Salary.Individual.Time := Fee.Individual.Time;
Salary.Individual.ID.FamilyName := 'Smith'
```

With Statement

The use of records as describes above does sometimes result in rather lengthy statements; it would often be easier if we could access individual fields in a record as if they were simple variables. This is the function of the **with** statement: it 'opens up' a record so that field identifiers may be used as variable identifiers.

A **with** statement consists of the reserved word **with** followed by a list of record variables separated by commas followed by the reserved word **do** and finally a statement.

Within a **with** statement, a field is designated only by its field identifier, i.e. without the record variable identifier:

```
with Salary do
begin
   Individual := NewEmployee;
   Cost := StandardRates;
end;
```

Records may be *nested* within **with** statements, i.e. records of records may be 'opened' as shown here:

```
with Salary, Individual, ID do
begin
   FamilyName := 'Smith';
   ChristianNames[1] := 'James';
end
```

This is equivalent to:

```
with Salary do with Individual do with ID do
   . . .
```

The maximum 'depth' of this nesting of **with** sentences, i.e. the maximum number of records which may be 'opened' within one block, depends on your implementation and is discussed in chapters 20, 21, and 22.

Variant Records

The syntax of a record type also provides for a variant part, i.e. alternative record structures which allows fields of a record to consist of a different number and different types of components, usually depending on the value of a *tag field*.

A variant part consists of a *tag-field* of a previously defined type, whose values determine the variant, followed by labels corresponding to each possible value of the tag field. Each label heads a *field list* which defines the type of the variant corresponding to the label.

Assuming the existence of the type:

```
Origin = (Citizen, Alien);
```

and of the types *Name* and *Date*, the following record allows the field *CitizenShip* to have different structures depending on whether the value of the field is *Citizen* or *Alien*:

```
type
  Person = record
             PersonName: Name;
             BirthDate: Date;
             case CitizenShip: Origin of
               Citizen: (BirthPlace: Name);
               Alien:   (CountryOfOrigin: Name;
                         DateOfEntry: Date;
                         PermittedUntil: Date;
                         PortOfEntry: Name);
           end;
```

In this variant record definition, the tag-field is an explicit field which may be selected and updated like any other field. Thus, if *Passenger* is a variable of type *Person*, statements like the following are perfectly legal:

```
Passenger.CitizenShip := Citizen;

with Passenger, PersonName do
  if CitizenShip = Alien then writeln(FamilyName);
```

The fixed part of a record, i.e. the part containing the common fields, must always precede the *variant part*. In the above example, the fields *PersonName* and *BirthDate* are the fixed fields. A record can only have one variant part. In a variant, the parentheses must be present, even if they will enclose nothing.

The maintenance of tag field values is the responsibility of the programmer and not of TURBO Pascal. Thus, in the *Person* type above, the field *DateOfEntry* can be accessed even if the value of the tag field *CitizenShip* is not *Alien*. Actually, the tag field identifier may be omitted altogether, leaving only the type identifier. Such record variants are known as *free unions*, as opposed to record variants with tag fields which are called *discriminated unions*. The use of free unions is infrequent and should only be practiced by experienced programmers.

Notes:

Chapter 12
SET TYPE

A **set** is a collection of related objects which may be thought of as a whole. Each object in such a set is called a *member* or an *element* of the set. Examples of sets could be:

1) All integers between 0 and 100
2) The letters of the alphabet
3) The consonants of the alphabet

Two sets are equal if and only if their elements are the same. There is no ordering involved, so the sets [1,3,5], [5,3,1] and [3,5,1] are all equal. If the members of one set are also members of another set, then the first set is said to be included in the second. In the examples above, 3) is included in 2).

There are three operations involving sets, similar to the operations addition, multiplication and subtraction operations on numbers:

The *union* (or sum) of two sets A and B (written A + B) is the set whose members are members of either A or B. For instance, the union of [1,3,5,7] and [2,3,4] is [1,2,3,4,5,7].

The *intersection* (or product) of two sets A and B (written A*B) is the set whose members are the members of both A and B. Thus, the intersection of [1,3,4,5,7] and [2,3,4] is [3,4].

The *relative complement* of B with respect to A (written A-B) is the set whose members are members of A but not of B. For instance, [1,3,5,7]-[2,3,4] is [1,5,7].

Set Type Definition

Although in mathematics there are no restrictions on the objects which may be members of a set, Pascal only offers a restricted form of sets. The members of a set must all be of the same type, called the *base type*, and the base type must be a simple type, i.e. any scalar type except real. A set type is introduced by the reserved words **set of** followed by a simple type.

Examples:
```
type
  DaysOfMonth = set of 0..31;
  WorkWeek = set of Mon..Fri;
  Letter = set of 'A'..'Z';
  AdditiveColors = set of (Red,Green,Blue);
  Characters = set of Char;
```

In TURBO Pascal, the maximum number of elements in a set is 256, and the ordinal values of the base type must be within the range 0 through 255.

Set Expressions

Set values may be computed from other set values through set expressions. Set expressions consist of set constants, set variables, set constructors, and set operators.

Set Constructors

A set constructor consists of one or more element specifications, separated by commas, and enclosed in square brackets. An element specification is an expression of the same type as the base type of the set, or a range expressed as two such expressions separated by two consecutive periods (..).

Examples:
```
['T','U','R','B','O']
[X,Y]
[X..Y]
[1..5]
['A'..'Z','a'..'z','0'..'9']
[1,3..10,12]
[]
```

The last example shows *the empty set*, which, as it contains no expressions to indicate its base type, is compatible with all set types. The set [1..5] is equivalent to the set [1,2,3,4,5]. If X > Y then [X..Y] denotes the empty set.

Set Operators

The rules of composition specify set operator precedence according to the following three classes of operators:

1)   *   Set intersection.

2)   +   Set union.
       −   Set difference.

3)   =   Test on equality.
       <>   Test on inequality.
     >=   *True* if all members of the second operand are included in the first operand.
     <=   *True* if all members of the first operand are included in the second operand.
     IN   Test on set membership. The second operand is of a set type, and the first operand is an expression of the same type as the base type of the set. The result is true if the first operand is a member of the second operand, otherwise it is false.

Set disjunction (when two sets contain no common members) may be expressed as:

```
A * B = [ ];
```

that is, the intersection between the two sets is the empty set. Set expressions are often useful to clarify complicated tests. For instance, the test:

```
if (Ch='T') or (Ch='U') or (Ch='R') or (Ch='B') or (Ch='O')
```

can be expressed much clearer as:

```
Ch in ['T','U','R','B','O']
```

And the test:

```
if (Ch >= '0') and (Ch <= '9') then ...
```

is better expressed as:

```
if Ch in['0'..'9'] then ...
```

Set Assignments

Values resulting from set expressions are assigned to set variables using the assignment operator `:=`.

Examples:
```
type
  ASCII = set of 0..127;
Var
  NoPrint,Print,AllChars: ASCII;
begin
  AllChars := [0..127];
  NoPrint := [0..31,127];
  Print := AllChars - NoPrint;
end.
```

Chapter 13
TYPED CONSTANTS

Typed constants are a TURBO specialty. A typed constant may be used exactly like a variable of the same type. Typed constants may thus be used as 'initialized variables', because the value of a typed constant is defined, whereas the value of a variable is undefined until an assignment is made. Care should be taken, of course, not to assign values to typed constants whose values are actually meant to be **constant**.

The use of a typed constant saves code if the constant is used often in a program, because a typed constant is included in the program code only once, whereas an untyped constant is included every time it is used.

Typed constants are defined like untyped constants (see page 48), except that the definition specifies not only the *value* of the constant but also the *type*. In the definition the typed constant identifier is succeeded by a colon and a type identifier, which is then followed by an equal sign and the actual constant.

Unstructured Typed Constants

An unstructured typed constant is a constant defined as one of the scalar types:

```
const
  NumberOfCars: Integer = 1267;
  Interest: Real = 12.67;
  Heading: string[7] = 'SECTION';
  Xon: Char = ^Q;
```

Contrary to untyped constants, a typed constant may be used in place of a variable as a variable parameter to a procedure or a function. As a typed constant is actually a variable with a constant value, it cannot be used in the definition of other constants or types. Thus, as *Min* and *Max* are typed constants, the following construct is **illegal**:

```
const
  Min: Integer = 0;
  Max: Integer = 50;
type
  Range: array[Min..Max] of integer
```

Structured Typed Constants

Structured constants comprise *array constants, record constants,* and *set constants.* They are often used to provide initialized tables and sets for tests, conversions, mapping functions, etc. The following sections describe each type in detail.

Array Constants

The definition of an array constant consists of the constant identifier succeeded by a colon and the type identifier of a previously defined array type followed by an equal sign and the constant value expressed as a set of constants separated by commas and enclosed in parentheses.

Examples:
```
type
  Status    = (Active,Passive,Waiting);
  StringRep = array[Status] of string[7];
const
  Stat: StringRep = ('active','passive','waiting');
```

The example defines the array constants *Stat,* which may be used to convert values of the scalar type *Status* into their corresponding string representations. The components of *Stat* are:

```
Stat[Active]  = 'active'
Stat[Passive] = 'passive'
Stat[Waiting] = 'waiting'
```

The component type of an array constant may be any type except *File* types and *Pointer* types. Character array constants may be specified both as single characters and as strings. Thus, the definition:

```
const
  Digits: array[0..9] of Char =
  ('0','1','2','3','4','5','6','7','8','9');
```

may be expressed more conveniently as:

```
const
  Digits: array[0..9] of Char = '0123456789';
```

Multi-dimensional Array Constants

Multi-dimensional array constants are defined by enclosing the constants of each dimension in separate sets of parentheses, separated by
commas. The innermost constants correspond to the rightmost dimen-
sions.

Example:
```
type
  Cube = array[0..1,0..1,0..1] of integer;
const
  Maze: Cube = (((0,1),(2,3)),((4,5),(6,7)));
begin
  Writeln(Maze[0,0,0],' = 0');
  Writeln(Maze[0,0,1],' = 1');
  Writeln(Maze[0,1,0],' = 2');
  Writeln(Maze[0,1,1],' = 3');
  Writeln(Maze[1,0,0],' = 4');
  Writeln(Maze[1,0,1],' = 5');
  Writeln(Maze[1,1,0],' = 6');
  Writeln(Maze[1,1,1],' = 7');
end.
```

Record Constants

The definition of a record constant consists of the constant identifier
succeeded by a colon and the type identifier of a previously defined
record type followed by an equal sign and the constant value expressed
as a list of field constants separated by semi-colons and enclosed in
parentheses.

Examples:
```
type
  Point      = record
                 X,Y,Z: integer;
               end;
  OS         = (CPM80,CPM86,MSDOS,Unix);
  UI         = (CCP,SomethingElse,MenuMaster);
  Computer   = record
                 OperatingSystems: array[1..4] of OS;
                 UserInterface: UI;
               end;
const
  Origo: Point   = (X:0; Y:0; Z:0);
  SuperComp: Computer =
               (OperatingSystems: (CPM80,CPM86,MSDOS,Unix);
               UserInterface: MenuMaster);
  Planel: array[1..3] of Point =
      ((X:1;Y:4;Z:5),(X:10;Y:-78;Z:45),(X:100;Y:10;Z:-7));
```

The field constants must be specified in the same order as they appear
in the definition of the record type. If a record contains fields of file types
or pointer types, then constants of that record type cannot be specified.
If a record constant contains a variant, then it is the responsibility of the
programmer to specify only the fields of the valid variant. If the variant
contains a tag field, then its value must be specified.

Set Constants

A set constant consists of one or more element specifications separated
by commas, and enclosed in square brackets. An element specification
must be a constant or a range expression consisting of two constants
separated by two consecutive periods (..).

Example:
```
type
  Up  = set of 'A'..'Z';
  Low = set of 'a'..'z';
const
  UpperCase: Up   = ['A'..'Z'];
  Vocals   : Low  = ['a','e','i','o','u','y'];
  Delimiter: set of Char =
               [' '..'/',':'..'?','['..''','{'..' '];
```

Chapter 14
FILE TYPES

Files provide a program with channels through which it can pass data. A file can either be a *disk file*, in which case data is written to and read from a magnetic device of some type, or a *logical device*, such as the pre-defined files *Input* and *Output* which refer to the computer's standard I/O channels; the keyboard and the screen.

A *file* consists of a sequence of components of equal type. The number of components in a file (the *size* of the file) is not determined by the definition of the file; instead the Pascal system keeps track of file accesses through a *file pointer*, and each time a component is written to or read from a file, the file pointer of that file is advanced to the next component. As all components of a file are of equal length, the position of a specific component can be calculated. Thus, the file pointer can be moved to any component in the file, providing random access to any element of the file.

File Type Definition

A file type is defined by the reserved words **file of** followed by the type of the components of the file, and a file identifier is declared by the same words followed by the identifier of a previously defined file type.

Examples:
```
type
  ProductName = string[80];
  Product = file of record
                  Name: ProductName;
                  ItemNumber: Real;
                  InStock: Real;
                  MinStock: Real;
                  Supplier: Integer;
              end;
Var
  ProductFile: Product;
  ProductNames: file of ProductName;
```

The component type of a file may be any type, except a file type. (that is, with reference to the example above, **file of** *Product* is **not** allowed). File variables may appear in neither assignments nor expressions.

Operations on Files

The following sections describe the procedures available for file handling. The identifier *FilVar* used throughout denotes a file variable identifier declared as described above.

Assign

Syntax: Assign(*FilVar, Str*);

Str is a string expression yielding any legal file name. This file name is assigned to the file variable *FilVar*, and all further operation on *FilVar* will operate on the disk file *Str*. Assign should never be used on a file which is in use.

Rewrite

Syntax: Rewrite(*FilVar*);

A new disk file of the name assigned to the file variable *FilVar* is created and prepared for processing, and the file pointer is set to the beginning of the file, i.e. component no. 0. Any previously existing file with the same name is erased. A disk file created by rewrite is initially empty, i.e. it contains no elements.

Reset

Syntax: Reset(*FilVar*);

The disk file of the name assigned to the file variable *FilVar* is prepared for processing, and the file pointer is set to the beginning of the file, i.e. component no. 0. *FilVar* must name an existing file, otherwise an I/O error occurs.

Read

Syntax: Read(*FilVar, Var*);

Var denotes one or more variables of the component type of *FilVar*, separated by commas. Each variable is read from the disk file, and following each read operation, the file pointer is advanced to the next component.

Write

Syntax: Write(*FilVar, Var*);

Var denotes one or more variables of the component type of *FilVar*, separated by commas. Each variable is written to the disk file, and following each write operation, the file pointer is advanced to the next component.

Seek

Syntax: Seek(*FilVar, n*);

Seek moves the file pointer is moved to the n'th component of the file denoted by *FilVar*. *n* is an integer expression. The position of the first component is 0. Note that in order to expand a file it is possible to *seek* one component beyond the last component. The statement

```
Seek(FilVar, FileSize(FilVar));
```

thus places the file pointer at the end of the file (*FileSize* returns the number of components in the file, and as the components are numbered from zero, the returned number is one greater than the number of the last component).

Flush

Syntax: Flush(*FilVar*);

Flush empties the internal sector buffer of the disk file *FilVar*, and thus assures that the sector buffer is written to the disk if any write operations have taken place since the last disk update. *Flush* also insures that the next read operation will actually perform a physical read from the disk file. *Flush* should never be used on a closed file.

Close

Syntax: Close(*FilVar*);

The disk file associated with *FilVar* is closed, and the disk directory is updated to reflect the new status of the file. Notice that it is necessary to *Close* a file, even if it has only been read from—you would otherwise quickly run out of file handles.

Erase

Syntax: Erase(*FilVar*);

The disk file associated with *FilVar* is erased. If the file is open, i.e. if the file has been reset or rewritten but not closed, it is good programming practice to *close* the file before erasing it.

Rename

Syntax: Rename(*FilVar, Str*);

The disk file associated with *FilVar* is renamed to a new name given by the string expression *Str*. The disk directory is updated to show the new name of the file, and further operations on *FilVar* will operate on the file with the new name. *Rename* should never be used on an open file.

Notice that it is the programmer's responsibility to assure that the file named by *Str* does not already exist. If it does, multiple occurrences of the same name may result. The following function returns *True* if the file name passed as a parameter exists, otherwise it returns *False*:

```
type
  Name=string[66];
  :
  :
function Exist(FileName: Name): boolean;
Var
  Fil: file;
begin
  Assign(Fil, FileName);
  {$I-}
  Reset(Fil);
  {$I+}
  Exist := (IOresult = 0)
end;
```

File Standard Functions

The following standard functions are applicable to files:

EOF

Syntax: EOF(*FilVar*);

A Boolean function which returns *True* if the file pointer is positioned at the end of the disk file, i.e. beyond the last component of the file. If not, *EOF* returns *False*.

FilePos

Syntax: FilePos(*FilVar*);

An integer function which returns the current position of the file pointer. The first component of a file is 0.

FileSize

Syntax: FileSize(*FilVar*);

An integer function which returns the size of the disk file expressed as the number of components in the file. If *FileSize(FilVar)* is zero, the file is empty.

Using Files

Before using a file, the *Assign* procedure must be called to assign the file name to a file variable. Before input and/or output operations are performed, the file must be opened with a call to *Rewrite* or *Reset*. This call will set the file pointer to point to the first component of the disk file, i.e. *FilePos(FilVar)* = 0. After *Rewrite*, *FileSize(FilVar)* is 0.

A disk file can be expanded only by adding components to the end of the existing file. The file pointer can be moved to the end of the file by executing the following sentence:

```
Seek(FilVar, FileSize(FilVar));
```

When a program has finished its input/output operations on a file, it should always call the *Close* procedure. Failure to do so may result in loss of data, as the disk directory is not properly updated.

The program below creates a disk file called *PRODUCTS.DTA*, and writes 100 records of the type *Product* to the file. This initializes the file for subsequent random access (i.e. records may be read and written anywhere in the file).

```
program InitProductFile;
const
  MaxNumberOfProducts = 100;
type
  ProductName = string[20];
  Product = record
              Name: ProductName;
              ItemNumber: Integer;
              InStock: Real;
              Supplier: Integer;
            end;
Var
  ProductFile: file of Product;
  ProductRec: Product;
  I: Integer;
begin
  Assign(ProductFile,'PRODUCT.DTA');
  Rewrite(ProductFile); {open the file and delete any data}
  with ProductRec do
  begin
    Name := ''; InStock := 0; Supplier := 0;
    for I := 1 to MaxNumberOfProducts do
    begin
      ItemNumber := I;
      Write(ProductFile,ProductRec);
    end;
  end;
  Close(ProductFile);
end.
```

The following program demonstrates the use of *Sseek* on random files. The program is used to update the *ProductFile* created by the program in the previous example.

```pascal
program UpDateProductFile;
const
  MaxNumberOfProducts = 100;
type
  ProductName = string[20];
  Product = record
              Name: ProductName;
              ItemNumber: Integer;
              InStock: Real;
              Supplier: Integer;
            end;
Var
  ProductFile: file of Product;
  ProductRec: Product;
  I, Pnr: Integer;
begin
  Assign(ProductFile,'PRODUCT.DTA'); Reset(ProductFile);
  ClrScr;
  Write('Enter product number (0= stop) '); Readln(Pnr);
  while Pnr in [1..MaxNumberOfProducts] do
  begin
    Seek(ProductFile,Pnr-1); Read(ProductFile,ProductRec);
    with ProductRec do
    begin
      Write('Enter name of product (',Name:20,')   ');
      Readln(Name);
      Write('Enter number in stock (',InStock:20:0,')   ');
      Readln(InStock);
      Write('Enter supplier number (',Supplier:20,')   ');
      Readln(Supplier);
      ItemNumber:=Pnr;
    end;
    Seek(ProductFile,Pnr-1);
    Write(ProductFile,ProductRec);
    ClrScr; Writeln;
    Write('Enter product number (0= stop) '); Readln(Pnr);
  end;
  Close(ProductFile);
end.
```

Text Files

Unlike all other file types, *text files* are not simply sequences of values of some type. Although the basic components of a text file are characters, they are structured into lines, each line being terminated by an *end-of-line* marker (a CR/LF sequence). The file is further ended by an *end-of-file* marker (a Ctrl-Z). As the length of lines may vary, the position of a given line in a file cannot be calculated. Text files can therefore only be processed sequentially. Furthermore, input and output cannot be performed simultaneously to a text file.

Operations on Text Files

A text file variable is declared by referring to the standard type identifier *Text*. Subsequent file operations must be preceded by a call to *Assign* and a call to *Reset* or *Rewrite* must furthermore precede input or output operations.

Rewrite is used to create a new text file, and the only operation then allowed on the file is the appending of new components to the end of the file. *Reset* is used to open an existing file for reading, and the only operation allowed on the file is sequential reading. When a new textfile is closed, an end-of-file mark is automatically appended to the file.

Character input and output on text files is made with the standard procedures *Read* and *Write*. Lines are processed with the special text file operators *Readln*, *Writeln*, and *Eoln*:

ReadLn

Syntax: Readln(*Filvar*);

Skips to the beginning of the next line, i.e. skips all characters up to and including the next CR/LF sequence.

WriteLn

Syntax: WriteLn(*Filvar*);

Writes a line marker, i.e. a CR/LF sequence, to the textfile.

Eoln

Syntax: Eoln(*Filvar*);

A Boolean function which returns *True* if the end of the current line has been reached, i.e. if the file pointer is positioned at the CR character of the CR/LF line marker. If *EOF(Filvar)* is true, *Eoln(Filvar)* is also true.

SeekEoln

Syntax: SeekEoln(*FilVar*);

Similar to *Eoln*, except that it skips blanks and TABs before it tests for an end-of-line marker. The type of the result is boolean.

SeekEof

Syntax: SeekEof(*FilVar*);

Similar to *EOF*, except that it skips blanks, TABs, and end-of-line markers (CR/LF sequences) before it tests for an end-of-file marker. The type of the result is boolean.

When applied to a text file, the *EOF* function returns the value *True*

if the file pointer is positioned at the end-of-file mark (the CTRL/Z character ending the file). The *Seek* and *Flush* procedures and the *FilePos* and *FileSize* functions are not applicable to text files.

The following sample program reads a text file from disk and prints it on the pre-defined device *Lst* which is the printer. Words surrounded by Ctrl-S in the file are printed underlined:

```
program TextFileDemo;
Var
  FilVar:        Text;
  Line,
  ExtraLine:     string[255];
  I:             Integer;
  UnderLine:     Boolean;
  FileName:      string[14];
begin
  UnderLine := False;
  Write('Enter name of file to list: ');
  Readln(FileName);
  Assign(FilVar,FileName);
  Reset(FilVar);
  while not Eof(FilVar) do
  begin
    Readln(FilVar,Line);
    I := 1; ExtraLine := '';
    for I := 1 to Length(Line) do
    begin
      if Line[I]<>^S then
      begin
        Write(Lst,Line[I]);
        if UnderLine then ExtraLine := ExtraLine+'_'
        else ExtraLine := ExtraLine+' ';
      end
      else UnderLine := not UnderLine;
    end;
    Write(Lst,^M); Writeln(Lst,ExtraLine);
  end; {while not Eof}
end.
```

Further extensions of the procedures *Read* and *Write*, which facilitate convenient handling of formatted input and output, are described on page 108.

Logical Devices

In TURBO Pascal, external devices such as terminals, printers, and modems are regarded as *logical devices* which are treated like text files. The following logical devices are available:

CON: The console device. Output is sent to the operating system's console output device, usually the CRT, and input is obtained from the console input device, usually the keyboard. Contrary to the TRM: device (see below), the CON: device provides buffered input. In short, this means that each *Read* or *Readln* from a textfile assigned to the CON: device will input an entire line into a line buffer, and that the operator is provided with a set of editing facilities during line input. For more details on console input, please refer to pages 105 and 108 .

TRM: The terminal device. Output is sent to the operating system's console output device, usually the CRT, and input is obtained from the console input device, usually the keyboard. Input characters are echoed, unless they are control characters. The only control character echoed is a carriage return (CR), which is echoed as CR/LF.

KBD: The keyboard device (input only). Input is obtained from the operating system's console input device, usually the keyboard. Input is not echoed.

LST: The list device (output only). Output is sent to the operating system's list device, typically the line printer.

AUX: The auxiliary device. In PC/MS-DOS, this is COM1:; in CP/M it is RDR: and PUN:.

USR: The user device. Output is sent to the user output routine, and input is obtained from the user input routine. For further details on user input and output, please refer to pages 209 , 241 , and 272 .

These logical devices may be accessed through the pre-assigned files discussed on page 105 or they may be assigned to file variables, exactly like a disk file. There is no difference between *Rewrite* and *Reset* on a file assigned to a logical device, *Close* performs no function, and an attempt to *Erase* such a file will cause an I/O error.

The standard functions *Eof* and *Eoln* operate differently on logical devices than on disk files. On a disk file, *Eof* returns *True* when the next character in the file is a Ctrl-Z, or when physical EOF is encountered, and *Eoln* returns *True* when the next character is a CR or a Ctrl-Z. Thus, *Eof* and *Eoln* are in fact 'look ahead' routines.

As you cannot look ahead on a logical device, *Eoln* and *Eof* operate on the *last* character read instead of on the *next* character. In effect, *Eof* returns *True* when the last character read was a Ctrl-Z, and *Eoln* returns *True* when the last character read was a CR or a Ctrl-Z. The following table provides an overview of the operation of *Eoln* and *Eof*:

	On Files	On Logical Devices
Eoln is true if is	**next** character CR or Ctrl-Z or if EOF is true	if **current** character is CR or Ctrl-Z
Eof is true if	**next** character is Ctrl-Z or if physical EOF is met	if **current** character is Ctrl-Z

Table 14-1: Operation of EOLN and Eof

Similarly, the *Readln* procedure works differently on logical devices than on disk files. On a disk file, *Readln* reads all characters up to and including the CR/LF sequence, whereas on a logical device it only reads up to and including the first CR. The reason for this is again the inability to 'look ahead' on logical devices, which means that the system has no way of knowing what character will follow the CR.

Standard Files

As an alternative to assigning text files to logical devices as described above, TURBO Pascal offers a number of pre-declared text files which have already been assigned to specific logical devices and prepared for processing. Thus, the programmer is saved the reset/rewrite and close processes, and the use of these standard files further saves code:

Input
> The primary input file. This file is assigned to either the CON: device or to the TRM: device (see below for further detail).

Output
> The primary output file. This file is assigned to either the CON: device or to the TRM: device (see below for further detail).

Con   Assigned to the console device (CON:).
Trm   Assigned to the terminal device (TRM:).
Kbd   Assigned to the keyboard device (KBD:).
Lst   Assigned to the list device (LST:).
Aux   Assigned to the auxiliary device (AUX:).
Usr   Assigned to the user device (USR:).

Notice that the use of *Assign, Reset, Rewrite*, and *Close* on these files is illegal.

When the *Read* procedure is used without specifying a file identifier, it always inputs a line, even if some characters still remain to be read from the line buffer, and it ignores Ctrl-Z, forcing the operator to terminate the line with RETURN. The terminating RETURN is not echoed, and internally the line is stored with a Ctrl-Z appended to the end of it. Thus, when less values are specified on the input line than there are parameters in the parameter list, any *Char* variables in excess will be set to Ctrl-Z, strings will be empty, and numeric variables will remain unaltered.

The **B** compiler directive is used to control this 'forced read' feature above. The default state is {$B + }, and in this state, read statements without a file variable will always cause a line to be input from the console. If a {$B-} compiler directive is placed at the beginning of the program (**before** the declaration part), the shortened version of read will act as if the input standard file had been specified, i.e.:

Read(v1,v2,...,vn) equals *Read(input,v1,v2,...,vn)*

and in this case, lines are only input when the line buffer has been emptied. The {$B-} state follows the definition of Standard Pascal I/O, whereas the default {$B + } state, not confirming to the standard in all aspects, provides better control of input operations.

If you don't want input echoed to the screen, you should read from the standard file *Kbd*:

```
Read(Kbd, Var)
```

As the standard files *Input* and *Output* are used very frequently, they are chosen by default if no file identifier is stated. The following list shows the abbreviated text file operations and their equivalents:

Write(Ch)	*Write(Output,Ch)*
Read(Ch)	*Read(Input,Ch)*
Writeln	*Writeln(Output)*
Readln	*Readln(Input)*
Eof	*Eof(Input)*
Eoln	*Eoln(Input)*

The following program shows the use of the standard file *Lst* to list the file *ProductFile* (see page 99) on the printer:

```pascal
program ListProductFile;
const
  MaxNumberOfProducts = 100;
type
  ProductName = string[20];
  Product = record
              Name: ProductName; ItemNumber: Integer;
              InStock: Real;
              Supplier: Integer;
            end;
Var
  ProductFile: file of Product;
  ProductRec: Product; I: Integer;
begin
  Assign(ProductFile,'PRODUCT.DTA'); Reset(ProductFile);
  for I := 1 to MaxNumberOfProducts do
  begin
    Read(ProductFile,ProductRec);
    with ProductRec do
    begin
      if Name<>'' then
        Writeln(Lst,'Item: ',ItemNumber:5,' ', Name:20,
                    ' From: ', Supplier:5,
                    ' Now in stock: ',InStock:0:0);
    end;
  end;
  Close(ProductFile);
end.
```

Text Input and Output

Input and output of data in readable form is done through *text files* as described on page 101. A text file may be assigned to any device, i.e. a disk file or one of the standard I/O devices. Input and output on text files is done with the standard procedures *Read, Readln, Write,* and *Writeln* which use a special syntax for their parameter lists to facilitate maximum flexibility of input and output.

In particular, parameters may be of different types, in which case the I/O procedures provide automatic data conversion to and from the basic *Char* type of text files.

If the first parameter of an I/O procedure is a variable identifier representing a text file, then I/O will act on that file. If not, I/O will act on the standard files *Input* and *Output*. See page 105 for more detail.

Read Procedure

The *Read* procedure provides input of characters, strings, and numeric data. The syntax of the *Read* statement is:

```
    Read(Var1,Var2,...,VarN)
or
    Read(FilVar,Var1,Var2,...,VarN)
```

where *Var1, Var2,...,VarN* are variables of type *Char, String, Integer* or *Real*. In the first case, the variables are input from the standard file *Input*, usually the keyboard. In the second case, the variables are input from the text file which is previously assigned to *FilVar* and prepared for reading.

With a variable of type *Char, Read* reads one character from the file and assigns that character to the variable. If the file is a disk file, *Eoln* is true if the next character is a CR or a Ctrl-Z, and *Eof* is true if the next character is a Ctrl-Z, or physical end-of-file is met. If the file is a logical device (including the standard files *Input* and *Output*), *Eoln* is true if the character read was a CR or if *Eof* is *True*, and *Eof* is true if the character read was a Ctrl-Z.

With a variable of type **string**, *Read* reads as many characters as allowed by the defined maximum length of the string, unless *Eoln* or *Eof* is reached first. *Eoln* is true if the character read was a CR or if *Eof* is *True*, and *Eof* is true if the last character read is a Ctrl-Z, or physical end-of-file is met.

With a numeric variable (*Integer* or *Real*), *Read* expects a string of characters which complies with the format of a numeric constant of the relevant type as defined on page 43 . Any blanks, TABs, CRs, or LFs preceding the string are skipped. The string must be no longer than 30 characters, and it must be followed by a blank, a TAB, a CR, or a Ctrl-Z. If the string does not conform to the expected format, an I/O error occurs. Otherwise the numeric string is converted to a value of the appropriate type and assigned to the variable. When reading from a disk file, and the input string is ended with a blank or a TAB, the next *Read* or *Readln* will start with the character immediately following that blank or TAB. For both disk files and logical devices, *Eoln* is true if the string was ended with a CR or a Ctrl-Z, and *Eof* is true if the string was ended with a Ctrl-Z.

A special case of numeric input is when *Eoln* or *Eof* is true at the beginning of the *Read* (e.g. if input from the keyboard is only a CR). In that case no new value is assigned to the variable, and the variable retains its former value.

If the input file is assigned to the console device (CON:), or if the standard file *Input* is used in the { $B + } mode (default), special rules apply to the reading of variables. On a call to *Read* or *Readln*, a line is input from the console and stored into a buffer, and the reading of variables then uses this buffer as the input source. This allows for editing during entry. The following editing facilities are available:

BACKSPACE and DEL
Backspaces one character position and deletes the character there. BACKSPACE is usually generated by pressing the key marked BS or BACKSPACE or by pressing Ctrl-H. DEL is usually generated by the key thus marked, or in some cases RUB or RUBOUT.

Esc and Ctrl-X
Backspaces to the beginning of the line and erases all characters input.

Ctrl-D
Recalls one character from the last input line.

Ctrl-R
Recalls the last input line.

RETURN and **Ctrl-M**
Terminates the input line and stores an end-of-line marker (a CR/LF sequence) in the line buffer. This code is generated by pressing the key marked RETURN or ENTER. The CR/LF is **not** echoed to the screen.

Ctrl-Z
Terminates the input line and stores an end-of-file marker (a Ctrl-Z character) in the line buffer.

The input line is stored internally with a Ctrl-Z appended to the end of it. Thus, if fewer values are specified on the input line than the number of variables in *Read*s parameter list, any *Char* variables in excess will be set to Ctrl-Z, *Strings* will be empty, and numeric variables will remain unchanged.

The maximum number of characters that can be entered on an input line from the console is 127 by default. However, you may lower this limit by assigning an integer in the range 0 through 127 to the predefined variable *BufLen*.

Example:
```
Write('File name (max. 14 chars): ');
BufLen:=14;
Read(FileName);
```

Notice that assignments to *BufLen* affect only the immediately following *Read*. After that, *BufLen* is restored to 127.

Readln Procedure

The *Readln* procedure is identical to the *Read* procedure, except that after the last variable has been read, the remainder of the line is skipped. I.e., all characters up to and including the next CR/LF sequence (or the next CR on a logical device) are skipped. The syntax of the procedure statement is:

```
    Readln(Varl,Var2,...,VarN)
or
    Readln(FilVar,Varl,Var2,...,VarN)
```

After a *Readln*, the following *Read* or *Readln* will read from the beginning of the next line. *Readln* may also be called without parameters:

```
    Readln
or
    Readln(FilVar)
```

in which case the remaining of the line is skipped. When *Readln* is reading from the console (standard file *Input* or a file assigned to CON:), the terminating CR **is** echoed to the screen as a CR/LF sequence, as opposed to *Read*.

Write Procedure

The *Write* procedure provides output of characters, strings, boolean values, and numeric values. The syntax of a *Write* statement is:

Write(Var1,Var2,...,VarN)
or
Write(FilVar,Var1,Var2,...,VarN)

where *Var1, Var2,...,VarN* (the *write parameters*) are variables of type *Char, String, Boolean, Integer* or *Real*, optionally followed by a colon and an integer expression defining the width of the output field. In the first case, the variables are output to the the standard file *Output*, usually the screen. In the second case, the variables are output to the text file which is previously assigned to *FilVar*.

The format of a *write parameter* depends on the type of the variable. In the following descriptions of the different formats and their effects, the symbols:

I, m, n	denote *Integer* expressions,
R	denotes a *Real* expression,
Ch	denotes a *Char* expression,
S	denotes a *String* expression, and
B	denotes a *Boolean expression*.

Write Parameters

Ch   The character *Ch* is output.

Ch:n The character *Ch* is output right-adjusted in a field which is *n* characters wide, i.e. *Ch* is preceded by $n - 1$ blanks.

S   The string *S* is output. Arrays of characters may also be output, as they are compatible with strings.

S:n The string *S* is output right-adjusted in a field which is *n* characters wide, i.e. *S* is preceded by $n - Length(S)$ blanks.

B   Depending on the value of *B*, either the word TRUE or the word FALSE is output.

B:n Depending on the value of *B*, either the word TRUE or the word FALSE is output right-adjusted in a field which is *n* characters wide.

I   The decimal representation of the value of *I* is output.

I:n The decimal representation of the value of *I* is output right-adjusted in a field which is *n* characters wide.

R   The decimal representation of the value of *R* is output in a field 18 characters wide, using floating point format. For $R > = 0.0$, the format is:

    ␣␣#.##########E*##

For R $<$ 0.0, the format is:

    ␣-#.##########E*##

where ␣ represents a blank, # represents a digit, and * represents either plus or minus.

R:n The decimal representation of the value of *R* is output, right adjusted in a field *n* characters wide, using floating point format. For $R > = 0.0$:

    `blanks#.digitsE*##`

For *R* < 0.0:

```
blanks-#.digitsE*##
```

where *blanks* represents zero or more blanks, *digits* represents from one to ten digits, # represents a digit, and * represents either plus or minus. As at least one digit is output after the decimal point, the field width is minimum 7 characters (8 for *R* < 0.0).

R:n:m The decimal representation of the value of *R* is output, right adjusted, in a field *n* characters wide, using fixed point format with *m* digits after the decimal point. No decimal part, and no decimal point, is output if *m* is 0. *m* must be in the range 0 through 24; otherwise floating point format is used. The number is preceded by an appropriate number of blanks to make the field width n.

Writeln Procedure

The *Writeln* procedure is identical to the *Write* procedure, except that a CR/LF sequence is output after the last value. The syntax of the *Writeln* statement is:

Writeln(Var1,Var1,Var2,...,VarN) or *Writeln(FilVar,Var1,Var2,...,VarN)*

A *Writeln* with no write parameters outputs an empty line consisting of a CR/LF sequence:

Writeln or *Writeln(FilVar)*

Untyped Files

Untyped files are low-level I/O channels primarily used for direct access to any disk file using a record size of 128 bytes.

In input and output operations to untyped files, data is transferred directly between the disk file and the variable, thus saving the space required by the sector buffer required by typed files. An untyped file variable therefore occupies less memory than other file variables. As an untyped file is furthermore compatible with any file, the use of an untyped file is therefore to be preferred if a file variable is required only for *Erase*, *Rename* or other non-input/output operations.

An untyped file is declared with the reserved word **file**:

```
var
   DataFile: file;
```

BlockRead / BlockWrite

All standard file handling procedures and functions except *Read*, *Write*, and *Flush* are allowed on untyped files. *Read* and *Write* are replaced by two special high-speed transfer procedures: *BlockRead* and *BlockWrite*. The syntax of a call to these procedures is:

BlockRead(FilVar, Var, Recs)
BlockWrite(FilVar, Var, Recs)

or

BlockRead(FilVar, Var, Recs, Result)
BlockWrite(FilVar, Var, Recs, Result)

where *FilVar* variable identifier of an untyped file, *Var* is any variable, and *Recs* is an integer expression defining the number of 128-byte records to be transferred between the disk file and the variable. The **optional** parameter *Result* returns the number of records actually transferred.

The transfer starts with the first byte occupied by the variable *Var*. The programmer must insure that the variable *Var* occupies enough space to accommodate the entire data transfer. A call to *BlockRead* or *BlockWrite* also advances the file pointer *Recs* records.

A file to be operated on by *BlockRead* or *BlockWrite* must first be prepared by *Assign* and *Rewrite* or *Reset*. *Rewrite* creates and opens a new file, and *Reset* opens an existing file. After processing, *Close* should be used to ensure proper termination.

The standard function *EOF* works as with typed files. So do standard functions *FilePos* and *FileSize* and standard procedure *Seek*, using a component size of 128 bytes (the record size used by *BlockRead* and *BlockWrite*).

The following program uses untyped files to copy files of any type. Notice the use of the optional fourth parameter on *BlockRead* to check the number of records actually read from the source file.

```
program  FileCopy;
const
  RecSize    = 128;
  BufSize    = 200;
var
  Source, Dest: File;
  SourceName,
  DestName:       string[14];
  Buffer:         array[1..RecSize,1..BufSize] of Byte;
  RecsRead:       Integer;
begin
  Write('Copy from: ');
  Readln(SourceName);
  Assign(Source, SourceName);
  Reset(Source);
  Write('      To: ');
  Readln(DestName);
  Assign(Dest, DestName);
  Rewrite(Dest);
  repeat
    BlockRead(Source,Buffer,BufSize,RecsRead);
    BlockWrite(Dest,Buffer,RecsRead);
  until RecsRead = 0;
  Close(Source); Close(Dest);
end.
```

I/O checking

The I compiler directive is used to control generation of runtime I/O error checking code. The default state is active, i.e. { $I + } which causes calls to an I/O check routine after each I/O operation. I/O errors then cause the program to terminate, and an error message indicating the type of error is displayed.

If I/O checking is passive, i.e. { $I − }, no run time checks are performed. An I/O error thus does not cause the program to stop, but suspends any further I/O until the standard function *IOresult* is called. When this is done, the error condition is reset and I/O may be performed again. It is now the programmer's responsibility to take proper action according to the type of I/O error. A zero returned by *IOresult* indicates a successful operation, anything else means that an error occurred during the last I/O operation. Appendix G lists all error messages and their Numbers. **Notice** that as the error condition is reset when IOresult is called, subsequent calls to IOresult will return zero until the next I/O error occurs.

The *IOresult* function is very convenient in situations where a program halt is an unacceptable result of an I/O error, like in the following example which continues to ask for a file name until the attempt to reset the file is successful (i.e. until an existing file name is entered):

```pascal
procedure OpenInFile;
begin
  repeat
    Write('Enter name of input file ');
    Readln(InFileName);
    Assign(InFile, InFileName);
    {$I-} Reset(InFile) {$I+} ;
    OK := (IOresult = 0);
    if not OK then
      Writeln('Cannot find file ',InFileName);
  until OK;
end;
```

When the I directive is passive (({ $I-}), the following standard procedures should be followed by a check of IOresult to ensure proper error handling:

* Append	Close	Read	Seek
Assign	Erase	ReadLn	Write
BlockRead	Execute	Rename	WriteLn
BlockWrite	Flush	Reset	
Chain	* GetDir	Rewrite	
* ChDir	* MkDir	* RmDir	

* PC-DOS/MS-DOS only.

Notes:

Chapter 15
POINTER TYPES

Variables discussed up to now have been *static*, i.e. their form and size is pre-determined, and they exist throughout the entire execution of the block in which they are declared. Programs, however, frequently need the use of a data structure which varies in form and size during execution. *Dynamic* variables serve this purpose as they are generated as the need arises and may be discarded after use.

Such dynamic variables are not declared in an explicit variable declaration like static variables, and they cannot be referenced directly by identifiers. Instead, a special variable containing the memory address of the variable is used to *point* to the variable. This special variable is called a pointer variable.

Defining a Pointer Variable

A pointer type is defined by the pointer symbol ^ succeeded by the type *identifier* of the dynamic variables which may be referenced by pointer variables of this type.

The following shows how to declare a record with associated pointers. The type *PersonPointer* is is declared as a *pointer to* variables of type *PersonRecord*:

```
type
   PersonPointer = ^PersonRecord;
   PersonRecord = record
                    Name: string[50];
                    Job: string[50];
                    Next: PersonPointer;
                  end;
Var
   FirstPerson, LastPerson, NewPerson: PersonPointer;
```

The variables *FirstPerson, LastPerson* and *NewPerson* are thus *pointer variables* which can point at records of type *PersonRecord*. As shown above, the type identifier in a pointer type definition may refer to an identifier which is not yet defined.

Allocating Variables (New)

Before it makes any sense to use any of these pointer variables we must, of course, have some variables to point at. New variables of any type are allocated with the standard procedure *New*. The procedure has one parameter which must be a pointer to variables of the type we want to create.

A new variable of type *PersonRecord* can thus be created by the statement:

```
New(FirstPerson);
```

which has the effect of having *FirstPerson* point at a dynamically allocated record of type *PersonRecord*.

Assignments between pointer variables can be made as long as both pointers are of identical type. Pointers of identical type may also be compared using the relational operators = and < >, returning a *Boolean* result (*True* or *False*).

The pointer value **nil** is compatible with all pointer types. **nil** points to no dynamic variable, and may be assigned to pointer variables to indicate the absence of a usable pointer. **nil** may also be used in comparisons.

Variables created by the standard procedure *New* are stored in a stack-like structure called the *heap*. The TURBO Pascal system controls the heap by maintaining a heap pointer which at the beginning of a program is initialized to the address of the first free byte in memory. On each call to *New*, the heap pointer is moved towards the top of free memory the number of bytes corresponding to the size of the new dynamic variable.

Mark and Release

When a dynamic variable is no longer required by the program, the standard procedures *Mark* and *Release* are used to reclaim the memory allocated to these variables. The *Mark* procedure assigns the value of the heap pointer to a variable. The syntax of a call to *Mark* is:

```
Mark(Var);
```

where *Var* is a pointer variable. The *Release* procedure sets the heap pointer to the address contained in its argument. The syntax is:

```
Release(Var);
```

where *Var* is a pointer variable, previously set by *Mark*. *Release* thus discards *all* dynamic variables above this address, and cannot release the space used by variables in the middle of the heap. If you want to do that, you should use *Dispose* (see page 124) instead of *Mark/Release*.

The standard function *MemAvail* is available to determine the available space on the heap at any given time. Further discussion is deferred to chapters 20, 21, and 22.

Using Pointers

Supposing we have used the *New* procedure to create a series of records of type *PersonRecord* (as in the example on the following page) and that the field *Next* in each record points at the next *PersonRecord* created, then the following statements will go through the list and write the contents of each record (*FirstPerson* points to the first person in the list):

```
while FirstPerson <> nil do
with FirstPerson^ do
begin
  Writeln(Name,' is a ',Job);
  FirstPerson := Next;
end;
```

FirstPerson^.Name may be read as *FirstPerson's.Name*, i.e. the field *Name* in the record pointed to by *FirstPerson*.

The following demonstrates the use of pointers to maintain a list of names and related job desires. Names and job desires will be read in until a blank name is entered. Then the entire list is printed. Finally, the memory used by the list is released for other use. The pointer variable *HeapTop* is used only for the purpose of recording and storing the initial value of the heap pointer. Its definition as a ^Integer (pointer to integer) is thus totally arbitrary.

```pascal
procedure Jobs;
type
  PersonPointer = ^PersonRecord;

  PersonRecord = record
                   Name: string[50];
                   Job: string[50];
                   Next: PersonPointer;
                 end;
Var
  HeapTop: ^Integer;
  FirstPerson, LastPerson, NewPerson: PersonPointer;
  Name: string[50];
begin
    FirstPerson := nil;
  Mark(HeapTop);
  repeat
    Write('Enter name:        ');
    Readln(Name);
    if Name <> '' then
    begin
      New(NewPerson);
      NewPerson^.Name := Name;
      Write('Enter profession: ');
      Readln(NewPerson^.Job);
      Writeln;
      if FirstPerson = nil then
        FirstPerson := NewPerson
      else
        LastPerson^.Next := NewPerson;
      LastPerson := NewPerson;
      LastPerson^.Next := nil;
    end;
  until Name='';
  Writeln;
  while FirstPerson <> nil do
  with FirstPerson^ do
  begin
      Writeln(Name,' is a ',Job);
      FirstPerson := Next;
  end;
  Release(HeapTop);
end.
```

Dispose

Instead of *Mark* and *Release*, standard Pascal's *Dispose* procedure may be used to reclaim space on the heap.

NOTICE that *Dispose* and *Mark/Release* use entirely different approaches to heap management - **and never shall the twain meet!** Any one program must use **either** *Dispose* **or** *Mark/Release* to manage the heap. Mixing them will produce unpredictable results.

The syntax is:

```
Dispose(Var);
```

where *Var* is a pointer variable.

Dispose allows dynamic memory used *by a specific pointer variable* to be reclaimed for new use, as opposed to *Mark* and *Release* which releases the entire heap *from the specified pointer variable and upward.*

Suppose you have a number of variables which have been allocated on the heap. The following figure illustrates the contents of the heap and the effect of *Dispose(Var3)* and *Mark(Var3)/ Release(Var3)* :

```
            Heap            After          After
                           Dispose      Mark/Release

         |--------|       |--------|      |--------|
         |  Var1  |       |  Var1  |      |  Var1  |
         |--------|       |--------|      |--------|
         |  Var2  |       |  Var2  |      |  Var2  |
         |--------|       |--------|      |--------|
         |  Var3  |       |        |      |        |
         |--------|       |--------|      |--------|
         |  Var4  |       |  Var4  |      |        |
         |--------|       |--------|      |--------|
         |  Var5  |       |  Var5  |      |        |
         |--------|       |--------|      |--------|
         |  Var6  |       |  Var6  |      |        |
         |--------|       |--------|      |--------|
HiMem    |  Var7  |       |  Var7  |      |        |
```

Figure 15-1: Using Dispose

After *Disposing* a pointer variable, the heap may thus consist of a number of memory areas in use interspersed by a number of free areas. Subsequent calls to *New* will use these if the new pointer variable fits into the space.

GetMem

The standard procedure *GetMem* is used to allocate space on the heap. Unlike *New*, which allocates as much space as required by the **type** pointed to by its argument, *GetMem* allows the programmer to control the amount of space allocated. *GetMem* is called with two parameters:

```
GetMem(PVar, I)
```

where *PVar* is any pointer variable, and *I* is an integer expression giving the number of bytes to be allocated.

FreeMem

Syntax: FreeMem;

The *FreeMem* standard procedure is used to reclaim an entire block of space on the heap. It is thus the counterpart of *GetMem*. *FreeMem* is called with two parameters:

```
FreeMem(PVar, I);
```

where *PVar* is any pointer variable, and *I* is an integer expression giving the number of bytes to be reclaimed, which must be **exactly** the number of bytes previously allocated to that variable by *GetMem*.

MaxAvail

Syntax: MaxAvail;

The *MaxAvail* standard function returns the size of the largest consecutive block of free space on the heap. On 16-bit systems this space is in in number of *paragraphs* (16 bytes each); on 8-bit systems it is in bytes. The result is an *Integer*, and if more than 32767 paragraphs/bytes are available, *MaxAvail* returns a negative number. The correct number of free paragraphs/bytes is then calculated as 65536.0 + *MaxAvail*. Notice the use of a real constant to generate a *Real* result, as the result is greater than *MaxInt*.

Hints

Note that no range checking is done on pointers. It is the responsibility of the programmer to ensure that a pointer points to a legal address.

If you have difficulties using pointers, a drawing of what you are tempting to do often clears up things.

Chapter 16
PROCEDURES AND FUNCTIONS

A Pascal program consists of one or more *blocks*, each of which may again consist of blocks, etc. One such block is a *procedure*, another is a *function* (in common called *subprograms*). Thus, a procedure is a separate part of a program, and it is activated from elsewhere in the program by a *procedure statement* (see page 56). A function is rather similar, but it computes and returns a value when its identifier, or *designator*, is encountered during execution (see page 54).

Parameters

Values may be passed to procedures and functions through *parameters*. Parameters provide a substitution mechanism which allows the logic of the subprogram to be used with different initial values, thus producing different results.

The procedure statement or function designator which invokes the subprogram may contain a list of parameters, called the *actual parameters*. These are passed to the *formal parameters* specified in the subprogram *heading*. The order of parameter passing is the order of appearance in the parameter lists. Pascal supports two different methods of parameter passing: by *value* and by *reference*, which determines the effect that changes of the formal parameters have on the actual parameters.

When parameters are passed *by value*, the formal parameter represents a local variable in the subprogram, and changes of the formal parameters have no effect on the actual parameter. The actual parameter may be any expression, including a variable, with the same type as the corresponding formal parameter. Such parameters are called a *value parameter* and are declared in the subprogram heading as in the following example. This and the following examples show procedure headings; see page 137 for a description of function headings.

```
procedure Example(Num1,Num2: Number; Str1,Str2: Txt);
```

Number and *Txt* are previously defined types (e.g. *Integer* and **string**[255]), and *Num1, Num2, Str1,* and *Str2* are the *formal parameters* to which the value of the *actual parameters* are passed. The types of the formal and the actual parameters must correspond.

Notice that the type of the parameters in the parameter part must be specified as a previously defined *type identifier*. Thus, the construct:

```
procedure Select(Model: array[1..500] of Integer);
```

is **not** allowed. Instead, the desired type should be defined in the **type** definition of the block, and the *type identifier* should then be used in the parameter declaration:

```
type
   Range = array[1..500] of Integer;

procedure Select(Model: Range);
```

When a parameter is passed *by reference*, the formal parameter in fact represents the actual parameter throughout the execution of the subprogram. Any changes made to the formal parameter is thus made to the actual parameter, which must therefore be a *variable*. Parameters passed by reference are called a *variable parameters*, and are declared as follows:

```
procedure Example(Var Num1,Num2: Number)
```

Value parameters and variable parameters may be mixed in the same procedure as in the following example:

```
procedure Example(Var Num1,Num2: Number; Str1,Str2: Txt);
```

in which *Num1* and *Num2* are variable parameters and *Str1* and *Str2* are value parameters.

All address calculations are done at the time of the procedure call. Thus, if a variable is a component of an array, its index expression(s) are evaluated when the subprogram is called.

Notice that **file** parameters must always be declared as variable parameters.

When a large data structure, such as an array, is to be passed to a sub-program as a parameter, the use of a variable parameter will save both time and storage space, as the only information then passed on to the subprogram is the address of the actual parameter. A value parameter would require storage for an extra copy of the entire data structure, and the time involved in copying it.

Relaxations on Parameter Type Checking

Normally, when using variable parameters, the formal and the actual parameters must match exactly. This means that subprograms employing variable parameters of type *String* will accept only strings of the exact length defined in the subprogram. This restriction may be overridden by the **V** compiler directive. The default active state { $V + } indicates strict type checking, whereas the passive state { $V-} relaxes the type checking and allows actual parameters of any string length to be passed, irrespective of the length of the formal parameters.

Example:
```
program Encoder;
{$V-}
type
  WorkString = string[255];
Var
  Line1: string[80];
  Line2: string[100];
procedure Encode(Var LineToEncode: WorkString);
Var I: Integer;
begin
  for I := 1 to Length(LineToEncode) do
    LinetoEncode[I] := Chr(Ord(LineToEncode[I])-30);
end;
begin
  Line1 := 'This is a secret message';
  Encode(Line1);
  Line2 := 'Here is another (longer) secret message';
  Encode(Line2);
end.
```

Untyped Variable Parameters

If the type of a formal parameter is not defined, i.e. the type definition is omitted from the parameter section of the subprogram heading, then that parameter is said to be *untyped*. Thus, the corresponding actual parameter may be any type.

The untyped formal parameter itself is incompatible with all types, and may be used only in contexts where the data type is of no significance, for example as a parameter to *Addr, BlockRead/Write, FillChar,* or *Move,* or as the address specification of **absolute** variables.

The *SwitchVar* procedure in the following example demonstrates the use of untyped parameters. It moves the contents of the variable *A1* to *A2* and the contents of *A2* to *A1*.

```
procedure SwitchVar(Var Alp,A2p; Size: Integer);
type
  A = array[1..MaxInt] of Byte;
Var
  A1: A absolute Alp;
  A2: A absolute A2p;
  Tmp: Byte;
  Count: Integer;
begin
  for Count := 1 to Size do
  begin
    Tmp := A1[Count];
    A1[Count] := A2[Count];
    A2[Count] := Tmp;
  end;
end;
```

Assuming the declarations:

```
type
  Matrix = array[1..50,1..25] of Real;
Var
  TestMatrix,BestMatrix:  Matrix;
```

then *SwitchVar* may be used to switch values between the two matrices:

```
SwitchVar(TestMatrix,BestMatrix, SizeOf(Matrix));
```

Procedures

A procedure may be either pre-declared (or 'standard') or user-declared, i.e. declared by the programmer. Pre-declared procedures are parts of the TURBO Pascal system and may be called with no further declaration. A user-declared procedure may be given the name of a standard procedure; but that standard procedure then becomes inaccessible within the scope of the user declared procedure.

Procedure Declaration

A procedure declaration consists of a procedure heading followed by a block which consists of a declaration part and a statement part.

The procedure heading consists of the reserved word **procedure** followed by an identifier which becomes the name of the procedure, optionally followed by a formal parameter list as described on page 127 .

Examples:
```
procedure LogOn;
procedure Position(X,Y: Integer);
procedure Compute(Var Data: Matrix; Scale: Real);
```

The declaration part of a procedure has the same form as that of a program. All identifiers declared in the formal parameter list and the declaration part are local to that procedure, and to any procedures within it. This is called the *scope* of an identifier, outside which they are not known. A procedure may reference any constant, type, variable, procedure, or function defined in an outer block.

The statement part specifies the action to be executed when the the procedure is invoked, and it takes the form of a compound statement (see page 57). If the procedure identifier is used within the statement part of the procedure itself, the procedure will execute recursively. **(CP/M-80 only:** Notice that the **A** compiler directive must be passive { $A-} when recursion is used, see Appendix C.)

The next example shows a program which uses a procedure and passes a parameter to this procedure. As the actual parameter passed to the procedure is in some instances a constant (a simple expression), the formal parameter must be a value parameter.

```
program Box;
Var
  I: Integer;
procedure DrawBox(X1,Y1,X2,Y2: Integer);
  Var I: Integer;
  begin
    GotoXY(X1,Y1);
    for I := X1 to X2 do write('-');
    for I := Y1+1 to Y2 do
    begin
      GotoXY(X1,I); Write('!');
      GotoXY(X2,I); Write('!');
    end;
    GotoXY(X1,Y2);
    for I := X1 to X2 do Write('-');
  end; { of procedure DrawBox }
begin
  ClrScr;
  for I := 1 to 5 do DrawBox(I*4,I*2,10*I,4*I);
  DrawBox(1,1,80,23);
end.
```

Often the changes made to the formal parameters in the procedure should also affect the actual parameters. In such cases *variable parameters* are used, as in the following example:

```
procedure Switch(Var A,B: Integer);
Var Tmp: Integer;
begin
  Tmp := A; A := B; B := Tmp;
end;
```

When this procedure is called by the statement:

```
Switch(I,J);
```

the values of **I** and **J** will be switched. If the procedure heading in **Switch** was declared as:

```
procedure Switch(A,B: Integer);
```

i.e. with a *value* parameter, then the statement `Switch(I,J)` would **not** change *I* and *J*.

Standard Procedures

TURBO Pascal contains a number of standard procedures. These are:

1) string handling procedures (described on pages 71 pp),
2) file handling procedures (described on pages 94, 101, and 114).
3) procedures for allocation of dynamic variables (described on pages 120 and 125), and
4) input and output procedures (described on pages 108 pp).

In addition to these, the following standard procedures are available, provided that the associated commands have been installed for your terminal (see pages 12 pp):

ClrEol

Syntax: ClrEol;

Clears all characters from the cursor position to the end of the line without moving the cursor.

ClrScr

Syntax: ClrScr;

Clears the screen and places the cursor in the upper left-hand corner. Beware that some screens also reset the video-attributes when clearing the screen, possibly disturbing any user-set attributes.

CrtInit

Syntax: CrtInit;

Sends the *Terminal Initialization String* defined in the installation procedure to the screen.

CrtExit

Syntax: CrtExit;

Sends the *Terminal Reset String* defined in the installation procedure to the screen.

Delay

Syntax: Delay(*Time*);

The *Delay* procedure creates a loop which runs for approx. as many milliseconds as defined by its argument *Time* which must be an integer. The exact time may vary somewhat in different operating environments.

DelLine

Syntax: DelLine;

Deletes the line containing the cursor and moves all lines below one line up.

InsLine

Syntax: InsLine;

Inserts an empty line at the cursor position. All lines below are moved one line down and the bottom line scrolls off the screen.

GotoXY

Syntax: GotoXY(*Xpos, Ypos*);

Moves the cursor to the position on the screen specified by the integer expressions *Xpos* (horizontal value, or *row*) and *Ypos* (vertical value, or *column*). The upper left corner (home position) is (1,1).

Exit

Syntax: Exit;

Exits the current block. When exit is executed in a subroutine, it causes the subroutine to return. When it is executed in the statement part of a program, it causes the program to terminate. A call to *Exit* may be compared to a **goto** statement addressing a label just before the **end** of a block.

Halt

Syntax: Halt;

Stops program execution and returns to the operating system.

In PC/MS-DOS, *Halt* may optionally pass a integer parameter specifying the return code of the program. *Halt* without a parameter corresponds to *Halt(O)*. The return code may be examined by the parent process using an MS-DOS system function call or through an ERRORLEVEL test in an MS-DOS batch file.

LowVideo

Syntax: LowVideo;

Sets the screen to the video attribute defined as 'Start of Low Video' in the installation procedure, i.e. 'dim' characters.

NormVideo

Syntax: NormVideo;

Sets the screen to the video attribute defined as 'Start of Normal Video' in the installation procedure, i.e. the 'normal' screen mode.

Randomize

Syntax: Randomize;

Initializes the random number generator with a random value.

Move

Syntax: Move(*var1*,*var2*,*Num*);

Does a mass copy directly in memory of a specified number of bytes. *var1* and *var2* are two variables of any type, and *Num* is an integer expression. The procedure copies a block of *Num* bytes, starting at the first byte occupied by *var1* to the block starting at the first byte occupied by *var2*. You may notice the absence of explicit 'moveright' and 'moveleft' procedures. This is because *Move* automatically handles possible overlap during the move process.

FillChar

Syntax: FillChar(*Var, Num, Value*);

Fills a range of memory with a given value. *Var* is a variable of any type, *Num* is an integer expression, and *Value* is an expression of type *Byte* or *Char*. *Num* bytes, starting at the first byte occupied by *Var*, are filled with the value *Value*.

Functions

Like procedures, functions are either standard (pre-declared) or declared by the programmer.

Function Declaration

A function declaration consists of a function *heading* and a *block* which is a declaration part followed by a statement part.

The function heading is equivalent to the procedure heading, except that the heading must define the *type* of the function result. This is done by adding a colon and a type to the heading as shown here:

```
function KeyHit: Boolean;
function Compute(Var Value: Sample): Real;
function Power(X,Y: Real): Real;
```

The result type of a function must be a scalar type (i.e. *Integer, Real, Boolean, Char,* declared scalar or subrange), a **string** type, or a pointer type.

The declaration part of a function is the same as that of a procedure.

The statement part of a function is a compound statement as described on page 57 . Within the statement part at least one statement assigning a value to the function identifier must occur. The last assignment executed determines the result of the function. If the function designator appears in the statement part of the function itself, the function will be invoked recursively. **(CP/M-80 only:** Notice that the **A** compiler directive must be passive { $A-} when recursion is used, see Appendix C.)

The following example shows the use of a function to compute the sum of a row of integers from **I** to **J**.

```
function RowSum(I,J: Integer): Integer;
  function SimpleRowSum(S: Integer): Integer;
  begin
    SimpleRowSum := S*(S+1) div 2;
  end;
begin
  RowSum := SimpleRowSum(J)-SimpleRowSum(I-1);
end;
```

The function *SimpleRowSum* is nested within the function *RowSum*. *SimpleRowSum* is therefore only available within the scope of *RowSum*.

The following program is the classical demonstration of the use of a recursive function to calculate the factorial of an integer number:

```
{$A-} {A- directive allows recursion in CP/M-80 version}
program Factorial;
Var Number: Integer;
function Factorial(Value: Integer): Real;
begin
  if Value = 0  then Factorial := 1
  else Factorial := Value * Factorial(Value-1);
end;
begin
  Read(Number);
  Writeln(^M,Number,'! = ',Factorial(Number));
end.
```

Note that the type used in the definition of a function type must be previously specified as a *type identifier*. Thus, the construct:

```
function LowCase(Line: UserLine): string[80];
```

is **not** allowed. Instead, a type identifier should be associated with the type *string[80]*, and that type identifier should then be used to define the function result type, for example:

```
type
  Str80 = string[80];
```

```
function LowCase(Line: UserLine): Str80;
```

Because of the implementation of the standard procedures *Write* and *Writeln*, a function using any of the standard procedures *Read, Readln, Write,* or *Writeln,* must **never** be called by an expression within a *Write* or *Writeln* statement. In 8-bit systems this is also true for the standard procedures *Str* and *Val.*

Standard Functions

The following standard (pre-declared) functions are implemented in TURBO Pascal:

1) string handling functions (described on pages 71 pp),
2) file handling functions (described on pages 94 and 101),
3) pointer related functions (described on pages 120 and 125).

Arithmetic Functions

Abs

Syntax: Abs(*Num*);

Returns the absolute value of *Num.* The argument *Num* must be either *Real* or *Integer,* and the result is of the same type as the argument.

ArcTan

Syntax: ArcTan(*Num*);

Returns the angle, in radians, whose tangent is *Num.* The argument *X* must be either *Real* or *Integer,* and the result is *Real.*

Cos

Syntax: Cos(*Num*);

Returns the cosine of *Num.* The argument *Num* is expressed in radians, and its type must be either *Real* or *Integer.* The result is of type *Real.*

Exp

Syntax: Exp(*Num*);

Returns the exponential of *Num*, i.e. *enum*. The argument *Num* must be either *Real* or *Integer*, and the result is *Real*.

Frac

Syntax: Frac(*Num*);

Returns the fractional part of *Num*, i.e. Frac(*Num*) = *Num* - Int(*Num*). The argument *Num* must be either *Real* or *Integer*, and the result is *Real*.

Int

Syntax: Int(*Num*);

Returns the integer part of *Num*, i.e. the greatest integer number less than or equal to *Num*, if *Num* $> =$ 0, or the smallest integer number greater than or equal to *Num*, if *Num* $<$ 0. The argument *Num* must be either *Real* or *Integer*, and the result is *Real*.

Ln

Syntax: Ln(*Num*);

Returns the natural logarithm of *Num*. The argument *Num* must be either *Real* or *Integer*, and the result is *Real*.

Sin

Syntax: Sin(*Num*);

Returns the sine of *Num*. The argument *Num* is expressed in radians, and its type must be either *Real* or *Integer*. The result is of type *Real*.

Sqr

Syntax: Sqr(*Num*);

Returns the square of *Num*, i.e. *Num* * *Num*. The argument *Num* must be either *Real* or *Integer*, and the result is of the same type as the argument.

Sqrt

Syntax: Sqrt(*Num*);

Returns the square root of *Num*. The argument *Num* must be either *Real* or *Integer*, and the result is *Real*.

Scalar Functions

Pred

Syntax: Pred(*Num*);

Returns the predecessor of *Num* (if it exists). *Num* is of any scalar type.

Succ

Syntax: Succ(*Num*);

Returns the successor of *Num* (if it exists). *Num* is of any scalar type.

Odd

Syntax: Odd(*Num*);

Returns boolean *True* is *Num* is an odd number, and *False* if *Num* is even. *Num* must be of type *Integer*.

Transfer Functions

The transfer functions are used to convert values of one scalar type to that of another scalar type. In addition to the following functions, the *retype* facility described on page 65 serves this purpose.

Chr

Syntax: Chr(*Num*);

Returns the character with the ordinal value given by the integer expression *Num*. Example: *Chr(65)* returns the character 'A'.

Ord

Syntax: Ord(*Var*);

Returns the ordinal number of the value *Var* in the set defined by the type *Var*. *Ord(Var)* is equivalent to *Integer(Var)* (see Type Conversions on page 65. *Var* may be of any scalar type, except *Real*, and the result is of type *Integer*.

Round

Syntax: Round(*Num*);

Returns the value of *Num* rounded to the nearest integer as follows: if *Num* $> = 0$, then *Round(Num) = Trunc(Num + 0.5)*, and if *Num* $<$ 0, then *Round(Num) = Trunc(Num − 0.5)* *Num* must be of type *Real*, and the result is of type *Integer*.

Trunc

Syntax: Trunc(*Num*);

Returns the greatest integer less than or equal to *Num*, if *Num* $> = 0$, or the smallest integer greater than or equal to *Num*, if *Num* $<$ 0. *Num* must be of type *Real*, and the result is of type *Integer*.

Miscellaneous Standard Functions

Hi

Syntax: Hi(*I*);

The low order byte of the result contains the high order byte of the value of the integer expression *I*. The high order byte of the result is zero. The type of the result is *Integer*.

KeyPressed

Syntax: KeyPressed

Returns boolean *True* if a key has been pressed at the console, and *False* if no key has been pressed. The result is obtained by calling the operating system console status routine.

Lo

Syntax: Lo(*I*);

Returns the low order byte of the value of the integer expression *I* with the high order byte forced to zero. The type of the result is *Integer*.

Random

Syntax: Random;

Returns a random number greater than or equal to zero and less than one. The type is *Real*.

Random(Num)

Syntax: Random(*Num*);

Returns a random number greater than or equal to zero and less than *Num*. *Num* and the random number are both *Integers*.

ParamCount

Syntax: ParamCount;

This integer function returns the number of parameters passed to the program in the command line buffer. Space and tab characters serve as separators.

ParamStr

Syntax: ParamStr(*N*);

This string function returns the *N*th parameter from the command line buffer.

SizeOf

Syntax: SizeOf(*Name*);

Returns the number of bytes occupied in memory by the variable or type *Name*. The result is of type *Integer*.

Swap

Syntax: Swap(*Num*);

The Swap function exchanges the high and low order bytes of its integer argument *Num* and returns the resulting value as an integer.

Example:
Swap($1234)   returns *$3412* (values in hex for clarity).

UpCase

Syntax: UpCase(*ch*);

Returns the uppercase equivalent of its argument *ch* which must be of type *Char*. If no uppercase equivalent exists, the argument is returned unchanged.

Forward References

A subprogram is **forward** declared by specifying its heading separately from the block. This separate subprogram heading is exactly as the normal heading, except that it is terminated by the reserved word **forward**. The block follows later within the same declaration part. Notice that the block is initiated by a copy of the heading, specifying only the name and no parameters, types, etc.

Example:
```
program Catch22;
Var
  X: Integer;
function Up(Var I: Integer): Integer; forward;
function Down(Var I: Integer): Integer;
begin
  I := I div 2; Writeln(I);
  if I <> 1 then I := Up(I);
end;
function Up;
begin
  while I mod 2 <> 0  do
  begin
    I := I*3+1; Writeln(I);
  end;
  I := Down(I);
end;
begin
  Write('Enter any integer: ');
  Readln(X);
  X := Up(X);
  Write('Ok. Program stopped again.');
end.
```

When the program is executed and if you enter e.g. *6* it outputs:

```
3
10
5
16
8
4
2
1
Ok. Program stopped again.
```

The above program is actually a more complicated version of the following program:

```
program Catch222;
Var
  X: Integer;
begin
  Write('Enter any integer: ');
  Readln(X);
  while X <> 1 do
  begin
    if X mod 2 = 0 then X := X div 2 else X := X*3+1;
    Writeln(X);
  end;
  Write('Ok. Program stopped again.');
end.
```

It may interest you to know that it cannot be proved if this small and very simple program actually **will** stop for any integer!

Chapter 17
INCLUDING FILES

The fact that the TURBO editor performs editing only within memory limits the size of source code handled by the editor. The I compiler directive can be used to circumvent this restriction, as it provides the ability to split the source code into smaller 'lumps' and put it back together at compile-time. The include facility also aids program clarity, as commonly used subprograms, once tested and debugged, may be kept as a 'library' of files from which the necessary files can be included in any other program.

The syntax for the I compiler directive is:

```
{$I filename}
```

where *filename* is any legal file name. Leading spaces are ignored and lower case letters are translated to upper case. If no file type is specified, the default type **.PAS** is assumed. This directive must be specified on a line by itself.

Examples:
```
{$Ifirst.pas}
{$I COMPUTE.MOD}
{$iStdProc }
```

Notice that a space must be left between the file name and the closing brace if the file does not have a three-letter extension; otherwise the brace will be taken as part of the name.

To demonstrate the use of the include facility, let us assume that in your 'library' of commonly used procedures and functions you have a file called *STUPCASE.FUN*. It contains the function *StUpCase* which is called with a character or a string as parameter and returns the value of this parameter with any lower case letters set to upper case.

File *STUPCASE.FUN:*

```
function StUpCase(St: AnyString): AnyString;
Var I: Integer;
begin
  for I := 1 to Length(St) do
    St[I] := UpCase(St[I]);
  StUpCase := St
end;
```

In any future program you write which requires this function to convert strings to upper case letters, you need only include the file at compile-time instead of duplicating it into the source code:

```
program Include Demo;
type
  InData= string[80];
  AnyString= string[255];
Var
  Answer: InData;
{$I STUPCASE.FUN}
begin
  ReadLn(Answer);
  Writeln(StUpCase(Answer));
end.
```

This method not only is easier and saves space; it also makes program updating quicker and safer, as any change to a 'library' routine will automatically affect all programs including this routine.

Notice that TURBO Pascal allows free ordering, and even multiple occurrences, of the individual sections of the declaration part. You may thus e.g. have a number of files containing various commonly used **type** definitions in your 'library' and include the ones required by different programs.

All compiler directives except **B** and **C** are local to the file in which they appear, i.e. if a compiler directive is set to a different value in an included file, it is reset to its original value upon return to the including file. **B** and **C** directives are always global. Compiler directives are described in Appendix C.

Include files cannot be nested, i.e. one include file cannot include yet another file and then continue processing.

Chapter 18
OVERLAY SYSTEM

The overlay system lets you create programs much larger than can be accommodated by the computer's memory. The technique is to collect a number of subprograms (procedures and functions) in one or more files separate from the main program file, which will then be loaded automatically one at a time into the **same** area in memory.

The following drawing shows a program using one overlay file with five overlay subprograms collected into one **overlay group**, thus sharing the same memory space in the main program:

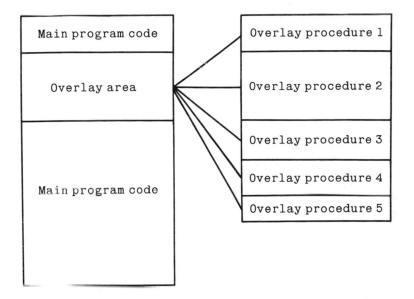

Figure 18-1 Principle of Overlay System

When an overlay procedure is called, it is automatically loaded into the overlay area reserved in the main program. This 'gap' is large enough to accommodate the largest of the overlays in the group. The space required by the main program is thus reduced by roughly the sum of all subprograms in the group less the largest of them.

In the example above, overlay procedure 2 is the largest of the five procedures and thus determines the size of the overlay area in the main code. When it is loaded into memory, it occupies the entire overlay area:

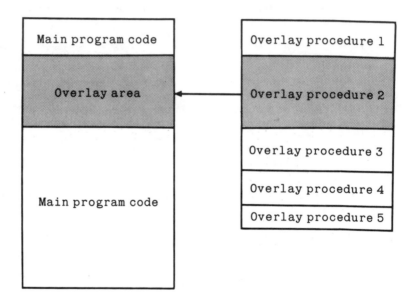

Figure 18-2: Largest Overlay Subprogram Loaded

The smaller subprograms are loaded into the same area of memory, each starting at the first address of the overlay area. Obviously they occupy only part of the overlay area; the remainder is unused:

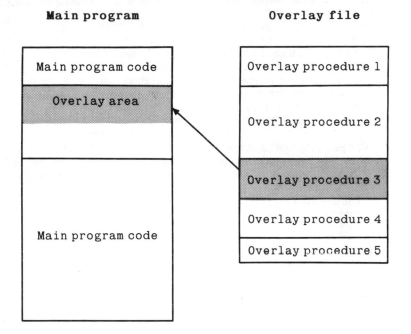

Figure 18-3: Smaller Overlay Subprogram Loaded

As procedures 1, 3, 4, and 5 execute in the same space as used by procedure 2, it is clear that they require no additional space in the main program. It is also clear that none of these procedures must ever call each other, as they are never present in memory simultaneously.

There could be many more overlay procedures in this group of overlays; in fact the total size of the overlay procedures could substantially exceed the size of the main program. And they would still require only the space occupied by the largest of them.

The tradeoff for this extra room for program code is the addition of disk access time each time a procedure is read in from the disk. With good planning, as discussed on page 155, this time is negligible.

Creating Overlays

Overlay subprograms are created automatically, simply by adding the reserved word **overlay** to the declaration of any procedure or function:

```
overlay procedure Initialize;
```
and
```
overlay function TimeOfDay: Time;
```

When the compiler meets such a declaration, code is no longer output to the main program file, but to a separate overlay file. The name of this file will be the same as that of the main program, and the type will be a number designating the overlay group, ranging form 000 through 099.

Consecutive overlay subprograms will be grouped together. I.e. as long as overlay subprograms are not separated by any other declaration, they belong to the same group and are placed in the same overlay file.

Example 1:
```
overlay procedure One;
begin
  :
end;

overlay procedure Two;
begin
  :
end;

overlay procedure Three;
begin
  :
end;
```

These three overlay procedures will be grouped together and placed in the same overlay file. If they are the first group of overlay subprograms in a program, the overlay file will be no. *000*.

The three overlay procedures in the following example will be placed in consecutive overlay files, *.000* and *.001*, because of the declaration of a non-overlay procedure *Count* separating overlay procedures *Two* and *Three*.

The separating declaration may be any declaration, for example a dummy **type** declaration, if you want to force a separation of overlay areas.

Example 2:
```
overlay procedure One;
begin
   :
end;

overlay procedure Two;
begin
   :
end;

procedure Count;
begin
   :
end

overlay procedure Three;
begin
   :
end;
```

A separate overlay area is reserved in the main program code for each overlay group, and the following files will be created:

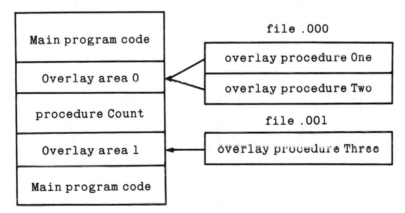

Figure 18-4: Multiple Overlay Files

Nested Overlays

Overlay subprograms may be nested, i.e. an overlay subprogram may itself contain overlay subprograms which may contain overlay subprograms, etc.

Example 3:
```
program OverlayDemo;
  :
  :
overlay procedure One;
begin
  :
end;

overlay procedure Two;
  overlay procedure Three;
  begin
    :
  end;
begin
  :
end;
  :
```

In this example, two overlay files will be created. File *.000* contains overlay procedures *One* and *Two*, and an overlay area is reserved in the main program to accommodate the largest of these. Overlay file *.001* contains overlay procedure *Three* which is local to overlay procedure *Two*, and an overlay area is created in the code of overlay procedure *Two*:

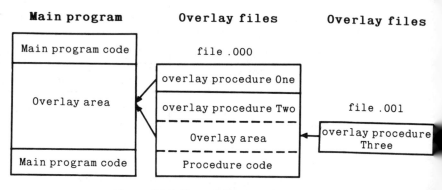

Figure 18-5: Nested Overlay Files

Automatic Overlay Management

An overlay subprogram is loaded into memory only when called. On each call to an overlay subprogram, a check is first made to see if that subprogram is already present in the overlay area. If not, it will automatically be read in from the appropriate overlay file.

Placing Overlay Files

During compilation, overlay files will be placed on the logged drive, i.e. on the same drive as the main program file (.COM or .CMD file).

During execution, the system normally expects to find its overlay files on the logged drive. This may be changed as described on pages 196 (PC/MS-DOS), 233 (CP/M-86), and 265 (CP/M-80).

Efficient Use of Overlays

The overlay technique, of course, adds overhead to a program by adding some extra code to manage the overlays, and by requiring disk accesses during execution. Overlays, therefore, should be carefully planned.

In order not to slow down execution excessively, an overlay subprogram should not be called too often, or - if one **is** called often - it should at least be called without intervening calls to other subprograms in the same overlay file in order to keep disk accesses at a minimum. The added time will of course vary greatly, depending on the actual disk configuration. A 5 1/4" floppy will add much to the run-time, a hard disk much less, and a RAM-disk, as used by many, very little.

To save as much space as possible in the main program, one group of overlays should contain as many individual subprograms as possible. From a pure space-saving point of view, the more subprograms you can put into a single overlay file, the better. The overlay space used in the main program needs only accommodate the largest of these subprograms - the rest of the subprograms have a free ride in the same area of memory. This must be weighed against the time considerations discussed above.

Restrictions Imposed on Overlays

Data Area

Overlay subprograms in the same group share the same area in memory and thus cannot be present simultaneously. They must therefore **not** call each other. Consequently, they may share the same data area which further adds to the space saved when using overlays (CP/M-80 version only).

In example 1 on page 152, none of the procedures may therefore call each other. In example 2, however, overlay procedures *One* and *Two* may call overlay procedure *Three*, and overlay procedure *Three* may call each of the other two, because they are in separate files and consequently in separate overlay areas in the main program.

Forward Declarations

Overlay subprograms may not be **forward** declared. This restriction is easily circumvented, however, by **forward** declaring an ordinary subprogram which then in turn calls the overlay subprogram.

Recursion

Overlay subprograms cannot be recursive. Also this restriction may be circumvented by declaring an ordinary recursive subprogram which then in turn calls the overlay subprogram.

Run-Time Errors

Run-time errors occurring in overlays are found as usual, and an address is issued by the error handling system. This address, however, is an address within the overlay area, and there is no way of knowing which overlay subprogram was actually active when the error occurred.

Run-time errors in overlays can therefore not always be readily found with the Options menu's 'Find run-time error' facility. What 'Find run-time error' will point out is the first occurrence of code at the specified address. This, of course, **may** be the place of the error, but the error may as well occur in a subsequent subprogram within the same overlay group.

This it not a serious limitation, however, as the type of error and the way it occurs will most often indicates in which subprogram the error happened. The way to locate the error precisely is then to place the suspected subprogram as the first subprogram of the overlay group. 'Find run-time error' will then work.

The best thing to do is not to place subprograms in overlays until they have been fully debugged!

Notes:

Chapter 19
IBM PC GOODIES

This chapter applies to the IBM PC-versions only, and the functions described can be expected to work on IBM PC and compatibles only! If you have problems on a compatible, it's not as compatible as you thought.

Screen Mode Control
TURBO provides a number of procedures to control the PC's various screen modes.

Windows
The window routines let you declare a smaller part of the screen to be your actual work area, protecting the rest of the screen from being overwritten.

Basic graphics
These built-in graphics routines let you plot points and draw lines in different colors.

Extended graphics
A set of external graphics routines allow for more advanced graphics. One simple statement includes these routines in your programs.

Turtlegraphics
The same external machine language file also provides you with turtle-graphics routines.

Sound
Standard procedures are provided which let you use the PC's sound capabilities in an easy way.

Keyboard
A number of the special keys of the IBM keyboard are installed as primary commands for the editor. These commands are listed on page 186, and you may add more if you wish. The secondary *WordStar* commands are still available.

Screen Mode Control

The IBM PC gives you a choice of screen modes, each with its own characteristics. Some display characters, some display graphics, and they all have different capabilities of showing colors. TURBO Pascal supports all these screen formats and provides an easy way of using them.

The following screen modes are available:

TextMode   25 lines of 40 or 80 characters
GraphColorMode   320x200 dots color graphics
GraphMode   320x200 dots black & white graphics (color on an RGB monitor)
HiRes   640x200 dots black + one color graphics

Text Modes

In text mode, the PC will display 25 lines of either 40 or 80 characters. The procedure to invoke this mode is named *TextMode* and is called as follows:

```
TextMode;
TextMode(BW40);    BW40 is an integer constant with the value 0
TextMode(C40);     C40 is an integer constant with the value 1
TextMode(BW80);    BW80 is an integer constant with the value 2
TextMode(C80);     C80 is an integer constant with the value 3
```

The first example with no parameters invokes the text mode which was active last, or the one that is currently active. The next two examples activate black and white text modes with 40 and 80 characters on each line. The final two examples activate color text modes with 40 and 80 characters on each line. Calling *TextMode* will clear the screen.

TextMode should be called before exiting a graphics program in order to return the system to text mode.

Color Modes

In the color text modes, each character may be chosen to be one of 16 colors, and the background may be one of 8 colors. The colors are referred to by the numbers 0 through 15. To make things easier, TURBO Pascal includes 16 pre-defined integer constants which may be used to identify colors by names:

Dark colors	Light colors
0: Black	**8**: DarkGray
1: Blue	**9**: LightBlue
2: Green	**10**: LightGreen
3: Cyan	**11**: LightCyan
4: Red	**12**: LightRed
5: Magenta	**13**: LightMagenta
6: Brown	**14**: Yellow
7: LightGray	**15**: White

Table 19-1: Text Mode Color Scale

Characters may be any of these colors, whereas the background may be any of the dark colors. Notice that some monitors do not recognize the intensity signal used to create the eight light colors. On such monitors, the light colors will be displayed as their dark equivalents.

TextColor

Syntax: TextColor(*Color*);

This procedure selects color of the **characters**. *Color* is an integer expression in the range 0 through 15, selecting character colors from the table given above.

Examples:
```
TextColor(1);              selects blue characters
TextColor(Yellow);         selects yellow characters
```

The characters may be made to blink by adding 16 to the color number. There is a pre-defined constant *Blink* for this purpose:

```
TextColor(Red + Blink);    selects red, blinking characters
```

TextBackground

> **Syntax:** TextBackground(*Color*);
>
> This procedure selects color of the **background**, that is, the cell immediately surrounding each character; the entire screen consists of 40 or 80 by 25 such cells. *Color* is an integer expression in the range 0 through 7, selecting character colors from the table given above.
>
> **Examples:**
> ```
> TextBackground(4);           selects red background
> TextBackground(Magenta);     selects magenta background
> ```

Cursor Position

> In text mode, two functions will tell you where the cursor is positioned on the screen:

WhereX

> **Syntax:** WhereX;
>
> This integer function returns the X-coordinate of the current cursor position.

WhereY

> **Syntax:** WhereY;
>
> This integer function returns the Y-coordinate of the current cursor position.

Graphics Modes

With a standard IBM graphics video board, or one that is compatible, TURBO will do graphics. Three modes are supported:

GraphColorMode   320x200 dots color graphics
GraphMode   320x200 dots black & white graphics
HiRes   640x200 dots black + one color graphics

The upper, left corner of the screen is coordinate 0,0. X coordinates stretch to the right, Y coordinates downward. All drawing is 'clip-ped', that is, anything displayed outside the screen will be ignored (except when the turtlegraphics' *Wrap* is in effect).

Activating one of the graphics modes will clear the screen. The standard procedure *ClrScr* works only in text mode, so the way to clear a graphics screen is to activate a graphics mode, possibly the one that's already active. With extended graphics and turtlegraphics, however, there is a *ClearScreen* procedure which clears the active window.

Graphics can be mixed with text. In 320 x 200 modes, the screen can display 40 x 25 characters and in 640 x 200 mode, it can display 80 x 25 characters.

The *TextMode* procedure should be called before exiting a graphics program in order to return the system to text mode, see page 160).

GraphColorMode

Syntax: GraphColorMode;

This standard procedure activates the 320x200 dots color graphics screen giving you X-coordinates between 0 and 319 and Y-coordinates between 0 and 199. Drawings may use colors selected from the palette described on page 165.

GraphMode

Syntax: GraphMode;

This standard procedure activates the 320x200 dots black and white graphics screen giving you X-coordinates between 0 and 319 and Y-coordinates between 0 and 199. On a RGB monitor like the IBM Color/Graphics Display, however, even this mode displays colors from a limited palette as shown on page 166.

HiRes

Syntax: HiRes;

This standard procedure activates the 640x200 dots high resolution graphics screen giving you X-coordinates between 0 and 639 and Y-coordinates between 0 and 199. In high resolutions graphics, the background (screen) is always black, and you draw in one color set by the *HiResColor* standard procedure.

HiResColor

Syntax: HiResColor(*Color*);

This standard procedure selects the color used for drawing in high resolution graphics. *Color* is an integer expression in the range 0 through 15. The background (screen) is always black. Changing *HiResColor* causes anything already on the screen to change to the new color.

Examples:
```
HiResColor(7);              selects light gray
HiResColor(Blue);           selects blue
```

This one color may be chosen from the following 16 colors:

Dark colors	Light colors
0: Black	**8**: DarkGray
1: Blue	**9**: LightBlue
2: Green	**10**: LightGreen
3: Cyan	**11**: LightCyan
4: Red	**12**: LightRed
5: Magenta	**13**: LightMagenta
6: Brown	**14**: Yellow
7: LightGray	**15**: White

Table 19-2: High Resolution Graphics Color Scale

Some monitors do not recognize the intensity signal used to create the eight light colors. On such monitors, the light colors will be dis-played as their dark equivalents.

Palette

Syntax: Palette(*N*);

This procedure activates the color palette indicated by the integer expression *N*. with a parameter specifying the number of the palette. Four color palettes exist, each containing three colors (1-3) and a fourth color (0) which is always equal to the background color (see later):

Color number:	0	1	2	3
Palette 0	Background	Green	Red	Brown
Palette 1	Background	Cyan	Magenta	LightGray
Palette 2	Background	LightGreen	LightRed	Yellow
Palette 3	Background	LightCyan	LightMagenta	White

Table 19-3: Color Palettes in Color Graphics

The graphics routines will use colors from this palette. They are called with a parameter in the range 0 through 3, and the color actually used is selected from the active palette:

`Plot(X,Y,2)`   will plot a red point when palette 0 is active.
`Plot(X,Y,3)`   will plot a yellow point when palette 2 is active.
`Plot(X,Y,0)`   will plot a point in the active background color, in effect erasing that point.

Once a drawing is on the screen, a change of palette will cause all colors on the screen to change to the colors of the new palette. Only three colors plus the color of the background may thus be displayed simultaneously.

The *GraphMode* supposedly displays only black and white graphics, but on on an RGB monitor, like the IBM Color/Graphics Display, even this mode displays the following limited palette:

Color number:	0	1	2	3
Palette 0	Background	Blue	Red	LightGray
Palette 1	Background	LightBlue	LightRed	White

Table 19-4: Color Palettes in B/W Graphics

GraphBackground

Syntax: GraphBackground(*Color*);

This standard procedure sets the the background color, that is the entire screen, to any of 16 colors. *Color* is an integer expression in the range 0 through 1

`GraphBackground(0);`   sets the screen to black
`GraphBackground(11);`   sets the screen to light cyan

The following color numbers and pre-defined constants are available:

Dark colors	Light colors
0: Black	**8**: DarkGray
1: Blue	**9**: LightBlue
2: Green	**10**: LightGreen
3: Cyan	**11**: LightCyan
4: Red	**12**: LightRed
5: Magenta	**13**: LightMagenta
6: Brown	**14**: Yellow
7: LightGray	**15**: White

Table 19-5: Graphics Background Color Scale

Some monitors do not recognize the intensity signal used to create the eight light colors. On such monitors, the light colors will be displayed as their dark equivalents.

Windows

TURBO Pascal lets you declare windows anywhere on the screen. When you write in such a window, the window behaves exactly as if you were using the entire screen, leaving the rest of the screen untouched.

Text Windows

The *Window* procedure allows you to define any area on the screen as the active window in text mode:

```
Window(X1,Y1,X2,Y2);
```

where X1 and Y1 are the absolute coordinates of the upper left corner of the window, X2 and Y2 are the absolute coordinates of the lower right corner. The minimum size of the text window is 2 columns by 2 lines.

The default window is *1,1,80,25* in 80-column modes and *1,1,40,25* in 40-column modes, that is, the entire screen.

All screen coordinates (except the window coordinates themselves) are relative to the active window. This means that after the statement:

```
Window(20,8,60,17);
```

which defines the center portion of the physical screen to be your active window, screen coordinates 1,1 (upper left corner) are now the upper left corner of the *window*, not of the physical screen:

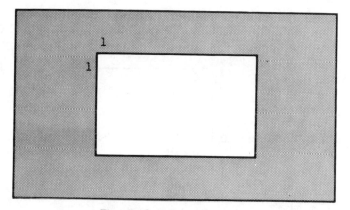

Figure 19-1: Text Windows

The screen outside the window is simply not accessible, and the window behaves as it were the entire screen. You may insert, delete, and scroll lines, and lines will wrap around if too long.

Graphics Windows

The *GraphWindow* procedure allows you to define an area of the screen as the active window in any of the graphics modes:

```
GraphWindow(X1,Y1,X2,Y2);
```

where X1 and Y1 are the absolute coordinates of the upper left corner of the window, X2 and Y2 are the absolute coordinates of the lower right corner.

The default graphics window is *0,0,319,199* in 320x200-dot modes and *0,0,639,199* in 640x200-dot mode, that is, the entire screen.

ALL screen coordinates are relative to the active *window*—not to the physical screen. For example, after:

```
GraphWindow(50,100,200,180);
```

coordinate 0,0 is in the upper left corner of the window.

Windows cause graphics to be 'clipped', that is, if you for example *Draw* between two coordinates outside the window, only the part of the line that falls within the window will be shown:

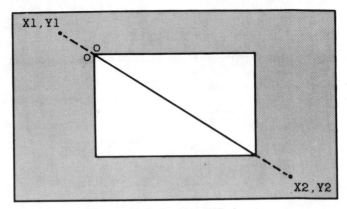

Figure 19-2: Graphics Windows

Basic Graphics

In each of the graphics modes, TURBO Pascal provides standard procedures which will plot points at specified coordinates and draw lines
between two coordinates:

Plot

Syntax: Plot(*X, Y, Color*);

Plots a point at the screen coordinates specified by *X* and *Y* in the color
specified by *Color*. *X, Y*, and *Color* are integer expressions.

Draw

Syntax: Draw(X1,Y1,X2,Y2,Color);

Draws a line between the screen coordinates specified by *X1, Y1* and
X2, Y2 in the color specified by *Color*. All parameters are integer expressions.

Extended Graphics

TURBO Pascal comes with a set of external machine language routines that can be included in TURBO programs during compilation. They provide extended graphics commands as described in the following.

The external graphics routines are contained in the file GRAPH.BIN. The file GRAPH.P contains the necessary **external** declarations, and the extended graphics routines are included in a TURBO program simply by using this statement to include the GRAPH.P file in the program:

```
{$I GRAPH.P }
```

ColorTable

Syntax: ColorTable(*C1,C2,C3,C4*);

ColorTable supplements *Palette* by defining a color 'translation table' which lets the current color of any given point determine the new color of that point when it is written again. The default color table value is (0,1,2,3), which means that when a point is written on the screen, it does not change the color that's already there:

color 0 becomes color 0
color 1 becomes color 1
color 2 becomes color 2
color 3 becomes color 3

The table (3,2,1,0) would cause

color 0 to become color 3
color 1 to become color 2
color 2 to become color 1
color 3 to become color 0

that is, all colors would be reversed. The *PutPic* procedure always uses the color table; all other draw procedures use the table if a color of −1 is specified, for example:

```
Plot(X,Y,-1);
```

Arc

Syntax: Arc(*X,Y,Angle,Radius,Color*);

Draws an arc of *Angle* degrees, starting at the position given by *X,Y*, with a radius given by *Radius*. If *Angle* is positive, the arc turns clockwise; if it is negative, the arc turns counterclockwise. If *Color* is from 0 through 3, the pen color is selected from the color palette (see page 165); if it is − 1, the color is selected from the color translation table defined by the *ColorTable* procedure (page 172).

Circle

Syntax: Circle(*X,Y,Radius,Color*);

Draws a circle in the color given by *Color* with its center at *X,Y* and a radius as specified by *Radius*.

The radius of the circle is the same in the horizontal and vertical axes. In 320 x 200 mode this draws a perfect circle, as the display is almost linear. In 640 x 200 mode, however, circles appear as ellipses.

If *Color* is from 0 through 3, the pen color is selected from the color palette (see page 165); if it is − 1, the color is selected from the color translation table defined by the *ColorTable* procedure (page 172).

GetPic

Syntax: GetPic(*Buffer,X1,Y1,X2,Y2*);

Copies the contents of a rectangular area defined by the integer expressions *X1,Y1,X2,Y2* into the variable *Buffer*, which may be of any type. The minimum buffer size in bytes required to store the image is calculated as:

320 x 200 modes:
  Size = ((Width + 3) div 4)*Height*2 + 6

640 x 200 modes:
  Size = ((Width + 7) div 8)*Height + 6

where:

Width = abs(x1-x2) + 1 and Height = abs(y1-y2) + 1

Note that it the responsibility of the programmer to ensure that the buffer is large enough to accommodate the entire transfer.

The first 6 bytes of the buffer constitute a three word header (three integers). After the transfer, the first word contains 2 in 320 x 200 mode or 1 in 640 x 200 mode The second word contains the width of the image and third contains the height. The remaining bytes contain the data. Data is stored with the leftmost pixels in the most significant bits of the bytes. At the end of each row, the remaining bits of the last byte are skipped.

PutPic

Syntax: PutPic(*Buffer,X,Y*);

Copies the contents of the variable *Buffer* onto a rectangular area on the screen. The integer expressions *X* and *Y* define the lower left-hand corner of the picture area. *Buffer* is a variable of any type, in which a picture has previously been stored by *GetPic*. Each bit in the buffer is converted to a color according to the color map before it is written to the screen.

GetDotColor

Syntax: GetDotColor(*X,Y*);

This integer function returns the color value of the dot located at coordinate *X,Y*. Values of 0 through 3 may be returned in 320 x 200 dot graphics, and 0 or 1 in 640 x 200 dot graphics. If *X,Y* is outside the window, *GetDotColor* returns − 1.

FillScreen

Syntax: FillScreen(*Color*);

Fills the entire active window with the color specified by the integer expression *Color*. If *Color* is in the range 0 through 3, the color will be selected from the color palette, if it is − 1, the color table will be used. This allows for dramatic effects; with a color table of *3,2,1,0*, for example, *FillScreen(* − *1)* will invert the entire image within the active window.

FillShape Procedure

Syntax: FillShape(*X, Y, FillColor, BorderColor*);

Fills an area of any shape with the color specified by the integer expression *FillColor* which must be in the range 0 through 3. The color translation table is not supported. The shape must be entirely enclosed by the color specified by *BorderColor*; if not, *FillShape* will 'spill' onto the area outside the shape. *X* and *Y* are the coordinates of a point within the image to be filled.

FillPattern

Syntax: FillPattern(*X1, Y1, X2, Y2, Color*);

Fills a rectangular area defined by the coordinates *X1, Y1, X2, Y2* with the pattern defined by the *Pattern* procedure. The pattern is replicated both horizontally and vertically to fill the entire area. Bits of value 0 cause no change to the display, whereas bits of value 1 cause a dot to be written using the color selected by *Color*.

Pattern

Syntax: Pattern(*P*);

Defines the pattern used by the *FillPattern* procedure. The pattern is an 8 x 8 matrix defined by the *P* parameter which must be of type **array**[0..7] **of** *Byte*. Each byte corresponds to a horizontal line in the pattern, and each bit corresponds to a pixel. The following shows some sample patterns and the hexadecimal value of each line in the matrix. A hyphen represents a binary 0, and an asterisk represents a binary 1.

```
- * - - - * - -    $44        * - * - * - * -    $AA
* - - - * - - -    $88        - * - * - * - *    $55
- - - * - - - *    $11        * - * - * - * -    $AA
- - * - - - * -    $22        - * - * - * - *    $55
- * - - - * - -    $44        * - * - * - * -    $AA
* - - - * - - -    $88        - * - * - * - *    $55
- - - * - - - *    $11        * - * - * - * -    $AA
- - * - - - * -    $22        - * - * - * - *    $55
```

To use the first pattern, the slanted lines, the following typed constant could be declared and passed as a parameter to *Pattern*:

```
const
  Lines: array[0..7] of Byte =
         ($44,$88,$11,$22,$44,$88,$11,$22);
```

When the pattern is used by the *FillPattern* procedure, low bits cause no change to the display, high bits cause a dot to be written.

Turtlegraphics

The external file GRAPH.BIN that contains the extended graphics routines mentioned in the previous section also contains the TURBO Turtlegraphics routines, so whenever you include the graphics declaration file GRAPH.P:

```
{$I GRAPH.P }
```

you also have access to the turtlegraphics described in the following.

TURBO Turtlegraphics is based on the 'turtle' concept devised by S. Papert and his co-workers at MIT. To make graphics easy for those of us who might have difficulty understanding cartesian coordinates, Papert et al. invented the idea of a 'turtle' that could 'walk' a given distance and turn through a specified angle, drawing a line as it went along. Very simple algorithms in this system can create more interesting images than an algorithm of the same length in cartesian coordinates.

Like the other graphics routines, turtlegraphics operate within a window. This window is set to the entire screen by default but the *Window* or *TurtleWindow* procedures can be used to define only part of the screen as the active graphics area, safeguarding the rest from being overwritten. Turtlegraphics and ordinary graphics can be used simultaneously, and they share a common window.

The TURBO Turtlegraphics routines operate on *turtle coordinates*. The turtle's *home* position (0,0) in this coordinate system is always in the middle of the active window, with positive values stretching to the right (X) and upwards (Y), and negative values stretching to the left (X) and downwards (Y):

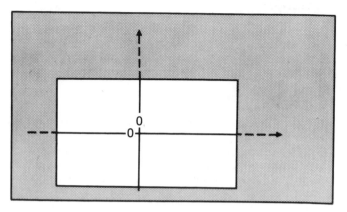

Figure 19-3: Turtle Coordinates

The range of coordinates on a full screen is:

320 x 200 modes: X = − 159..0..160, Y = − 99..0..100
640 x 200 mode: X = − 319..0..320, Y = − 99..0..100

but the actual range will be limited to the size of the active window. Coordinates outside the active window are legal, but will be ignored. This means that drawings are 'clipped' to the limits of the active window.

Back

Syntax: Back(*Dist*);

Moves the turtle backwards the distance given by the integer expression *Dist* from its current position in the direction opposite to the the turtle's current heading while drawing a line in the current pen color (if *Dist* is is negative, the turtle moves forwards).

ClearScreen

Syntax: ClearScreen;

This procedure clears the active window and homes the turtle.

Forwd

Syntax: Forwd(*Dist*);

Moves the turtle forwards the distance given by the integer expression *Dist* from its current position in the direction the turtle is currently facing, while drawing a line in the current pen color (if *Dist* is is negative, the turtle moves backwards).

Heading

Syntax: Heading;

The *Heading* function returns an integer in the range 0..359 giving the direction in which the turtle is currently pointing. 0 is upwards, and increasing angles represent headings in clockwise direction.

HideTurtle

Syntax: HideTurtle;

Hides the turtle, so that it is not shown on the screen. This is the initial state of the turtle, so to see the turtle, you must first call the *ShowTurtle* procedure.

Home

Syntax: Home;

This procedure puts the turtle to its home position at turtle coordinates 0,0 (the middle of the active window), and points it in heading 0 (upwards).

NoWrap

Syntax: NoWrap;

This procedure disables the turtle from 'wrapping', that is, re-appear ing at the opposite side of the active window if it exceeds the window boundary. *NoWrap* is the system's initial value.

PenDown

Syntax: PenDown;

This procedure 'puts the pen down' so that when the turtle moves, it draws a line. This is the initial status of the pen.

PenUp

Syntax: PenUp;

This procedure 'lifts the pen' so the turtle moves without drawing a line.

SetHeading

Syntax: SetHeading(*Angle*);

Turns the turtle to the angle specified by the integer expression *Angle*. 0 is upwards, and increasing angles represent clockwise rotation. If *Angle* is not in the range 0..359, it is converted into a number in that range.

Four integer constants are pre-defined to easily turn the turtle in the four main directions: *North* = 0 (up), *East* = 90 (right), *South* = 180, and *West* = 270 (left).

SetPenColor

Syntax: SetPenColor(*Color*);

Selects the color of the 'pen', that is, the color that will be used for drawing when the turtle moves. *Color* is an integer expression yielding a value between − 1 and 3. If *Color* is from 0 through 3, the pen color is selected from the color palette (see page 165); if it is − 1, the color is selected from the color translation table defined by the *ColorTable* procedure (page 172).

SetPosition

Syntax: SetPosition(*X, Y*);

Moves the turtle to the location with coordinates given by the integer expressions *X* and *Y* without drawing a line.

ShowTurtle

Syntax: ShowTurtle;

Displays the turtle as a small triangle. The turtle is initially **hidden**, so to see the turtle, you must first call this procedure.

TurnLeft

Syntax: TurnLeft(*Angle*);

Turns the turtle *Angle* degrees from its current direction. Positive angles turn the turtle to the left, negative angles turn it to the right.

TurnRight

Syntax: TurnRight(*Angle*);

Turns the turtle *Angle* degrees from its current direction. Positive angles turn the turtle to the right, negative angles turn it to the left.

TurtleWindow

Syntax: TurtleWindow(*X, Y, W, H*);

The *TurtleWindow* procedure defines an area of the screen as the active graphics area in any of the graphics modes, exactly as does the *Window* procedure. *TurtleWindow*, however, lets you define the window in terms of *turtle coordinates*, which are more natural to use in turtlegraphics. *X* and *Y* are the screen coordinates of the center of the window; *W* is its width, and *H* is its height.

The default TurtleWindow is *159,99,320,200* in 320x200-dot modes and *319,99,640,200* in 640x200-dot mode, that is, the entire screen. If the turtlewindow is defined to fall partly outside the physical screen, it is clipped the edges of the physical screen.

Turtlegraphics are 'clipped' to the active window, that is, if you move the turtle outside the active window, it will not be shown and it will not draw.

When the window is set (whether by *TurtleWindow* or by *Window*, the turtle is initialized to its *Home* position and heading. Changing screen mode resets the window to the entire screen.

Turtlegraphics operate *in turtle coordinates*. The turtle's *home* position (0,0) in this coordinate system is always in the middle of the active window, with positive values stretching to the right (X) and upwards (Y), and negative values stretching to the left (X) and downwards (Y):

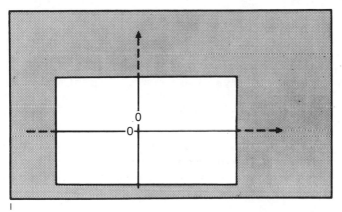

Figure 19-4: Turtle Coordinates

The range of coordinates on a full screen is:

320 x 200 modes: X = -159..0..160, Y = -99..0..100
640 x 200 mode: X = -319..0..320, Y = -99..0..100

but the actual range will be limited to the size of the active window.

Coordinates outside the active window are legal, but will be ignored. This means that drawings are 'clipped' to the limits of the active window, and anything drawn outside of the active window is lost.

TurtleThere

Syntax: TurtleThere;

This boolean function returns *True* if the turtle is visible in the active window (after a *ShowTurtle*), otherwise it returns *False*.

TurtleDelay

Syntax: TurtleDelay(Ms);

This procedure sets a delay in milliseconds between each step of the turtle. Normally, there is no delay.

Wrap

Syntax: Wrap;

After a call to this procedure, the turtle will re-appear at the opposite side of the active window when it exceeds the window boundary. Use *NoWrap* to return to normal.

Xcor

Syntax: Xcor;

This function returns the integer value of the turtle's current X-coordinate.

Ycor

Syntax: Ycor;

This function returns the integer value of the turtle's current Y-coordinate.

Sound

The PC's speaker is accessed through the standard procedure *Sound*:

```
Sound(I);
```

where *I* is an integer expression specifying the frequency in Hertz. The specified frequency will be emitted until the speaker is turned off with a call to the *NoSound* standard procedure:

```
NoSound
```

The following example program will emit a 440-Hertz beep for half a second:

```
begin
  Sound(440);
  Delay(500);
  NoSound;
end.
```

Editor Command Keys

In addition to the *WordStar* commands, the editing keys of IBM PC keyboard have been implemented as primary commands. This means that while e.g. Ctrl-E, Ctrl-X, Ctrl-S, and Ctrl-D still move the cursor up, down, left, and right, you may also use the arrows on the numeric keypad. The following table provides an overview of available editing keys, their functions, and their *WordStar*-command equivalents:

ACTION	PC-KEY	COMMAND
Character left	Left arrow	Ctrl-S
Character right	Right arrow	Ctrl-D
Word left	Ctrl-left arrow	Ctrl-A
Word right	Ctrl-right arrow	Ctrl-F
Line up	Up arrow	Ctrl-E
Line down	Down arrow	Ctrl-X
Page up	PgUp	Ctrl-R
Page down	PgDn	Ctrl-C
To left on line	Home	Ctrl-Q-S
To right on line	End	Ctrl-Q-D
To top of page	Ctrl-Home	Ctrl-Q-E
To bottom of page	Ctrl-End	Ctrl-Q-X
To top of file	Ctrl-PgUp	Ctrl-Q-R
To end of file	Ctrl-PgDn	Ctrl-Q-C
Insert mode on/off	Ins	Ctrl-V
Mark block begin	F7	Ctrl-K-B
Mark block end	F8	Ctrl-K-K
Tab	<TAB>	Ctrl-I

Table 19-6: IBM PC Keyboard Editing Keys

Note that while maintaining *WordStar* compatibility in the commands, some function keys have different meanings in *WordStar* and TURBO.

Chapter 20
PC-DOS AND MS-DOS

This chapter describes features of TURBO Pascal specific to the PC-DOS and MS-DOS implementations. It presents two kinds of information:

1)   Things you should know to make efficient use of TURBO Pascal. Pages 187 through 209.

2)   The rest of the chapter describes things which are of interest only to experienced programmers, such as machine language routines, technical aspects of the compiler, etc.

Tree-Structured Directories

On the Main Menu

The DOS structured directories are supported by TURBO's main menu:

```
Logged drive: A
Active directory: \

Work file:
Main file:

Edit      Compile  Run    Save
Dir       Quit  compiler  Options

Text:      0 bytes
Free: 62903 bytes

> ■
```

Figure 20-1: TURBO Main Menu

Notice the addition of the **A** command which lets you change the Active directory using the same path description as with the CHDIR command of DOS. The currently active directory is shown after the colon.

DOS uses a backslash: \ to refer to the ROOT directory, as shown in the example. The rest of directories have names just like files, that is a 1-8 letter name optionally followed by a period and a 1-3 letter type. Each directory can contain ordinary files or other directories.

Files in this system of directories are referenced by a **path** name in addition to the file name. A path name consists of the names of the directories leading to the file, separated by backslashes. The complete reference to a file called INVADERS.PAS in the directory TURBO is thus:

```
\TURBO\INVADERS.PAS
```

The first backslash indicates that the path starts from the root directory. If you were logged on some other directory, and you wanted to move to the TURBO directory, you would press **A** and enter:

```
\TURBO
```

In every sub-directory you will see two special entries in a DIR listing: . and .. The one period serves to identify this directory as a sub-directory. The two periods is a reference to the directory's 'parent' directory. These two periods may be used in a directory path; if, for example, you are logged on a sub-directory of TURBO, you may return to TURBO by pressing **A** and then entering the two periods.

Directory-related procedures

TURBO Pascal provides the following procedures to manipulate the tree-structured directories of MS-DOS.

ChDir

Syntax: ChDir(*St*);

Changes the current directory to the path specified by the string expression *St*. Also changes the logged drive if *St* contains a file name. For example:

```
ChDir('B:\PROG');
```

MkDir

Syntax: MkDir(*St*);

Creates a new sub-directory as specified by the path given by the string expression *St*. The last item in the path must be an non-existing filename.

RmDir

Syntax: RmDir(*St*);

Removes the sub-directory specified by the path given by the string expression *St*.

GetDir

Syntax: GetDir(*Dr,St*);

Returns the current directory of the drive indicated by *Dr* in the string variable *St*. *Dr* is an integer expression where 0 = logged drive, 1 = A, etc.

Compiler Options

The **O** command selects the following menu from which you may view and change some default values of the compiler. It also provides a helpful function to find runtime errors in programs compiled into object code files.

```
compile -> Memory
           Com-file
           cHn-file

command line Parameter:

Find run-time error  Quit
```

Figure 20-2: Options Menu

Memory / Com file / cHn-file

The three commands **M**, **C**, and **H** select the compiler mode, i.e. where to put the code which results from the compilation. **M**emory is the default mode. When active, code is produced in memory and resides there ready to be activated by a **R**un command.

Com-file is selected by pressing **C**. The arrow moves to point to this line. The compiler writes code to a file with the same name as the Work file (or Main file, if specified) and the file type .COM. This file contains the program code and Pascal runtime library, and may be activated by typing its name at the console.

c**H**ain-file is selected by pressing **H**. The arrow moves to point to this line. The compiler writes code to a file with the same name as the Work file (or Main file, if specified) and the file type .CHN. This file contains the program code but no Pascal library and must be activated from another TURBO Pascal program with the *Chain* procedure (see page 193).

When the **C**om or c**H**n mode is selected, four additional lines will appear on the screen:

```
minimum cOde segment size:    XXXX paragraphs (max.YYYY)
minimum Data segment size:    XXXX paragraphs (max.YYYY)
mInimum free dynamic memory: XXXX paragraphs
mAximum free dynamic memory: XXXX paragraphs
```

Figure 20-3: Memory Usage Menu

Tho use of these commands is described in the following sections.

Minimum Code Segment Size

The **O**-command is used to set the minimum size of the code segment for a .COM using *Chain* or *Execute*. As discussed on page 193 , *Chain* and *Execute* do not change the base addresses of the code, data, and stack segments, and a 'root' program using *Chain* or *Execute* must therefore allocate segments of sufficient size to accommodate the largest segments in any *Chained* or *Executed* program.

Consequently, when compiling a 'root' program, you must set the value of the *Minimum Code Segment Size* to at least the same value as the largest code segment size of the programs to be chained/executed from that root. The required values are obtained from the status printout terminating any compilation. The values are in hexadecimal and specify number of paragraphs, a paragraph being 16 bytes.

Minimum Data Segment Size

The **D**-command is used to set the minimum size of the data segment for a .COM using *Chain* or *Execute*. As discussed above, a 'root' program using these commands must allocate segments of sufficient size to accommodate the largest data of any *Chained* or *Executed* program.

Consequently, when compiling a 'root' program, you must set the value of the *Minimum Data Segment Size* to at least the same value as the largest data segment size of the programs to be chained/executed from that root. The required values are obtained from the status printout terminating any compilation. The values are in hexadecimal and specify number of paragraphs, a paragraph being 16 bytes.

Minimum Free Dynamic Memory

This value specifies the minimum memory size required for stack and heap. The value is in hexadecimal and specifies a number of paragraphs, a paragraph being 16 bytes.

Maximum Free Dynamic Memory

This value specifies the maximum memory size allocated for stack and heap. It must be used in programs which operate in a multi-user environment to assure that the program does not allocate the entire free memory. The value is in hexadecimal and specifies a number of paragraphs, a paragraph being 16 bytes.

Command Line Parameters

The **P**-command lets you enter one or more parameters which are passed to your program when running it in **M**emory mode, just as if they had been entered on the DOS command line. These parameters may be accessed through the *ParamCount* and *ParamStr* functions.

Find Run-time Error

When you run a program compiled in memory, and a run-time error occurs, the editor is invoked, and the error is automatically pointed out. This, of course, is not possible if the program is in a .COM file or an .CHN file. Run time errors then print out the error code and the value of the program counter at the time of the error:

```
Run-time error 01, PC=1B56
Program aborted
```

Figure 20-4: Run-time Error Message

To find the place in the source text where the error occurred, enter the **F** command. When prompted for the address, enter the address given by the error message:

```
Enter PC: 1B56
```

Figure 20-5: Find Run-time Error

The place in the source text is now found and pointed out exactly as if the error had occurred while running the program in memory.

Notice that locating errors in programs using overlays can be a bit more tricky, as explained on page 196.

Standard Identifiers

The following standard identifiers are unique to the DOS implementations:

CSeg	*LongFilePos*	*MemW*	*PortW*
DSeg	*LongFileSize*	*MsDos*	*SSeg*
Intr	*LongSeek*	*Ofs*	*Seg*

Chain and Execute

TURBO Pascal provides two procedures *Chain* and *Execute* which allow TURBO programs to activate other TURBO programs. The syntax of the procedure calls are:

Chain(*FilVar*)
Execute(*FilVar*)

where *FilVar* is a file variable of any type, previously assigned to a disk file with the standard procedure *Assign*. If the file exists, it is loaded into memory and executed.

The *Chain* procedure is used only to activate special TURBO Pascal .CHN files, i.e. files compiled with the cHn-file option selected on the Options menu (see page 190). Such a file contains only program code; no Pascal library, it uses the Pascal library already present in memory.

The *Execute* procedure is used to activate any TURBO Pascal .COM file.

If the disk file does not exist, an I/O error occurs. This error is treated as described on page 116. When the I compiler directive is passive (($I-)), program execution continues with the statement following the failed *Chain* or *Execute* statement, and the *IOresult* function must be called prior to further I/O.

Data can be transferred from the current program to the chained program either by *shared global variables* or by *absolute address variables*.

To ensure overlapping, shared global variables should be declared as the very first variables in both programs, and they must be listed in the same order in both declarations. Furthermore, both programs must be compiled to the same size of code and data segments (see page 191). When these conditions are satisfied, the variables will be placed at the same address in memory by both programs, and as TURBO Pascal does not automatically initialize its variables, they may be shared.

Example:
Program *MAIN.COM:*

```
program Main;
var
   Txt:       string[80];
   CntPrg:    file;

begin
   Write('Enter any text: '); Readln(Txt);
   Assign(CntPrg, 'ChrCount.chn');
   Chain(CntPrg);
end.
```

Program *CHRCOUNT.CHN:*

```
program ChrCount;
var
  Txt:         string[80];
  NoOfChar,
  NoOfUpc,
  I:           Integer;

begin
  NoOfUpc := 0;
  NoOfChar := Length(Txt);
  for I := 1 to length(Txt) do
    if Txt[I] in ['A'..'Z'] then NoOfUpc := Succ(NoOfUpc);
  Write('No of characters in entry: ',NoOfChar);
  Writeln('. No of upper case characters: ', NoOfUpc,'.');
end.
```

If you want a TURBO program to determine whether it was invoked by eXecute or directly from the DOS command line, you should use an **absolute** variable at address *Cseg:$80*. This is the command line length byte, and when a program is called from DOS, it contains a value between 0 and 127. When eXecuting a program, therefore, the calling program should set this variable to something higher than 127. When you then check the variable in the called program, a value between 0 and 127 indicates that the program was called from DOS, a higher value that it was called from another TURBO program.

Chaining and eXecuting TURBO programs does not alter the memory allocation state. The base addresses and sizes of the code, data and stack segments are not changed; *Chain* and *Execute* only replace the program code in the code segment. 'Alien' programs, therefore, cannot be initiated from a TURBO program.

It is important that the first program which executes a *Chain* statement allocates enough memory for the code, data, and stack segments to accommodate largest .CHN program. This is done by using the **Options** menu to change the minimum code, data and free memory sizes (see page 190).

Note that neither *Chain* nor *Execute* can be used in direct mode, that is, from a program run with the compiler options switch in position **Memory** (page 190).

Overlays

During execution, the system normally expects to find its overlay files on the logged drive and current directory. The *OvrPath* procedure may be used to change this default value.

OvrPath Procedure

Syntax: OvrPath(*Path*);

where *Path* is a string expression specifying a subdirectory path (see page 188 for an explanation of DOS directory paths). On subsequent calls to overlay files, the files will be expected in the specified directory. Once an overlay file has been opened in one directory, future calls to the same file will look in the same directory. The path may optionally specify a drive (*A:*, *B:*, etc.).

The current directory is identified by a single period. *OvrPath('.')* thus causes overlay files to be sought on the current directory.

Example :
```
program OvrTest;

overlay procedure ProcA;
begin
  Writeln('Overlay A');
end;

overlay procedure ProcB;
begin
  Writeln('Overlay B');
end;

procedure Dummy;
begin
  {Dummy procedure to separate the overlays
   into two groups}
end;

overlay procedure ProcC;
begin
  Writeln('Overlay C');
end;
```

```
begin
  OvrPath('\sub1');
  ProcA;
  OvrPath('.');
  ProcC;
  OvrPath('\sub1');
  ProcB;
end.
```

The first call to *OvrPath* specifies overlays to be sought on the subdirectory *sub1*. The call to *ProcA* therefore causes the first overlay file (containing the two overlay procedures *ProcA* and *ProcB* to be opened on this directory.

Next, the *OvrPath('.')* statement specifies that following overlays are to be found on the current directory. The call to *ProcC* opens the second overlay file here.

The following *ProcB* statement calls an overlay procedure in the first overlay file; and to ensure that it is sought on the *sub1* directory, the *OvrPath('\sub1')* statement must be executed before the call.

Files

File Names

A file name in DOS consists of a path of directory names, separated by backslashes, leading up to the desired directory, followed by the actual file name:

Drive:\ *Dirname*\ ... \ *Dirname*\ *Filename*

If the path begins with a backslash, it starts in the root directory; otherwise, it starts in the logged drive.

The *Drive* and path specification is optional. If omitted, the file is assumed to reside on the logged drive.

The *FileName* consists of a name of one through eight letters or digits, optionally followed by a period and a file type of one through three letters or digits.

Number of Open Files

The number of files that may be open at the same time is controlled through the **F** compiler directive. The default setting is {$F16}, which means that up to 16 files may be open at any one time. If, for instance, a {$F24} directive is placed at the beginning of a program (**before** the declaration part), up to 24 files may be open concurrently. The F compiler directive does not limit the number of files that may be declared in a program; it only sets a limit to the number of files that may be open at the same time.

Note that even though the F compiler directive has been used to allocate sufficient file space, you may still experience a 'too many open files' error condition, if the operating system runs out of file buffers. If that happens, you should supply a higher value for the 'files = xx' parameter in the CONFIG.SYS file. The default value is usually 8. For further detail, please refer to your MS-DOS documentation.

Extended File Size

The following three additional file routines exist to accommodate the extended range of records in DOS. These are:

LongFileSize function,
LongFilePosition function, and
LongSeek procedure

They correspond to their *Integer* equivalents *FileSize*, *FilePosition*, and *Position* but operate with *Reals*. The functions thus return results of type *Real*, and the second parameter of the *LongSeek* procedure must be an expression of type *Real*.

File of Byte

In the CP/M implementations, access to non-TURBO files (except text files) must be done through untyped files because the two first bytes of typed TURBO files always contain the number of components in the file. This is not the case in the DOS versions, however, and a non-turbo file may therefore be declared as a **file of byte** and accessed randomly with *Seek*, *Read*, and *Write*.

Flush Procedure

The *Flush* procedure has no effect with typed files in DOS, as DOS typed file variables do not employ a sector buffer.

Truncate Procedure

Syntax: Truncate(*FilVar*);

This procedure truncates the file identified by *FilVar* at the current position of the file pointer, that is, records beyond the file pointer are cut away. *Truncate* also prepares the file for subsequent output.

Text Files

Buffer Size

The text file buffer size is 128 bytes by default. This is adequate for most applications, but heavily I/O-bound programs, as for example a copy program, will benefit from a larger buffer, as it will reduce disk head movement.

You are therefore given the option to specify the buffer size when declaring a text file:

```
VAR   TextFile: Text[$800];
```

declares a text file variable with a buffer size of 2K bytes.

Append Procedure

Syntax: Append(*FilVar*);

The disk file assigned to the file variable *FilVar* is opened, and the file pointer is moved to the end of the file. The only operation allowed after *Append* is appending of new components.

Flush Procedure

The *Flush* procedure causes the file buffer to be flushed when used with text files.

Logical Devices

The following additional logical devices are provided:

INP: Refers to the MS-DOS standard input file (standard handle number 0).

OUT: Refers to the MS-DOS standard output file (standard handle number 1).

ERR: Refers to the MS-DOS standard error output file (standard handle number 2).

These devices may also be used with typed and untyped files.

The MS-DOS operating system itself also provides a number of logical devices, for instance 'CON', 'LST' and 'AUX'. TURBO Pascal will treat these devices as if they were disk files, with one exception: when a text file is opened, using *Reset, Rewrite* or *Append*, TURBO Pascal asks MS-DOS for the status of the file. If MS-DOS reports that the file is a device, TURBO Pascal disables the buffering that normally occurs on textfiles, and all I/O operations on the file are done on a character by character basis.

The D compiler option may be used to disable this check. The default state of the D option is {$D + }, and in this state, device checks are made. In the {$D − } state, no checks are made and all device I/O operations are buffered. In this case, a call to the flush standard procedure will ensure that the characters you have written to a file have actually been sent to it.

I/O redirection

PC/MS-DOS TURBO Pascal supports the I/O redirection feature provided by the MS-DOS operating system. In short, I/O redirection allows you to use disk files as the standard input source and/or standard output destination. Furthermore, a program supporting I/O redirection can be used as a *filter* in a *pipe*. Details on I/O redirection, filters, and pipes, are found in the MS-DOS documentation.

I/O redirection is enabled through the **G** (get) and **P** (put) compiler directives. The G directive controls the input file and the P directive controls the output file. The G and P directives both require an integer argument, which defines the size of the input or output buffer. The default buffer sizes are zero, and with these, *Input* and *Output* will refer to the *CON:* or the *TRM:* device.

If a non-zero input buffer is defined, for instance {$G256}, the standard *Input* file will refer to the MS-DOS standard input handle. Likewise, if a non-zero output buffer is defined, for instance {$P1024}, the standard *Output* file will refer to the MS-DOS standard output handle. The **D** compiler directive (see page 201) applies to such non-zero-buffer *Input* and *Output* files. The P and G compiler directives must be placed at the beginning of a program to have any effect, i.e. before the declaration part.

The following program demonstrates re-directed I/O. It will read characters from the standard input file, keep a count of each alphabetical character (A through Z), and output a frequency distribution graph to the standard output file:

```
{$G512,P512,D-}
program CharacterFrequencyCounter;
const
  Bar    = #223;
var
  Count:    array[65..90] of Real;
  Ch:       Char;
  I,Graph:  Integer;
  Max,
  Total:    Real;
begin
  Max := 0; Total := 0;
  for I := 65 to 90 do Count[I] := 0;
  while not EOF do
  begin
    Read(Ch);
    if Ord(Ch) > 127 then Ch := Chr(Ord(Ch)-128);
    Ch := UpCase(Ch);
    if Ch in ['A'..'Z'] then
    begin
      Count[Ord(Ch)] := Count[Ord(Ch)] +1;
      if Count[Ord(Ch)] > Max then Max := Count[Ord(Ch)];
      Total := Total +1;
    end;
  end;
  Writeln('    Count    %');
  for I := 65 to 90 do
  begin
    Write(Chr(I),':    ',Count[I]:5:0,
          Count[I]*100/Total:5:0,'  ');
    for Graph := 1 to Round(Count[I]*63/Max) do
      Write(Bar);
    Writeln;
  end;
  Writeln('Total', Total:5:0);
end.
```

If the program is compiled into a file called COUNT.COM, then the MS-DOS command:

    COUNT < TEXT.DOC > CHAR.CNT

will read the file TEXT.DOC and output the graph to the file CHAR.CNT.

Absolute Variables

Variables may be declared to reside at specific memory addresses, and are then called **absolute**. This is done by adding to the variable declaration the reserved word **absolute** followed by two *Integer* constants specifying a segment and an offset at which the variable is to be located:

```
var
  Abc: Integer absolute $0000:$00EE;
  Def: Integer absolute $0000:$00F0;
```

The first constant specifies the segment base address, and the second constant specifies the offset within that segment. The standard identifiers *CSeg* and *DSeg* may be used to place variables at absolute addresses within the code segment (CSeg) or the data segment (DSeg):

```
Special: array[1..CodeSize] absolute CSeg:$05F3;
```

Absolute may also be used to declare a variable "on top" of another variable, i.e. that a variable should start at the same address as another variable. When **absolute** is followed by the identifier of a variable or parameter, the new variable will start at the address of that variable parameter.

Example:
```
var
  Str: string[32];
  StrLen: Byte absolute Str;
```

This declaration specifies that the variable *StrLen* should start at the same address as the variable *Str*, and as the first byte of a string variable contains the length of the string, *StrLen* will contain the length of *Str*. Notice that an **absolute** variable declaration may only specify one identifier.

Further details on space allocation for variables are found on page 216.

Absolute Address Functions

The following functions are provided for obtaining information about program variable addresses and system pointers.

Addr

Syntax: Addr(*Name*);

Returns the address in memory of the first byte of the variable with the identifier *Name*. If *Name* is an array, it may be subscripted, and if *Name* is a record, specific fields may be selected. The value returned is a 32 bit pointer consisting of a segment address and an offset.

Ofs

Syntax: Ofs(*Name*);

Returns the offset in the segment of memory occupied by the first byte of the variable, procedure or function with the identifier *Name*. If *Name* is an array, it may be subscripted, and if *Name* is a record, specific fields may be selected. The value returned is an *Integer*.

Seg

Syntax: Seg(*Name*);

Returns the address of the segment containing the first byte of the variable with the identifier *Name*. If *Name* is an array, it may be subscripted, and if *Name* is a record, specific fields may be selected. The value returned is an *Integer*.

Cseg

Syntax: Cseg;

Returns the base address of the **C**ode segment. The value returned is an *Integer*.

Dseg

Syntax: Dseg;

Returns the base address of the **D**ata segment. The value returned is an *Integer*.

Sseg

Syntax: Sseg;

Returns the base address of the **S**tack segment. The value returned is an *Integer*.

Predefined Arrays

TURBO Pascal offers four predefined arrays of type *Byte*, called *Mem*, *MemW*, *Port* and *PortW* which are used to access CPU memory and data ports.

Mem Array

The predefined arrays *Mem* and *MemW* are used to access memory. Each component of the array *Mem* is a byte, and each component of the array

Wmem is a word (two bytes, LSB first). The index must be an address specified as the segment base address and an offset separated by a colon and both of type *Integer*.

The following statement assigns the value of the byte located in segment 0000 at offset $0081 to the variable *Value*

```
Value:=Mem[0000:$0081];
```

While the following statement:

```
MemW[Seg(Var):Ofs(Var)]:=Value;
```

places the value of the *Integer* variable *Value* in the memory location occupied by the two first bytes of the variable *Var*.

Port Array

The *Port* and *PortW* array are used to access the data ports of the 8086/88 CPU. Each element of the array represents a data port, with the index corresponding to port numbers. As data ports are selected by 16-bit addresses the index type is *Integer*. When a value is assigned to a component of *Port* or *PortW* it is output to the port specified. When a component of port is referenced in an expression, its value is input from the port specified. The components of the *Port* array are of type *Byte* and the components of *PortW* are of type *Integer*.

Example:
```
Port[56]:=10;
```

The use of the port array is restricted to assignment and reference in expressions only, i.e. components of *Port* and *PortW* cannot be used as variable parameters to procedures and functions. Furthermore, operations referring to the entire port array (reference without index) are not allowed.

With Statements

With statements may be nested to a maximum of 9 levels.

Pointer Related Items

MemAvail

The standard function *MemAvail* is available to determine the available space on the heap at any given time. The result is an *Integer* specifying the number of available *paragraphs* on the heap (a *paragraph* is 16 bytes).

Pointer Values

In very special circumstances it can be of interest to assign a specific value to a pointer variable *without using another pointer variable* or it can be of interest to obtain the actual value of a pointer variable.

Assigning a Value to a Pointer

The standard function *Ptr* can be used to assign specific values to a pointer variable. The function returns a 32 bit pointer consisting of a segment address and an offset.

Example:
```
Pointer:=Ptr(Cseg,$80);
```

Obtaining The Value of a Pointer

A pointer value is represented as a 32 bit entity and the standard function *Ord* can therefore **not** be used to obtain its value. Instead the functions *Ofs* and *Seg* must be used.

The following statement obtains the value of the pointer *P* (which is a segment address and an offset):

```
SegmentPart:=Seg(P^);
OffsetPart:=Ofs(P^);
```

DOS Function Calls

For the purpose of making DOS system calls, TURBO Pascal introduces a procedure *MsDos*, which has a record as parameter:

```
MsDos(Record);
```

Details on DOS system calls and BIOS routines are found in the IBM DOS Technical Reference Manual.

The parameter to *MsDos* must be of the type:

```
record
  AX,BX,CX,DX,BP,SI,DI,DS,ES,Flags: Integer;
end;
```

or, alternatively:

```
record case Integer of
    1: (AX,BX,CX,DX,BP,SI,DI,DS,ES,Flags: Integer);
    2: (AL,AH,BL,BH,CL,CH,DL,DH          : Byte);
  end;
```

Before TURBO makes the DOS system call, the registers AX, BX, CX, DX, BP, SI, DI, DS, and ES are loaded with the values specified in the record parameter. When DOS has finished operation the *MsDos* procedure will restore the registers to the record thus making any results from DOS available.

The following example shows how to use an MsDos function call to get the time from DOS:

```
procedure Timer(var Hour,Min,Sec,Frac:Integer);
type
  RegPack   =   record
                  AX,BX,CX,DX,BP,SI,DI,DS,ES,Flags: Integer;
                end;
var
  Regs:       Regpack;
```

```
begin
  with Regs do
  begin
    AX := $2C00;
    MsDos(Regs);
    Hour := hi(CX);
    Min  := lo(CX);
    Sec  := hi(DX);
    Frac := lo(DX);
  end;
  :
  :
  :
end;    { procedure Timer }
```

User Written I/O Drivers

For some applications it is practical for a programmer to define his own input and output drivers, i.e. routines which perform input and output of characters to and from an external device. The following drivers are part of the TURBO environment, and used by the standard I/O drivers (although they are not available as standard procedures or functions):

function *ConSt*: boolean; { 11 }
function *ConIn*: Char; { 8 }
procedure *ConOut* (Ch: Char); { 2 }
procedure *LstOut* (Ch: Char); { 5 }
procedure *AuxOut* (Ch: Char); { 4 }
function *AuxIn*: Char; { 3 }
procedure *UsrOut* (Ch: Char); { 2 }
function *UsrIn*: Char; { 8 }

The *ConSt* routine is called by the function *KeyPressed*, the *ConIn* and *ConOut* routines are used by the CON:, TRM:, and KBD: devices, the *LstOut* routine is used by the LST: device, the *AuxOut* and *AuxIn* routines are used by the AUX: device, and the *UsrOut* and *UsrIn* routines are used by the USR: device.

By default, these drivers are assigned to the DOS system calls as showed in curly brackets in the above listing of drivers.

This, however, may be changed by the programmer by assigning the address of a self-defined driver procedure or a driver function to one of the following standard variables:

Variable	Contains the address of the
ConStPtr	*ConSt* function
ConInPtr	*ConIn* function
ConOutPtr	*ConOut* procedure
LstOutPtr	*LstOut* procedure
AuxOutPtr	*AuxOut* procedure
AuxInPtr	*AuxIn* function
UsrOutPtr	*UsrOut* procedure
UsrInPtr	*UsrIn* function

A user defined driver procedure or driver function must match the definitions given above, i.e. a *ConSt* driver must be a boolean function, a *ConIn* driver must be a char function, etc.

External Subprograms

The reserved word **external** is used to declare external procedures and functions, typically procedures and functions written in machine code.

The reserved word **external** must be followed by a string constant specifying the name of a file in which executable machine code for the external procedure or function must reside. The default file type is *.COM*.

During compilation of a program containing external functions or procedures, the associated files are loaded and placed in the object code. As it is impossible to know in advance exactly *where* in the object code the external code will be placed this code **must** be relocatable, and no references must be made to the data segment. Furthermore the external code must save the registers BP, CS, DS and SS and restore these before executing the RET instruction.

An external subprogram has no *block*, i.e. no declaration part and no statement part. Only the subprogram heading is specified, immediately followed by the reserved word **external** and a filename specifying where to find the executable code for the subprogram.

Example:
```
procedure DiskReset; external 'DSKRESET';
function IOstatus: boolean; external 'IOSTAT';
```

An external file may contain code for more than one subprogram. The first subprogram is declared as described above, and the following are declared by specifying the identifier of the first subprogram followed by an an integer constant specifying an offset, enclosed in square brackets. The entry point of each subprogram is the address of the first subprogram plus the offset.

Example:
```
procedure Com1; external 'SERIAL.BIN';
function Com1Stat: Boolean; external Com1[3];
procedure Com1In: Char; external Com1[6];
procedure Com1Out: Char; external Com1[9];
```

The above example loads the file SERIAL.BIN into the program code, and defines four procedures called *Com1*, *Com1Stat*, *Com1In*, and *Com1Out* with entry points at the base address of the external code plus 0, 3, 6 and 9, respectively. When an external file contains several subprograms, the first part of the code is typically a jump table, as assumed in the example. In that way, the entry points of the subprograms remain unchanged if the external file is modified.

Parameters may be passed to external subprograms, and the syntax is exactly the same as that of calls to ordinary procedures and functions:

```
procedure Plot(X,Y: Integer); external 'PLOT';
procedure QuickSort(var List: PartNo); external 'QS';
```

External subprograms and parameter passing is discussed further on page 221.

In-line Machine Code

TURBO Pascal features the **inline** statements as a very convenient way of inserting machine code instructions directly into the program text. An inline statement consists of the reserved word **inline** followed by one or more *code elements* separated by slashes and enclosed in parentheses.

A code element is built from one or more data elements, separated by plus (+) or minus (−) signs. A data element is either an integer constant, a variable identifier, a procedure identifier, a function identifier, or a location counter reference. A location counter reference is written as an asterisk (*).

Example:
```
inline (10/$2345/count+1/sort-*+2);
```

Each code element generates one byte or one word (two bytes) of code. The value of the byte or the word is calculated by adding or subtracting the values of the data elements according to the signs that separate them. The value of a variable identifier is the address (or offset) of the variable. The value of a procedure or function identifier is the address (or offset) of the procedure or function. The value of a location counter reference is the address (or offset) of the location counter, i.e. the address at which to generate the next byte of code.

A code element will generate one byte of code if it consists of integer constants only, and if its value is within the 8-bit range (0..255). If the value is outside the 8-bit range, or if the code element refers to variable, procedure, or function identifiers, or if the code element contains a location counter reference, one word of code is generated (least significant byte first).

The ' < ' and ' > ' characters may be used to override the automatic size selection described above. If a code element starts with a ' < ' character, only the least significant byte of the value is coded, even if it is a 16-bit value. If a code element starts with a ' > ' character, a word is always coded, even though the most significant byte is zero.

Example:
```
inline (<$1234/>$44);
```

This **inline** statement generates three bytes of code: $34, $44, $00.

The value of a variable identifier use in a **inline** statement is the offset address of the variable within its base segment. The base segment of global variables (i.e. variables declared in the main program block) is the data segment, which is accessible through the DS register. The base segment of local variables (i.e. variables declared within the current subprogram) is the stack segment, and in this case the variable offset is relative to the BP (base page) register, the use of which automatically causes the stack segment to be selected. The base segment of typed constants is the code segment, which is accessible through the CS register. **inline** statements should not attempt to access variables that are not declared in the main program nor in the current subprogram.

The following example of an inline statement generates machine code that will convert all characters in its string argument to upper case.

```
procedure UpperCase(var Strg: Str);
{Str is type String[255]}
begin
  inline
    ($C4/$BE/Strg/          {       LES  DI,Strg[BP]               }
     $26/$8A/$0D/           {       MOV  CL,ES:[DI]                }
     $FE/$C1/               {       INC  CL                        }
     $FE/$C9/               { L1:   DEC  CL                        }
     $74/$13/               {       JZ   L2                        }
     $47/                   {       INC  DI                        }
     $26/$80/$3D/$61/       {       CMP  ES:BYTE PTR [DI],'a'}
     $72/$F5/               {       JB   L1                        }
     $26/$80/$3D/$7A/       {       CMP  ES:BYTE PTR [DI],'z'}
     $77/$EF/               {       JA   L1                        }
     $26/$80/$2D/$20/       {       SUB  ES:BYTE PTR [DI],20H}
     $EB/$E9);              {       JMP  SHORT L1                  }
                            { L2:                                   }
end;
```

Inline statements may be freely mixed with other statements throughout the statement part of a block, and **inline** statements may use all CPU registers. **Note**, however, that the contents of the registers BP, SP, DS, and SS must be the same on exit as on entry.

Interrupt Handling

A TURBO Pascal interrupt routine must manually preserve registers AX, BX, CX, DX, SI, DI, DS and ES. This is done by placing the following in-line statement as the first statement of the procedure:

```
inline ($50/$53/$51/$52/$56/$57/$1E/$06/$FB);
```

The last byte ($FB) is an STI instruction which enables further interrupts - it may or may not be required. The following inline statement must be the last statement in the procedure:

```
inline ($07/$1F/$5F/$5E/$5A/$59/$5B/$58/$8B/$E5/$5D/$CF);
```

This restores the registers and reloads the stack pointer (SP) and the base page register (BP). The last byte ($CF) is an IRET instruction which overrides the RET instruction generated by the compiler.

An interrupt service procedure must not employ any I/O operations using the standard procedures and functions of TURBO Pascal, as the BDOS is not re-entrant. The programmer must initialize the interrupt vector used to activate the interrupt service routine.

Intr procedure

Syntax: Intr(*InterruptNo, Result*)

This procedure initializes the registers and flags as specified in the parameter *Result* which must be of type:

```
Result = record
            AX,BX,CX,DX,BP,SI,DI,DS,ES,Flags: Integer;
         end;
```

It then makes the software interrupt given by the parameter *interruptNo* which must be an *Integer* constant. When the interrupt service routine returns control to your program, *Result* will contain any values returned from the service routine.

Note that the data segment register DS, used to access global variables, will not have the correct value when the interrupt service routine is entered. Therefore, global variables cannot be directly accessed. *Typed constants*, however, are available, as they are stored in the code segment. The way to access global variables in the interrupt service routine is therefore to store the value of *Dseg* in a typed constant in the main program. This typed constant can then be accessed by the interrupt handler and used to set its DS register.

Internal Data Formats

In the following descriptions, the symbol @ denotes the offset of the first byte occupied by a variable of the given type within its segment. The segment base address can be determined by using the standard function *Seg*.

Global and *local variables*, and *typed constants* occupy different segments as follows:

Global variables reside in the data segment and the offset is relative to the DS register.

Local variables reside in the stack segment and the offset is relative to the BP register.

Typed constants reside in the code segment and the offset is relative to the CS register.

All variables are contained within their base segment.

Basic Data Types

The basic data types may be grouped into structures (arrays, records, and disk files), but this structuring will not affect their internal formats.

Scalars

The following scalars are all stored in a single byte: *Integer* subranges with both bounds in the range 0..255, booleans, chars, and declared scalars with less than 256 possible values. This byte contains the ordinal value of the variable.

The following scalars are all stored in two bytes: *Integers*, *Integer* subranges with one or both bounds not within the range 0..255, and declared scalars with more than 256 possible values. These bytes contain a 2's complement 16-bit value with the least significant byte stored first.

Reals

Reals occupy 6 bytes, giving a floating point value with a 40-bit mantissa and an 8-bit 2's exponent. The exponent is stored in the first byte and the mantissa in the next five bytes with the least significant byte first:

@	Exponent
@ + 1	LSB of mantissa
:	
@ + 5	MSB of mantissa

The exponent uses binary format with an offset of $80. Hence, an exponent of $84 indicates that the value of the mantissa is to be multiplied by $2 \char94 (\$84-\$80) = 2 \char94 4 = 16$. If the exponent is zero, the floating point value is considered to be zero.

The value of the mantissa is obtained by dividing the 40-bit unsigned integer by $2 \char94 40$. The mantissa is always normalized, i.e. the most significant bit (bit 7 of the fifth byte) should be interpreted as a 1. The sign of the mantissa is stored in this bit, however, a 1 indicating that the number is negative, and a 0 indicating that the number is positive.

Strings

A string occupies as many bytes as its maximum length plus one. The first byte contains the current length of the string. The following bytes contains the string with the first character stored at the lowest address. In the table shown below, **L** denotes the current length of the string, and *Max* denotes the maximum length:

@	Current length (L)
@ + 1	First character
@ + 2	Second character
:	
@ + L	Last character
@ + L + 1	Unused
:	
@ + Max	Unused

Sets

An element in a *Set* occupies one bit, and as the maximum number of elements in a set is 256, a set variable will never occupy more than 32 bytes (256/8).

If a set contains less than 256 elements, some of the bits are bound to be zero at all times and need therefore not be stored. In terms of memory efficiency, the best way to store a set variable of a given type would then be to "cut off" all insignificant bits, and rotate the remaining bits so that the first element of the set would occupy the first bit of the first byte. Such rotate operations, however, are quite slow, and TURBO therefore employs a compromise: Only bytes which are statically zero (i.e. bytes of which no bits are used) are not stored. This method of compression is very fast and in most cases as memory efficient as the rotation method.

The number of bytes occupied by a set variable is calculated as (*Max* **div** 8) − (*Min* **div** 8) + 1, where *Max* and *Min* are the upper and lower bounds of the base type of that set. The memory address of a specific element *E* is:

MemAddress = @ + (*E* **div** 8) − (*Min* **div** 8)

and the bit address within the byte at *MemAddress* is:

BitAddress = *E* **mod** 8

where *E* denotes the ordinal value of the element.

Pointers

A pointer consists of four bytes containing a segment base address and an offset. The two least significant bytes contains the offset and the two most significant bytes the base address. Both are stored in memory using byte reversed format, i.e. the least significant byte is stored first. The value **nil** corresponds to two zero words.

Data Structures

Data structures are built from the basic data types using various structuring methods. Three different structuring methods exist: Arrays, records, and disk files. The structuring of data does not in any way affect the internal formats of the basic data types.

Arrays

The components with the lowest index values are stored at the lowest memory address. A multi-dimensional array is stored with the rightmost dimension increasing first, e.g. given the array

```
Board: array[1..8,1..8] of Square
```

you have the following memory layout of its components:

```
lowest address:    Board[1,1]
                   Board[1,2]
                    :
                   Board[1,8]
                   Board[2,1]
                   Board[2,2]
                    :
                    :
Highest address:   Board[8,8]
```

Records

The first field of a record is stored at the lowest memory address. If the record contains no variant parts, the length is given by the sum of the lengths of the individual fields. If a record contains a variant, the total number of bytes occupied by the record is given by the length of the fixed part plus the length of largest of its variant parts. Each variant starts at the same memory address.

Disk Files

Disk files are different from other data structures in that data is not stored in internal memory but in a file on an external device. A disk file is controlled through a file interface block (FIB).

File Interface Blocks

The following table shows the format of a FIB:

@ + 0	File handle (LSB).
@ + 1	File handle (MSB).
@ + 2	Record length (LSB) or flags byte.
@ + 3	Record length (MSB) or character buffer.
@ + 4	Buffer offset (LSB).
@ + 5	Buffer offset (MSB).
@ + 6	Buffer size (LSB).
@ + 7	Buffer size (MSB).
@ + 8	Buffer pointer (LSB).
@ + 9	Buffer pointer (MSB).
@ + 10	Buffer end (LSB).
@ + 11	Buffer end (MSB).
@ + 12	First byte of file path.
:	
@ + 75	Last byte of file path.

The word at @ + 0 and @ + 1 contains the 16-bit file handle returned by MS-DOS when the file was opened (or 0FFFFH when the file is closed). For typed and untyped files, the word at @ + 2 and @ + 3 contains the record length in bytes (zero if the file is closed), and bytes @ + 4 to @ + 11 are unused.

For text files, the format of the flags byte at @ + 2 is:

Bit 0..3	File type.
Bit 5	Pre-read character flag.
Bit 6	Output flag.
Bit 7	Input flag.

File type 0 denotes a disk file, and 1 through 5 denote the TURBO Pascal logical I/O devices (CON:, KBD:, LST:, AUX:, and USR:). Bit 5 is set if the character buffer contains a pre-read character, bit 6 is set if output is allowed, and bit 7 is set if input is allowed.

The four words from @ + 4 to @ + 11 store the offset address of the buffer, its size, the offset of the next character to read or write, and the offset of the first byte after the buffer. The buffer always resides in the same segment as the FIB, usually starting at @ + 76. When a textfile is assigned to a logical device, only the flags byte and the character buffer are used.

The file path is an ASCII string (a string terminated by a zero byte) of up to 63 characters.

Random Access Files

A random access file consists of a sequence of records, all of the same length and same internal format. To optimize file storage capacity, the records of a file are totally contiguous.

TURBO saves no information about the record length. The programmer must therefore see to it that a random access file is accessed with the correct record length.

The size returned by the standard function *Filesize* is obtained from the DOS directory.

Text Files

The basic components of a text file are characters, but a text file is furthermore divided into *lines*. Each line consists of any number of characters ended by a CR/LF sequence (ASCII $0D/ $0A). The file is terminated by a Ctrl-Z (ASCII $1B).

Parameters

Parameters are transferred to procedures and functions via the stack which is addressed through SS:SP.

On entry to an **external** subroutine, the top of the stack always contains the return address within the code segment (a word). The parameters, if any, are located below the return address, i.e. at higher addresses on the stack.

If an external function has the following subprogram header:

function Magic(**var** R: Real; S: string5): Integer;

then the stack upon entry to *Magic* would have the following contents:

```
< Function result         >
< Segment base address of R  >
< Offset address of R     >
< First character of S    >
:
< Last character of S     >
< Length of S             >
< Return address          >  SP
```

An external subroutine should save the Base Page register (BP) and then copy the Stack Pointer SP into the Base Page register in order to be able to refer to parameters. Furthermore the subroutine should reserve space on the stack for local workarea. This can be obtained by the following instructions:

```
PUSH  BP
MOV   BP,SP
SUB   SP,WORKAREA
```

The last instruction will have the effect of adding the following to the stack:

```
< Return address             >  BP
< The saved BP register      >
< First byte of local workarea >
:
< Last byte of local work area >  SP
```

Parameters are accessed via the BP register.

The following instruction will load length of the string into the AL register:

```
MOV  AL,[BP-1]
```

Before executing a RET instruction the subprogram must reset the Stack Pointer and Base Page register to their original values. When executing the RET the parameters may be removed by giving RET a parameter specifying how many bytes to remove. The following instructions should therefore be used when exiting from a subprogram:

```
MOV  SP,BP
POP  BP
RET  NoOfBytesToRemove
```

Variable Parameters

With a variable (**var**) parameter, two words are transferred on the stack giving the base address and offset of the first byte occupied by the actual parameter.

Value Parameters

With value parameters, the data transferred on the stack depends upon the type of the parameter as described in the following sections.

Scalars

Integers, Booleans, Chars and declared scalars (i.e. all scalars except *Reals*) are transferred on the stack as a word. If the variable occupies only one byte when it is stored, the most significant byte of the parameter is zero.

Reals

A real is transferred on the stack using six bytes.

Strings

When a string is at the top of the stack, the topmost byte contains the length of the string followed by the characters of the string.

Sets

A set always occupies 32 bytes on the stack (set compression only applies to the loading and storing of sets).

Pointers

A pointer value is transferred on the stack as two words containing the base address and offset of a dynamic variable. The value NIL corresponds to two zero words.

Arrays and Records

Even when used as value parameters, *Array* and *Record* parameters are not actually transferred on the stack. Instead, two words containing the base address and offset of the first byte of the parameter are transferred. It is then the responsibility of the subroutine to use this information to make a local copy of the variable.

Function Results

User written **external** functions must remove all parameters and the function result from the stack when they return.

User written **external** functions must return their results exactly as specified in the following:

Values of scalar types, except *Reals*, must be returned in the AX register. If the result Is only one byte then AH should be set to zero. Boolean functions must return the function value by setting the Z flag (Z = *False*, NZ = *True*).

Reals must be returned on the stack with the exponent at the lowest address. This is done by not removing the function result variable when returning.

Sets must be returned on the top of the stack according to the format described on page 223. On exit SP must point at the byte containing the string length.

Pointer values must be returned in DX:AX.

The Heap and The Stacks

During execution of TURBO Pascal program the following segments are allocated for the program:

a Code Segment,
a Data Segment, and
a Stack Segment

Two stack-like structures are maintained during execution of a program: tho *hoap* and tho *stack*.

The heap is used to store dynamic variables, and is controlled with the standard procedures *New, Mark,* and *Release*. At the beginning of a program, the heap pointer *HeapPtr* is set to low memory in the stack segment and the heap grows upwards towards the stack. The pre-defined variable *HeapPtr* contains the value of the heap pointer and allows the programmer to control the position of the heap.

The stack is used to store local variables, intermediate results during evaluation of expressions and to transfer parameters to procedures and functions. At the beginning of a program, the stack pointer is set to the address of the top of the stack segment.

On each call to the procedure *New* and on entering a procedure or function, the system checks for collision between the heap and the recursion stack. If a collision has occurred, an execution error results, unless the **K** compiler directive is passive ({ $K-}).

Memory Management

When a TURBO program is executed, three segments are allocated for the program: A code segment, a data segment, and a stack segment.

Code segment (CS is the code segment register):

```
CS:0000 - CS:00FF    MS-DOS base page.
CS:0100 - CS:EOFR    Run-time library code.
CS:EOFR - CS:EOFP    Program code.
CS:EOFP - CS:EOFC    Unused.
```

Data segment (DS is the data segment register):

```
DS:0000 - DS:EOFW    Run-time library workspace.
DS:EOFW - DS:EOFM    Main program block variables.
DS:EOFM - DS:EOFD    Unused.
```

The unused areas between (CS:EOFP-CS:EOFC and DS:EOFM-DS:EOFD) are allocated only if a minimum cOde segment size larger than the required size is specified at compilation. The sizes of the code and data segments never exceed 64K bytes each.

The stack segment is slightly more complicated, as it may be larger than 64K bytes. On entry to the program the stack segment register (SS) and the stack pointer (SP) is loaded so that SS:SP points at the very last byte available in the entire segment. During execution of the program SS is never changed but SP may move downwards until it reaches the bottom of the segment, or 0 (corresponding to 64K bytes of stack) if the stack segment is larger than 64K bytes.

The heap grows from low memory in the stack segment towards the actual stack residing in high memory. Each time a variable is allocated on the heap, the heap pointer (which is a double word variable maintained by the TURBO run-time system) is moved upwards, and then normalized, so that the offset address is always between $0000 and $000F. Therefore, the maximum size of a single variable that can be allocated on the heap is 65521 bytes (corresponding to $10000 less $000F). The total size of all variables allocated on the heap is however only limited by the amount of memory available. The heap pointer is available to the programmer through the *HeapPtr* standard identifier. *HeapPtr* is a typeless pointer which is compatible with all pointer types. Assignments to *HeapPtr* should be exercised only with extreme care.

Chapter 21
CP/M-86

This chapter describes features of TURBO Pascal specific to the CP/M-86 implementation. It presents two kinds of information:

1)   Things you should know to make efficient use of TURBO Pascal. Pages 227 through 240.

2)   The rest of the chapter describes things which are of interest only to experienced programmers, such as machine language routines, technical aspects of the compiler, etc.

Compiler Options

The **O** command selects the following menu from which you may view and change some default values of the compiler. It also provides a helpful function to find runtime errors in programs compiled into object code files.

```
compile -> Memory
           Cmd-file
           cHn-file

command line Parameter:

Find run-time error   Quit
```

Figure 21-1: Options Menu

Memory / Cmd file / cHn-file

The three commands **M**, **C**, and **H** select the compiler mode, i.e. where to put the code which results from the compilation. **Memory** is the default mode. When active, code is produced in memory and resides there ready to be activated by a **Run** command.

Cmd-file is selected by pressing **C**. The arrow moves to point to this line. The compiler writes code to a file with the same name as the Work file (or Main file, if specified) and the file type .CMD. This file contains the program code and Pascal runtime library, and may be activated by typing its name at the console.

cHain-file is selected by pressing **H**. The arrow moves to point to this line. The compiler writes code to a file with the same name as the Work file (or Main file, if specified) and the file type .CHN. This file contains the program code but no Pascal library and must be activated from another TURBO Pascal program with the *Chain* procedure (see page 231).

When the **C**md or c**H**n mode is selected, four additional lines will appear on the screen:

```
minimum cOde segment size:   XXXX paragraphs (max.YYYY)
minimum Data segment size:   XXXX paragraphs (max.YYYY)
mInimum free dynamic memory: XXXX paragraphs
mAximum free dynamic memory: XXXX paragraphs
```

Figure 21-2: Memory Usage Menu

The use of these commands are described in the following sections.

Minimum Code Segment Size

The **O**-command is used to set the minimum size of the code segment for a .CMD using *Chain* or *Execute*. As discussed on page 231, *Chain* and *Execute* do not change the base addresses of the code, data, and stack segments, and a 'root' program using *Chain* or *Execute* must therefore allocate segments of sufficient size to accommodate the largest segments in any *Chained* or *Executed* program.

Consequently, when compiling a 'root' program, you must set the value of the *Minimum Code Segment Size* to at least the same value as the largest code segment size of the programs to be chained/executed from that root. The required values are obtained from the status printout terminating any compilation. The values are in hexadecimal and specify number of paragraphs, a paragraph being 16 bytes.

Minimum Data Segment Size

The **D**-command is used to set the minimum size of the data segment for a .CMD using *Chain* or *Execute*. As discussed above, a 'root' program using these commands must allocate segments of sufficient size to accommodate the largest data of any *Chained* or *Executed* program.

Consequently, when compiling a 'root' program, you must set the value of the *Minimum Data Segment Size* to at least the same value as the largest data segment size of the programs to be chained/executed from that root. The required values are obtained from the status printout terminating any compilation. The values are in hexadecimal and specify number of paragraphs, a paragraph being 16 bytes.

Minimum Free Dynamic Memory

This value specifies the minimum memory size required for stack and heap. The value is in hexadecimal and specifies a number of paragraphs, a paragraph being 16 bytes.

Maximum Free Dynamic Memory

This value specifies the maximum memory size allocated for stack and heap. It must be used in programs which operate in a multi-user environment like Concurrent CP/M-86 to assure that the program does not allocate the entire free memory. The value is in hexadecimal and specifies a number of paragraphs, a paragraph being 16 bytes.

Command Line Parameters

The **P**-command lets you enter one or more parameters which are passed to your program when running it in **M**emory mode, just as if they had been entered on the DOS command line. These parameters may be accessed through the *ParamCount* and *ParamStr* functions.

Find Runtime Error

When you run a program compiled in memory, and a runtime error occurs, the editor is invoked, and the error is automatically pointed out. This, of course, is not possible if the program is in a .CMD file or an .CHN file. Run time errors then print out the error code and the value of the program counter at the time of the error:

```
Run-time error 01, PC=1B56
Program aborted
```

Figure 21-3: Run-time Error Message

To find the place in the source text where the error occurred, enter the **F** command. When prompted for the address, enter the address given by the error message:

```
Enter PC: 1B56
```

Figure 21-4: Find Run-time Error

The place in the source text is now found and pointed out exactly as if the error had occurred while running the program in memory.

Notice that locating errors in programs using overlays can be a bit more tricky, as explained on page 156.

Standard Identifiers

The following standard identifiers are unique to the 16-bit implementations:

Bdos	Intr	Ofs	Seg
CSeg	MemW	PortW	SSeg
DSeg			

Chain and Execute

TURBO Pascal provides two procedures *Chain* and *Execute* which allow TURBO programs to activate other TURBO programs. The syntax of the procedure calls are:

Chain(*FilVar*)
Execute(*FilVar*)

where *FilVar* is a file variable of any type, previously assigned to a disk file with the standard procedure *Assign*. If the file exists, it is loaded into memory and executed.

The *Chain* procedure is used only to activate special TURBO Pascal .CHN files, i.e. files compiled with the cHn-file option selected on the Options menu (see page 190). Such a file contains only program code; no Pascal library, it uses the Pascal library already present in memory.

The *Execute* procedure is used to activate any TURBO Pascal .CMD file.

If the disk file does not exist, an I/O error occurs. This error is treated as described on page 116. When the I compiler directive is passive (({$I-}), program execution continues with the statement following the failed *Chain* or *Execute* statement, and the *IOresult* function must be called prior to further I/O.

Data can be transferred from the current program to the chained program either by *shared global variables* or by *absolute address variables*.

To ensure overlapping, shared global variables should be declared as the very first variables in both programs, and they must be listed in the same order in both declarations. Furthermore, both programs must be compiled to the same size of code and data segments (see pages 228 and 229). When these conditions are satisfied, the variables will be placed at the same address in memory by both programs, and as TURBO Pascal does not automatically initialize its variables, they may be shared.

Example:
Program *MAIN.CMD:*

```
program Main;
var
  Txt:       string[80];
  CntPrg:    file;

begin
  Write('Enter any text: '); Readln(Txt);
  Assign(CntPrg, 'ChrCount.chn');
  Chain(CntPrg);
end.
```

Program *CHRCOUNT.CHN:*

```
program ChrCount;
var
  Txt:       string[80];
  NoOfChar,
  NoOfUpc,
  I:         Integer;

begin
  NoOfUpc := 0;
  NoOfChar := Length(Txt);
  for I := 1 to length(Txt) do
    if Txt[I] in ['A'..'Z'] then NoOfUpc := Succ(NoOfUpc);
  Write('No of characters in entry: ',NoOfChar);
  Writeln('. No of upper case characters: ', NoOfUpc,'.');
end.
```

If you want a TURBO program to determine whether it was invoked by eXecute or directly from the CP/M command line, you should use an **absolute** variable at address *Dseg:$80*. This is the command line length byte, and when a program is called from CP/M, it contains a value between 0 and 127. When eXecuting a program, therefore, the calling program should set this variable to something higher than 127. When you then check the variable in the called program, a value between 0 and 127 indicates that the program was called from CP/M, a higher value that it was called from another TURBO program.

Chaining and eXecuting TURBO programs does not alter the memory allocation state. The base addresses and sizes of the code, data and stack segments are not changed; *Chain* and *Execute* only replace the program code in the code segment. 'Alien' programs, therefore, cannot be initiated from a TURBO program.

It is important that the first program which executes a *Chain* statement allocates enough memory for the code, data, and stack segments to accommodate largest .CHN program. This is done by using the Options menu to change the minimum code, data and free memory sizes (see page 190).

Note that neither *Chain* nor *Execute* can be used in direct mode, that is, from a program run with the compiler options switch in position **Memory** (page 190).

Overlays

During execution, the system normally expects to find its overlay files on the logged drive. The *OvrDrive* procedure may be used to change this default value.

OvrDrive Procedure

Syntax: OvrDrive(*Drive*);

where *Drive* is an integer expression specifying a drive (0 = logged drive, 1 = A:, 2 = B:, etc.). On subsequent calls to overlay files, the files will be expected on the specified drive. Once an overlay file has been opened on one drive, future calls to the same file will look on the same drive.

Example:
```
program OvrTest;

overlay procedure ProcA;
begin
  Writeln('Overlay A');
end;
```

```
overlay procedure ProcB;
begin
  Writeln('Overlay B');
end;

procedure Dummy;
begin
  {Dummy procedure to separate the overlays
   into two groups}
end;

overlay procedure ProcC;
begin
  Writeln('Overlay C');
end;

begin
  OvrDrive(2);
  ProcA;
  OvrDrive(0);
  ProcC;
  OvrDrive(2);
  ProcB;
end.
```

The first call to *OvrDrive* specifies overlays to be sought on the B: drive. The call to *ProcA* therefore causes the first overlay file (containing the two overlay procedures *ProcA* and *ProcB* to be opened here.

Next, the *OvrDrive(0)* statement specifies that following overlays are to be found on the logged drive. The call to *ProcC* opens the second overlay file here.

The following *ProcB* statement calls an overlay procedure in the first overlay file; and to ensure that it is sought on the B: drive, the *OvrDrive(2)* statement must be executed before the call.

Files

File Names

A file name in CP/M consists of one through eight letters or digits, optionally followed by a period and a file type of one through three letters or digits:

Drive:Name.Type

Untyped Files

An optional second parameter on *Reset* and *ReWrite* may be used to specify the block size to be used by *BlockRead* and *BlockWrite*. For example:

```
Assign(InFile,'INDATA');
Reset(InFile,BlockSize);
```

where *BlockSize* is an integer expression.

Text Files

The *Seek* and *Flush* procedures and the *FilePos* and *FileSize* functions are not applicable to CP/M text files.

Buffer Size

The text file buffer size is 128 bytes by default. This is adequate for most applications, but heavily I/O-bound programs, as for example a copy program, will benefit from a larger buffer, as it will reduce disk head movement.

You are therefore given the option to specify the buffer size when declaring a text file:

```
VAR
   TextFile: Text[$1000];
```

declares a text file variable with a buffer size of 4K bytes.

Absolute Variables

Variables may be declared to reside at specific memory addresses, and
are then called **absolute**. This is done by adding to the variable declaration
the reserved word **absolute** followed by two *Integer* constants specifying a segment and an offset at which the variable is to be located:

```
var
  Abc: Integer  absolute $0000:$00EE;
  Def: Integer  absolute $0000:$00F0;
```

The first constant specifies the segment base address, and the second
constant specifies the offset within that segment. The standard
identifiers *CSeg* and *DSeg* may be used to place variables at absolute
addresses within the code segment (CSeg) or the data segment (DSeg):

```
Patch: array[1..PatchSize] of byte absolute CSeg:$05F3;
```

Absolute may also be used to declare a variable "on top" of another
variable, i.e. that a variable should start at the same address as another
variable. When **absolute** is followed by the identifier of a variable or
parameter, the new variable will start at the address of that variable
parameter.

Example:
```
var
  Str: string[32];
  StrLen: Byte absolute Str;
```

This declaration specifies that the variable *StrLen* should start at the
same address as the variable *Str*, and as the first byte of a string variable contains the length of the string, *StrLen* will contain the length of
Str. Notice that an **absolute** variable declaration may only specify one
identifier.

Further details on space allocation for variables are found on page 246.

Absolute Address Functions

The following functions are provided for obtaining information about program variable addresses and system pointers.

Addr

Syntax: Addr(*Name*)

Returns the address in memory of the first byte of the variable with the identifier *Name*. If *Name* is an array, it may be subscripted, and if *Name* is a record, specific fields may be selected. The value returned is a 32 bit pointer consisting of a segment address and an offset.

Ofs

Syntax: Ofs(*Name*)

Returns the offset in the segment of memory occupied by the first byte of the variable, procedure or function with the identifier *Name*. If *Name* is an array, it may be subscripted, and if *Name* is a record, specific fields may be selected. The value returned is an *Integer*.

Seg

Syntax: Seg(*Name*)

Returns the address of the segment containing the first byte of the variable with the identifier *Name*. If *Name* is an array, it may be subscripted, and if *Name* is a record, specific fields may be selected. The value returned is an *Integer*. To obtain the segment address of a procedure or function, use the CSEG function.

Cseg

Syntax: Cseg

Returns the base address of the Code segment. The value returned is an *Integer*.

Dseg

Syntax: Dseg

Returns the base address of the **D**ata segment. The value returned is an *Integer*.

Sseg

Syntax: Sseg

Returns the base address of the **S**tack segment. The value returned is an *Integer*.

Predefined Arrays

TURBO Pascal offers four predefined arrays of type *Byte*, called *Mem*, *MemW*, *Port* and *PortW* which are used to access CPU memory and data ports.

Mem Array

The predefined arrays *Mem* and *MemW* are used to access memory. Each component of the array *Mem* is a byte, and each component of the array *Wmem* is a word (two bytes, LSB first). The index must be an address specified as the segment base address and an offset separated by a colon and both of type *Integer*.

The following statement assigns the value of the byte located in segment 0000 at offset $0081 to the variable *Value*

```
Value:=Mem[0000:$0081];
```

While the following statement:

```
MemW[Seg(Var):Ofs(Var)]:=Value;
```

places the value of the *Integer* variable *Value* in the memory location occupied by the two first bytes of the variable *Var*.

Port Array

The *Port* and *PortW* array are used to access the data ports of the 8086/88 CPU. Each element of the array represents a data port, with the index corresponding to port numbers. As data ports are selected by 16-bit addresses the index type is *Integer*. When a value is assigned to a component of *Port* or *PortW* it is output to the port specified. When a component of port is referenced in an expression, its value is input from the port specified. The components of the *Port* array are of type *Byte* and the components of *PortW* are of type *Integer*.

Example:
```
Port[56]:=10;
```

The use of the port array is restricted to assignment and reference in expressions only, i.e. components of *Port* and *PortW* cannot be used as variable parameters to procedures and functions. Furthermore, operations referring to the entire port array (reference without index) are not allowed.

With Statements

With statements may be nested to a maximum of 9 levels.

Pointer Related Items

MemAvail

The standard function *MemAvail* is available to determine the available space on the heap at any given time. The result is an *Integer* specifying the number of available *paragraphs* on the heap (a *paragraph* is 16 bytes).

Pointer Values

In very special circumstances it can be of interest to assign a specific value to a pointer variable *without using another pointer variable* or it can be of interest to obtain the actual value of a pointer variable.

Assigning a Value to a Pointer

The standard function *Ptr* can be used to assign specific values to a pointer variable. The function returns a 32 bit pointer consisting of a segment address and an offset.

Example:
```
Pointer:=Ptr(Cseg,$80);
```

Obtaining The Value of a Pointer

A pointer value is represented as a 32 bit entity and the standard function *Ord* can therefore **not** be used to obtain its value. Instead the functions *Ofs* and *Seg* must be used.

The following statement obtains the value of the pointer *P* (which is a segment address and an offset):

```
SegmentPart:=Seg(P^);
OffsetPart:=Ofs(P^);
```

Function Calls

For the purpose of calling the CP/M-86 BDOS, TURBO Pascal introduces a procedure *Bdos*, which has a record as parameter.

Details on BDOS and BIOS routines are found in the *CP/M-86 Operating System Manual* published by Digital Research.

The parameter to *Bdos* must be of the type:

```
record
  AX,BX,CX,DX,BP,SI,DI,DS,ES,Flags: Integer;
end;
```

Before TURBO calls the BDOS, the registers AX, BX, CX, DX, BP, SI, DI, DS, and ES are loaded with the values specified in the record parameter. When the BDOS has finished operation the *Bdos* procedure will restore the registers to the record thus making any results from the BDOS available.

User Written I/O Drivers

For some applications it is practical for a programmer to define his own input and output drivers, i.e. routines which perform input and output of characters to and from an external device. The following drivers are part of the TURBO environment, and used by the standard I/O drivers (although they are not available as standard procedures or functions):

function	*ConSt*: boolean; { 6 }
function	*ConIn*: Char; { 6 }
procedure	*ConOut*(Ch: Char); { 6 }
procedure	*LstOut*(Ch: Char); { 5 }
procedure	*AuxOut*(Ch: Char); { 4 }
function	*AuxIn*: Char; { 3 }
procedure	*UsrOut*(Ch: Char); { 6 }
function	*UsrIn*: Char; { 6 }

The *ConSt* routine is called by the function *KeyPressed*, the *ConIn* and *ConOut* routines are used by the CON:, TRM:, and KBD: devices, the *LstOut* routine is used by the LST: device, the *AuxOut* and *AuxIn* routines are used by the AUX: device, and the *UsrOut* and *UsrIn* routines are used by the USR: device.

By default, these drivers are assigned to the BDOS functions as showed in curly braces in the above listing of drivers.

This, however, may be changed by the programmer by assigning the address of a self-defined driver procedure or a driver function to one of the following standard variables:

Variable	Contains the address of the
ConStPtr	*ConSt* function
ConInPtr	*ConIn* function
ConOutPtr	*ConOut* procedure
LstOutPtr	*LstOut* procedure
AuxOutPtr	*AuxOut* procedure
AuxInPtr	*AuxIn* function
UsrOutPtr	*UsrOut* procedure
UsrInPtr	*UsrIn* function

A user defined driver procedure or driver function must match the definitions given above, i.e. a *ConSt* driver must be a boolean function, a *ConIn* driver must be a char function, etc.

External Subprograms

The reserved word **external** is used to declare external procedures and functions, typically procedures and functions written in machine code.

The reserved word **external** must be followed by a string constant specifying the name of a file in which executable machine code for the external procedure or function must reside.

During compilation of a program containing external functions or procedures the associated files are loaded and placed in the object code. Since it is impossible to know beforehand exactly *where* in the object code the external code will be placed this code **must** be relocatable, and no references must be made to the data segment. Furthermore the external code must save the registers BP, CS, DS and SS and restore these before executing the RET instruction.

An external subprogram has no *block*, i.e. no declaration part and no statement part. Only the subprogram heading is specified, immediately followed by the reserved word **external** and a filename specifying where to find the executable code for the subprogram.

The type of the filename is *.CMD*. Only the code segment of a .CMD file is loaded.

Example:
```
procedure DiskReset; external 'DSKRESET';
function IOstatus: boolean; external 'IOSTAT';
```

Parameters may be passed to external subprograms, and the syntax is exactly the same as that of calls to ordinary procedures and functions:

```
procedure Plot(X,Y: Integer); external 'PLOT';
procedure QuickSort(var List: PartNo); external 'QS';
```

External subprograms and parameter passing is discussed further on page 252.

In-line Machine Code

TURBO Pascal features the **inline** statements as a very convenient way of inserting machine code instructions directly into the program text. An inline statement consists of the reserved word **inline** followed by one or more *code elements* separated by slashes and enclosed in parentheses.

A code element is built from one or more data elements, separated by plus (+) or minus (−) signs. A data element is either an integer constant, a variable identifier, a procedure identifier, a function identifier, or a location counter reference. A location counter reference is written as an asterisk (*).

Example:
```
inline (10/$2345/count+1/sort-*+2);
```

Each code element generates one byte or one word (two bytes) of code. The value of the byte or the word is calculated by adding or subtracting the values of the data elements according to the signs that separate them. The value of a variable identifier is the address (or offset) of the variable. The value of a procedure or function identifier is the address (or offset) of the procedure or function. The value of a location counter reference is the address (or offset) of the location counter, i.e. the address at which to generate the next byte of code.

A code element will generate one byte of code if it consists of integer constants only, and if its value is within the 8-bit range (0..255). If the value is outside the 8-bit range, or if the code element refers to variable, procedure, or function identifiers, or if the code element contains a location counter reference, one word of code is generated (least significant byte first).

The ' < ' and ' > ' characters may be used to override the automatic size selection described above. If a code element starts with a ' < ' character, only the least significant byte of the value is coded, even if it is a 16-bit value. If a code element starts with a ' > ' character, a word is always coded, even though the most significant byte is zero.

Example:
```
inline (<$1234/>$44);
```

This **inline** statement generates three bytes of code: $34, $44, $00.

The value of a variable identifier use in a **inline** statement is the offset address of the variable within its base segment. The base segment of global variables (i.e. variables declared in the main program block) is the data segment, which is accessible through the DS register. The base segment of local variables (i.e. variables declared within the current sub-program) is the stack segment, and in this case the variable offset is relative to the BP (base page) register, the use of which automatically causes the stack segment to be selected. The base segment of typed constants is the code segment, which is accessible through the CS register. **inline** statements should not attempt to access variables that are not declared in the main program nor in the current subprogram.

The following example of an inline statement generates machine code that will convert all characters in its string argument to upper case.

```
procedure UpperCase(var Strg: Str);
{Str is type String[255]}
begin
  inline
    ($C4/$BE/Strg/      {      LES  DI,Strg[BP]         }
     $26/$8A/$0D/        {      MOV  CL,ES:[DI]           }
     $FE/$C1/            {      INC  CL                   }
     $FE/$C9/            { L1:  DEC  CL                   }
     $74/$13/            {      JZ   L2                   }
     $47/                {      INC  DI                   }
     $26/$80/$3D/$61/    {      CMP  ES:BYTE PTR [DI],'a'}
     $72/$F5/            {      JB   L1                   }
     $26/$80/$3D/$7A/    {      CMP  ES:BYTE PTR [DI],'z'}
     $77/$EF/            {      JA   L1                   }
     $26/$80/$2D/$20/    {      SUB  ES:BYTE PTR [DI],20H}
     $EB/$E9);           {      JMP  SHORT L1             }
                         { L2:                            }
end;
```

Inline statements may be freely mixed with other statements throughout the statement part of a block, and **inline** statements may use all CPU registers. **Note**, however, that the contents of the registers BP, SP, DS, and SS must be the same on exit as on entry.

Interrupt Handling

A TURBO Pascal interrupt routine must manually preserve registers AX, BX, CX, DX, SI, DI, DS and ES. This is done by placing the following in-line statement as the first statement of the procedure:

```
inline ($50/$53/$51/$52/$56/$57/$1E/$06/$FB);
```

The last byte ($FB) is an STI instruction which enables further interrupts - it may or may not be required. The following inline statement must be the last statement in the procedure:

```
inline ($07/$1F/$5F/$5E/$5A/$59/$5B/$58/$8B/$E5/$5D/$CF);
```

This restores the registers and reloads the stack pointer (SP) and the base page register (BP). The last byte ($CF) is an IRET instruction which overrides the RET instruction generated by the compiler.

An interrupt service procedure must not employ any I/O operations using the standard procedures and functions of TURBO Pascal, as the BDOS is not re-entrant. The programmer must initialize the interrupt vector used to activate the interrupt service routine.

Intr procedure

Syntax: Intr(*InterruptNo, Result*)

This procedure initializes the registers and flags as specified in the parameter *Result* which must be of type:

```
Result = record
            AX,BX,CX,DX,BP,SI,DI,DS,ES,Flags: Integer;
         end;
```

It then makes the software interrupt given by the parameter *interruptNo* which must be an *Integer* constant. When the interrupt service routine returns control to your program, *Result* will contain any values returned from the service routine.

Note that the data segment register DS, used to access global variables, will not have the correct value when the interrupt service routine is entered. Therefore, global variables cannot be directly accessed. *Typed constants*, however, are available, as they are stored in the code segment. The way to access global variables in the interrupt service routine is therefore to store the value of *Dseg* in a typed constant in the main program. This typed constant can then be accessed by the interrupt handler and used to set its DS register.

Internal Data Formats

In the following descriptions, the symbol @ denotes the offset of the first byte occupied by a variable of the given type within its segment. The segment base address can be determined by using the standard function *Seg*.

Global and *local variables*, and *typed constants* occupy different segments as follows:

Global variables reside in the data segment and the offset is relative to the DS register.

Local variables reside in the stack segment and the offset is relative to the BP register.

Typed constants reside in the code segment and the offset is relative to the CS register.

All variables are contained within their base segment.

Basic Data Types

The basic data types may be grouped into structures (arrays, records, and disk files), but this structuring will not affect their internal formats.

Scalars

The following scalars are all stored in a single byte: *Integer* subranges with both bounds in the range 0..255, booleans, chars, and declared scalars with less than 256 possible values. This byte contains the ordinal value of the variable.

The following scalars are all stored in two bytes: *Integers*, *Integer* subranges with one or both bounds not within the range 0..255, and declared scalars with more than 256 possible values. These bytes contain a 2's complement 16-bit value with the least significant byte stored first.

Reals

Reals occupy 6 bytes, giving a floating point value with a 40-bit mantissa and an 8-bit 2's exponent. The exponent is stored in the first byte and the mantissa in the next five bytes with the least significant byte first:

@	Exponent
@ + 1	LSB of mantissa
:	
@ + 5	MSB of mantissa

The exponent uses binary format with an offset of $80. Hence, an exponent of $84 indicates that the value of the mantissa is to be multiplied by 2 ^($84-$80) = 2 ^4 = 16. If the exponent is zero, the floating point value is considered to be zero.

The value of the mantissa is obtained by dividing the 40-bit unsigned integer by 2^40. The mantissa is always normalized, i.e. the most significant bit (bit 7 of the fifth byte) should be interpreted as a 1. The sign of the mantissa is stored in this bit, however, a 1 indicating that the number is negative, and a 0 indicating that the number is positive.

Strings

A string occupies as many bytes as its maximum length plus one. The first byte contains the current length of the string. The following bytes contains the string with the first character stored at the lowest address. In the table shown below, **L** denotes the current length of the string, and *Max* denotes the maximum length:

@	Current length (*L*)
@ + 1	First character
@ + 2	Second character
:	
@ + *L*	Last character
@ + *L* + 1	Unused
:	
@ + *Max*	Unused

Sets

An element in a *Set* occupies one bit, and as the maximum number of elements in a set is 256, a set variable will never occupy more than 32 bytes (256/8).

If a set contains less than 256 elements, some of the bits are bound to be zero at all times and need therefore not be stored. In terms of memory efficiency, the best way to store a set variable of a given type would then be to "cut off" all insignificant bits, and rotate the remaining bits so that the first element of the set would occupy the first bit of the first byte. Such rotate operations, however, are quite slow, and TURBO therefore employs a compromise: Only bytes which are statically zero (i.e. bytes of which no bits are used) are not stored. This method of compression is very fast and in most cases as memory efficient as the rotation method.

The number of bytes occupied by a set variable is calculated as (*Max* **div** 8) − (*Min* **div** 8) + 1, where *Max* and *Min* are the upper and lower bounds of the base type of that set. The memory address of a specific element *E* is:

MemAddress = @ + (*E* **div** 8) − (*Min* **div** 8)

and the bit address within the byte at MemAddress is:

BitAddress = *E* **mod** 8

where *E* denotes the ordinal value of the element.

Pointers

A pointer consists of four bytes containing a segment base address and an offset. The two least significant bytes contains the offset and the two most significant bytes the base address. Both are stored in memory using byte reversed format, i.e. the least significant byte is stored first. The value **nil** corresponds to two zero words.

Data Structures

Data structures are built from the basic data types using various structuring methods. Three different structuring methods exist: Arrays, records, and disk files. The structuring of data does not in any way affect the internal formats of the basic data types.

Arrays

The components with the lowest index values are stored at the lowest memory address. A multi-dimensional array is stored with the rightmost dimension increasing first, e.g. given the array

```
Board: array[1..8,1..8] of Square
```

you have the following memory layout of its components:

```
lowest address:    Board[1,1]
                   Board[1,2]
                   :
                   Board[1,8]
                   Board[2,1]
                   Board[2,2]
                   :
                   :
Highest address:   Board[8,8]
```

Records

The first field of a record is stored at the lowest memory address. If the record contains no variant parts, the length is given by the sum of the lengths of the individual fields. If a record contains a variant, the total number of bytes occupied by the record is given by the length of the fixed part plus the length of largest of its variant parts. Each variant starts at the same memory address.

Disk Files

Disk files are different from other data structures in that data is not stored in internal memory but in a file on an external device. A disk file is controlled through a file interface block (FIB).

File Interface Blocks

The table below shows the format of a FIB:

@ + 0	Flags byte.
@ + 1	Character buffer.
@ + 2	Number of records (LSB) or buffer offset (LSB).
@ + 3	Number of records (MSB) or buffer offset (MSB).
@ + 4	Record length (LSB) or buffer size (LSB).
@ + 5	Record length (MSB) or buffer size (MSB).
@ + 6	Buffer pointer (LSB).
@ + 7	Buffer pointer (MSB).
@ + 8	Current record (LSB) or buffer end (LSB).
@ + 9	Current record (MSB) or buffer end (LSB).
@ + 10	Unused.
@ + 11	Unused.
@ + 12	First byte of CP/M FCB.
:	
@ + 47	Last byte of CP/M FCB.
@ + 48	First byte of sector buffer.
:	
@ + 175	Last byte of sector buffer.

The format of the flags byte at @ + 0 is:

Bit 0..3   File type.
Bit 4   Read semaphore.
Bit 5   Write semaphore or pre-read character flag.
Bit 6   Output flag.
Bit 7   Input flag.

File type 0 denotes a disk file, and 1 through 5 denote the TURBO Pascal logical I/O devices (CON:, KBD:, LST:, AUX:, and USR:). For typed files, bit 4 is set if the contents of the sector buffer is undefined, and bit 5 is set if data has been written to the sector buffer. For textfiles, bit 5 is set if the character buffer contains a pre-read character. Bit 6 is set if output is allowed, and bit 7 is set if input is allowed.

For typed and untyped files, the four words from @ + 2 to @ + 9 store the number of records in the file, the record length in bytes, the sector buffer pointer, and the current record number. For typed files, the sector buffer pointer stores an offset (0..127) in the sector buffer at @ + 48. The FIB of an untyped file has no sector buffer, and so the sector buffer pointer is not used.

For text files, the four words from @ + 2 to @ + 9 store the offset address of the buffer, its size, the offset of the next character to read or write, and the offset of the first byte after the buffer. The buffer always resides in the same segment as the FIB, usually starting at @ + 48. The size of a textfile FIB may be larger than indicated, depending on the size of the buffer. When a textfile is assigned to a logical device, only the flags byte and the character buffer are used.

Random Access Files

A random access file consists of a sequence of records, all of the same length and same internal format. To optimize file storage capacity, the records of a file are totally contiguous. The first four bytes of the first sector of a file contains the number of records in the file and the length of each record in bytes. The first record of the file is stored starting at the fourth byte.

sector 0, byte 0:	Number of records (LSB)
sector 0, byte 1:	Number of records (MSB)
sector 0, byte 2:	Record length (LSB)
sector 0, byte 3:	Record length (MSB)

Text Files

The basic components of a text file are characters, but a text file is furthermore divided into *lines*. Each line consists of any number of characters ended by a CR/LF sequence (ASCII $0D/ $0A). The file is terminated by a Ctrl-Z (ASCII $1B).

Parameters

Parameters are transferred to procedures and functions via the stack which is addressed through SS:SP.

On entry to an **external** subroutine, the top of the stack always contains the return address within the code segment (a word). The parameters, if any, are located below the return address, i.e. at higher addresses on the stack.

If an external function has the following subprogram header:

function Magic(**var** R: Real; S: string5): Integer;

then the stack upon entry to *Magic* would have the following contents:

```
< Function result          >
< Segment base address of R >
< Offset address of R       >
< First character of S      >
:
< Last character of S       >
< Length of S               >
< Return address            > SP
```

An external subroutine should save the Base Page register (BP) and then copy the Stack Pointer SP into the Base Page register in order to be able to refer to parameters. Furthermore the subroutine should reserve space on the stack for local workarea. This can be obtained by the following instructions:

```
PUSH  BP
MOV   BP,SP
SUB   SP,WORKAREA
```

The last instruction will have the effect of adding the following to the stack:

```
< Return address                     >  BP
< The saved BP register              >
< First byte of local workarea       >
:
< Last byte of local work area >  SP
```

Parameters are accessed via the BP register.

The following instruction will load length of the string into the AL register:

```
MOV   AL,[BP+4]
```

Before executing a RET instruction the subprogram must reset the Stack Pointer and Base Page register to their original values. When executing the RET the parameters may be removed by giving RET a parameter specifying how many bytes to remove. The following instructions should therefore be used when exiting from a subprogram:

```
MOV   SP,BP
POP   BP
RET   NoOfBytesToRemove
```

Variable Parameters

With a variable (**var**) parameter, two words are transferred on the stack giving the base address and offset of the first byte occupied by the actual parameter.

Value Parameters

With value parameters, the data transferred on the stack depends upon the type of the parameter as described in the following sections.

Scalars

Integers, Booleans, Chars and declared scalars (i.e. all scalars except *Reals*) are transferred on the stack as a word. If the variable occupies only one byte when it is stored, the most significant byte of the parameter is zero.

Reals

A real is transferred on the stack using six bytes.

Strings

When a string is at the top of the stack, the topmost byte contains the length of the string followed by the characters of the string.

Sets

A set always occupies 32 bytes on the stack (set compression only applies to the loading and storing of sets).

Pointers

A pointer value is transferred on the stack as two words containing the base address and offset of a dynamic variable. The value NIL corresponds to two zero words.

Arrays and Records

Even when used as value parameters, *Array* and *Record* parameters are not actually transferred on the stack. Instead, two words containing the base address and offset of the first byte of the parameter are transferred. It is then the responsibility of the subroutine to use this information to make a local copy of the variable.

Function Results

User written **external** functions must remove all parameters and the function result from the stack when they return.

User written **external** functions must return their results exactly as specified in the following:

Values of scalar types, except *Reals*, must be returned in the AX register. If the result is only one byte then AH should be set to zero. Boolean functions must return the function value by setting the Z flag (Z = *False*, NZ = *True*).

Reals must be returned on the stack with the exponent at the lowest address. This is done by not removing the function result variable when returning.

Sets must be returned on the top of the stack according to the format described on page 254. On exit SP must point at the byte containing the string length.

Pointer values must be returned in the DX:AX.

The Heap and The Stacks

During execution of TURBO Pascal program the following segments are allocated for the program:

a Code Segment,
a Data Segment, and
a Stack Segment

Two stack-like structures are maintained during execution of a program: the *heap* and the *stack*.

The heap is used to store dynamic variables, and is controlled with the standard procedures *New, Mark,* and *Release*. At the beginning of a program, the heap pointer *HeapPtr* is set to low memory in the stack segment and the heap grows upwards towards the stack. The pre-defined variable *HeapPtr* contains the value of the heap pointer and allows the programmer to control the position of the heap.

The stack is used to store local variables, intermediate results during evaluation of expressions and to transfer parameters to procedures and functions. At the beginning of a program, the stack pointer is set to the address of the top of the stack segment.

On each call to the procedure *New* and on entering a procedure or function, the system checks for collision between the heap and the recursion stack. If a collision has occurred, an execution error results, unless the **K** compiler directive is passive (({ $K-}).

Memory Management

When a TURBO program is executed, three segments are allocated for the program: A code segment, a data segment, and a stack segment.

Code segment (CS is the code segment register):

```
CS:0000 - CS:EOFR    Run-time library code.
CS:EOFR - CS:EOFP    Program code.
CS:EOFP - CS:EOFC    Unused.
```

Data segment (DS is the data segment register):

```
DS:0000 - DS:00FF    CP/M-86 base page.
DS:0100 - DS:EOFW    Run-time library workspace.
DS:EOFW - DS:EOFM    Main program block variables.
DS:EOFM - DS:EOFD    Unused.
```

The unused areas between (CS:EOFP-CS:EOFC and DS:EOFM-DS:EOFD) are allocated only if a minimum cOde segment size larger than the required size is specified at compilation. The sizes of the code and data segments never exceed 64K bytes each.

The stack segment is slightly more complicated, as it may be larger than 64K bytes. On entry to the program the stack segment register (SS) and the stack pointer (SP) is loaded so that SS:SP points at the very last byte available in the entire segment. During execution of the program SS is never changed but SP may move downwards until it reaches the bottom of the segment, or 0 (corresponding to 64K bytes of stack) if the stack segment is larger than 64K bytes.

The heap grows from low memory in the stack segment towards the actual stack residing in high memory. Each time a variable is allocated on the heap, the heap pointer (which is a double word variable maintained by the TURBO run-time system) is moved upwards, and then normalized, so that the offset address is always between $0000 and $000F. Therefore, the maximum size of a single variable that can be allocated on the heap is 65521 bytes (corresponding to $10000 less $000F). The total size of all variables allocated on the heap is however only limited by the amount of memory available.

The heap pointer is available to the programmer through the *HeapPtr* standard identifier. *HeapPtr* is a typeless pointer which is compatible with all pointer types. Assignments to *HeapPtr* should be exercised only with extreme care.

Memory Management

Notes:

Chapter 22
CP/M-80

This chapter describes features of TURBO Pascal specific to the 8-bit CP/M-80 implementation. It presents two kinds of information:

1) Things you should know to make efficient use of TURBO Pascal. Pages 259 through 272.

2) The rest of the chapter describes things which are only of interest to experienced programmers, such as machine language routines, technical aspects of the compiler, etc.

eXecute Command

You will find an additional command on the main TURBO menu in the CP/M-80 version: eXecute. It lets you run other programs from within TURBO Pascal, for example copying programs, word processors - in fact anything that you can run from your operating system. When entering **X**, you are prompted:

Command: ■

You may now enter the name of any program which will then load and run normally. Upon exit from the program, control is re-transferred to TURBO Pascal, and you return to the TURBO prompt > .

compiler Options

The **O** command selects the following menu on which you may view and change some default values of the compiler. It also provides a helpful function to find runtime errors in programs compiled into object code files.

```
compile -> Memory
            Com-file
            cHn-file

command line Parameter:

Find run-time error   Quit
```

Figure 22-1: Options Menu

Memory / Com file / cHn-file

The three commands **M**, **C**, and **H** select the compiler mode, i.e. where to put the code which results from the compilation.

Memory is the default mode. When active, code is produced in memory and resides there ready to be activated by a **R**un command.

Com-file is selected by pressing **C**. The arrow moves to point to this line. When active, code is written to a file with the same name as the Work file (or Main file, if specified) and the file type .COM. This file contains the program code and Pascal runtime library, and may be activated by typing its name at the console. Programs compiled this way may be larger than programs compiled in memory, as the program code itself does not take up memory during compilation, and as program code starts at a lower address.

c**H**ain-file is selected by pressing **H**. The arrow moves to point to this line. When active, code is written to a file with the same name as the Work file (or Main file, if specified) and the file type .CHN. This file contains the program code but no Pascal library and must be activated from another TURBO Pascal program with the *Chain* procedure (see page 263).

When **C**om or c**H**n mode is selected, the menu is expanded with the following two lines:

```
Start address: XXXX (min YYYY)
End   address: XXXX (max YYYY)
```

Figure 22-2: Start and End Addresses

Start Address

The Start address specifies the address (in hexadecimal) of the first byte of the code. This is normally the end address of the Pascal library plus one, but may be changed to a higher address if you want to set space aside e.g. for absolute variables to be shared by a series of chained programs.

When you enter an **S**, you are prompted to enter a new Start address. If you just hit < RETURN >, the minimum value is assumed. Don't set the Start address to anything less than the minimum value, as the code will then overwrite part of the Pascal library.

End Address

The End address specifies the highest address available to the program (in hexadecimal). The value in parentheses indicate the top of the TPA on your computer, i.e. BDOS minus one. The default setting is 700 to 1000 bytes less to allow space for the loader which resides just below BDOS when executing programs from TURBO.

If compiled programs are to run in a different environment, the **End** address may be changed to suit the TPA size of that system. If you anticipate your programs to run on a range of different computers, it will be wise to set this value relatively low, e.g. C100 (48K), or even A100 (40K) if the program is to run under MP/M.

When you enter an **E**, you are prompted to enter a End address. If you just hit < RETURN > , the default value is assumed (i.e. top of TPA less 700 to 1000 bytes). If you set the **E**nd address higher than this, the resulting programs cannot be executed from TURBO, as they will overwrite the TURBO loader; and if you set it higher than the TPA top, the resulting programs will overwrite part of BDOS if run on your machine.

Command Line Parameters

The **P**-command lets you enter one or more parameters which are passed to your program when running it in **M**emory mode, just as if they had been entered on the DOS command line. These parameters may be accessed through the *ParamCount* and *ParamStr* functions.

Find Runtime Error

When you run a program compiled in memory, and a runtime error occurs, the editor is invoked, and the error is automatically pointed out. This, of course, is not possible if the program is in a .COM file or an .CHN file. Run time errors then print out the error code and the value of the program counter at the time of the error, e.g.:

```
Run-time error 01, PC=1B56
Program aborted
```

Figure 22-3: Run-time Error Message

To find the place in the source text where the error occurred, enter the **F** command on the **O**ptions menu. When prompted for the address, enter the address given by the error message:

```
Enter PC: 1B56
```

Figure 22-4: Find Run-time Error

The place in the source text is now found and pointed out exactly as if the error had occurred while running the program in memory.

Standard Identifiers

The following standard identifiers are unique to the CP/M-80 implementation:

Bios	*Bdos*	*RecurPtr*
BiosHL	*BdosHL*	*StackPtr*

Chain and Execute

TURBO Pascal provides two standard procedures: *Chain* and *Execute* which allow you to activate other programs from a TURBO program. The syntax of these procedure calls is:

```
Chain(FilVar)
Execute(FilVar)
```

where *FilVar* is a file variable of any type, previously assigned to a disk file with the standard procedure *Assign*. If the file exists, it is loaded into memory and executed.

The *Chain* procedure is used only to activate special TURBO Pascal .CHN files, i.e. files compiled with the cHn-file option selected on the **O**ptions menu (see page 260). Such a file contains only program code; no Pascal library. It is loaded into memory and executed at the start address of the current program, i.e. the address specified when the current program was compiled. It then uses the Pascal library already present in memory. Thus, the current program and the chained program must use the same start address.

The *Execute* procedure may be used to execute any .COM file, i.e. any file containing executable code. This could be a file created by TURBO Pascal with the **C**om-option selected on the **O**ptions menu (see page 260). The file is loaded and executed at address $100, as specified by the CP/M standard.

If the disk file does not exist, an I/O error occurs. This error is treated as described on page 116. If the **I** compiler directive is passive (($I-)), program execution continues with the statement following the failed *Chain* or *Execute* statement, and the *IOresult* function must be called prior to further I/O.

Data can be transferred from the current program to the chained program either by *shared global variables* or by *absolute address variables*.

To ensure overlapping, shared global variables should be declared as the very first variables in both programs, and they must be listed in the same order in both declarations. Furthermore, both programs must be compiled to the same memory size (see page 261). When these conditions are satisfied, the variables will be placed at the same address in memory by both programs, and as TURBO Pascal does not automatically initialize its variables, they may be shared.

Example:
Program *MAIN.COM:*

```
program Main;
var
  Txt:        string[80];
  CntPrg:     file;
begin
  Write('Enter any text: '); Readln(Txt);
  Assign(CntPrg, 'ChrCount.chn');
  Chain(CntPrg);
end.
```

Program *CHRCOUNT.CHN:*

```
program ChrCount;
var
  Txt:        string[80];
  NoOfChar,
  NoOfUpc,
  I:          Integer;
begin
  NoOfUpc := 0;
  NoOfChar := Length(Txt);
  for I := 1 to length(Txt) do
    if Txt[I] in ['A'..'Z'] then NoOfUpc := Succ(NoOfUpc);
  Write('No of characters in entry: ',NoOfChar);
  Writeln('. No of upper case characters: ', NoOfUpc,'.');
end.
```

If you want a TURBO program to determine whether it was invoked by eXecute or directly from the DOS command line, you should use an **absolute** variable at address *$80*. This is the command line length byte, and when a program is called from CP/M, it contains a value between 0 and 127. When eXecuting a program, therefore, the calling program should set this variable to something higher than 127. When you then check the variable in the called program, a value between 0 and 127 indicates that the program was called from CP/M, a higher value that it was called from another TURBO program.

Note that neither *Chain* nor *Execute* can be used in direct mode, i.e. from a program run with the compiler options switch in position **Memory** (page 260).

Overlays

During execution, the system normally expects to find its overlay files on the logged drive. The *OvrDrive* procedure may be used to change this default value.

OvrDrive Procedure

Syntax: OvrDrive(*Drive*)

where *Drive* is an integer expression specifying a drive (0 = logged drive, 1 = A:, 2 = B:, etc.). On subsequent calls to overlay files, the files will be expected on the specified drive. Once an overlay file has been opened on one drive, future calls to the same file will look on the same drive.

Example :
```
program OvrTest;

overlay procedure ProcA;
begin
  Writeln('Overlay A');
end;

overlay procedure ProcB;
begin
  Writeln('Overlay B');
end;
```

```
procedure Dummy;
begin
  {Dummy procedure to separate the overlays
   into two groups}
end;

overlay procedure ProcC;
begin
  Writeln('Overlay C');
end;

begin
  OvrDrive(2);
  ProcA;
  OvrDrive(0);
  ProcC;
  OvrDrive(2);
  ProcB;
end.
```

The first call to *OvrDrive* specifies overlays to be sought on the B: drive. The call to *ProcA* therefore causes the first overlay file (containing the two overlay procedures *ProcA* and *ProcB* to be opened here.

Next, the *OvrDrive(0)* statement specifies that following overlays are to be found on the logged drive. The call to *ProcC* opens the second overlay file here.

The following *ProcB* statement calls an overlay procedure in the first overlay file; and to ensure that it is sought on the B: drive, the *OvrDrive(2)* statement must be executed before the call.

Files

File Names

A file name in CP/M consists of one through eight letters or digits, optionally followed by a period and a file type of one through three letters or digits:

Drive:Name.Type

Text Files

The *Seek* and *Flush* procedures and the *FilePos* and *FileSize* functions are not applicable to CP/M text files.

Absolute Variables

Variables may be declared to reside at specific memory addresses, and are then called **absolute**. This is done by adding the reserved word **absolute** and an address expressed by an integer constant to the variable declaration.

Example:
```
var
IObyte: Byte absolute $0003;
CmdLine: string[127] absolute $80;
```

Absolute may also be used to declare a variable "on top" of another variable, i.e. that a variable should start at the same address as another variable. When **absolute** is followed by the variable (or parameter) identifier, the new variable will start at the address of that variable (or parameter).

Example:
```
var
Str: string[32];
StrLen: Byte absolute Str;
```

The above declaration specifies that the variable *StrLen* should start at the same address as the variable *Str*, and since the first byte of a string variable gives the length of the string, *StrLen* will contain the length of *Str*. Notice that only one identifier may be specified in an **absolute** declaration, i.e. the construct:

```
Identl, Ident2: Integer absolute $8000
```

is **illegal**. Further details on space allocation for variables are given on pages 278 and 288.

Addr Function

Syntax: Addr(*name*);

Returns the address in memory of the first byte of the type, variable, procedure, or function with the identifier *name*. If *name* is an array, it may be subscribed, and if *name* is a record, specific fields may be selected. The value returned is of type *Integer*.

Predefined Arrays

TURBO Pascal offers two predefined arrays of type *Byte*, called *Mem* and *Port*, which are used to directly access CPU memory and data ports.

Mem Array

The predeclared array *Mem* is used to access memory. Each component of the array is a *Byte*, and indexes correspond to addresses in memory. The index type is *Integer*. When a value is assigned to a component of *Mem*, it is stored at the address given by the index expression. When the *Mem* array is used in an expression, the byte at the address specified by the index is used.

Examples:
```
Mem[WsCursor] := 2;
Mem[WsCursor+1] := $1B;
Mem[WsCursor+2] := Ord(' ');
IObyte := Mem[3];
Mem[Addr+Offset] := Mem[Addr];
```

Port Array

The *Port* array is used to access the data ports of the Z-80 CPU. Each element of the array represents a data port with indexes corresponding to port numbers. As data ports are selected by 8-bit addresses, the index type is *Byte*. When a value is assigned to a component of *Port*, it is output to the port specified. When a component of *Port* is referenced in an expression, its value is input from the port specified.

The use of the port array is restricted to assignment and reference in expressions only, i.e. components of *Port* cannot function as variable parameters to procedures and functions. Furthermore, operations referring to the entire *Port* array (reference without index) are not allowed.

Array Subscript Optimization

The **X** compiler directive allows the programmer to select whether array subscription should be optimized with regard to execution speed or to code size. The default mode is active, i.e. { **$X +** }, which causes execution speed optimization. When passive, i.e. { **$X-**}, the code size is minimized.

With Statements

The default 'depth' of nesting of *With* statements is 2, but the **W** directive may be used to change this value to between 0 and 9. For each block, *With* statements require two bytes of storage for each nesting level allowed. Keeping the nesting to a minimum may thus greatly affect the size of the data area in programs with many subprograms.

Pointer Related Items

MemAvail

The standard function *MemAvail* is available to determine the available space on the heap at any given time. The result is an *Integer*, and if more than 32767 bytes is available, *MemAvail* returns a negative number. The correct number of free bytes is then calculated as 65536.0 + *MemAvail*. Notice the use of a real constant to generate a *Real* result, as the result is greater than *GMaxInt*. Memory management is discussed in further detail on page 288.

Pointers and Integers

The standard functions *Ord* and *Ptr* provide direct control of the address contained in a pointer. *Ord* returns the address contained in its pointer argument as an *Integer*, and *Ptr* converts its *Integer* argument into a pointer which is compatible with all pointer types.

These functions are extremely valuable in the hands of an experienced programmer as they allow a pointer to point to anywhere in memory. If used carelessly, however, they are very dangerous, as a dynamic variable may be made to overwrite other variables, or even program code.

CP/M Function Calls

For the purpose of calling CP/M BDOS and BIOS routines, TURBO Pascal introduces two standard procedures: *Bdos* and *Bios*, and four standard functions: *Bdos, BdosHL, Bios,* and *BiosHL*.

Details on BDOS and BIOS routines are found in the *CP/M Operating System Manual* published by Digital Research.

Bdos procedure and function

Syntax: Bdos(*Func* {, *Param* });

The *Bdos* **procedure** is used to invoke CP/M BDOS routines. *Func* and *Param* are integer expressions. *Func* denotes the number of the called routine and is loaded into the C register. *Param* is optional and denotes a parameter which is loaded into the DE register pair. A call to address 5 then invokes the BDOS.

The *Bdos* **function** is called like the procedure and returns an *Integer* result which is the value returned by the BDOS in the A register.

BdosHL function

Syntax: BdosHL(*Func* {, *Param* });

This function is exactly similar to the *Bdos* function above, except that the result is the value returned in the HL register pair.

Bios procedure and function

Syntax: Bios(*Func* {, *Param* });

The *Bios* **procedure** is used to invoke BIOS routines. *Func* and *Param* are integer expressions. *Func* denotes the number of the called routine, with 0 meaning the WBOOT routine, 1 the CONST routine, etc. I.e. the address of the called routine is *Func* * 3 plus the WBOOT address contained in addresses 1 and 2. *Param* is optional and denotes a parameter which is loaded into the BC register pair prior to the call.

The *Bios* **function** is called like the procedure and returns an integer result which is the value returned by the BIOS in the A register.

BiosHL function

Syntax: BiosHL(*Func* {, *Param* });

This function is exactly similar to the *Bios* function above, except that the result is the value returned in the HL register pair.

User Written I/O Drivers

For some applications it is practical for a programmer to define his own input and output drivers, i.e. routines which perform input and output of characters to and from external devices. The following drivers are part of the TURBO environment, and used by the standard I/O drivers (although they are not available as standard procedures or functions):

```
function    ConSt: boolean;
function    ConIn: Char;
procedure   ConOut (Ch: Char);
procedure   LstOut (Ch: Char);
procedure   AuxOut (Ch: Char);
function    AuxIn: Char;
procedure   UsrOut (Ch: Char);
function    UsrIn: Char;
```

The *ConSt* routine is called by the function *KeyPressed*, the *ConIn* and *ConOut* routines are used by the CON:, TRM:, and KBD: devices, the *LstOut* routine is used by the LST: device, the *AuxOut* and *AuxIn* routines are used by the AUX: device, and the *UsrOut* and *UsrIn* routines are used by the USR: device.

By default, these drivers use the corresponding BIOS entry points of the CP/M operating system, i.e. *ConSt* uses CONST, *ConIn* uses CONIN, *ConOut* uses CONOUT, *LstOut* uses LIST, *AuxOut* uses PUNCH, *AuxIn* uses READER, *UsrOut* uses CONOUT, and *UsrIn* uses CONIN. This, however, may be changed by the programmer by assigning the address of a self-defined driver procedure or a driver function to one of the following standard variables:

Variable	Contains the address of the
ConStPtr	*ConSt* function
ConInPtr	*ConIn* function
ConOutPtr	*ConOut* procedure
LstOutPtr	*LstOut* procedure
AuxOutPtr	*AuxOut* procedure
AuxInPtr	*AuxIn* function
UsrOutPtr	*UsrOut* procedure
UsrInPtr	*UsrIn* function

A user defined driver procedure or driver function must match the definitions given above, i.e. a *ConSt* driver must be a *Boolean* function, a *ConIn* driver must be a *Char* function, etc.

External Subprograms

The reserved word **external** is used to declare external procedures and functions, typically procedures and functions written in machine code.

An external subprogram has no *block*, i.e. no declaration part and no statement part. Only the subprogram heading is specified, immediately followed by the reserved word **external** and an integer constant defining the memory address of the subprogram:

```
procedure DiskReset; external $EC00;
function IOstatus: boolean; external $D123
```

Parameters may be passed to external subprograms, and the syntax is exactly the same as that of calls to ordinary procedures and functions:

```
procedure Plot(X,Y: Integer); external $F003;
procedure QuickSort(var List: PartNo); external $1C00;
```

Parameter passing to external subprograms is discussed further on page 283.

In-line Machine Code

TURBO Pascal features the **inline** statements as a very convenient way of inserting machine code instructions directly into the program text. An inline statement consists of the reserved word **inline** followed by one or more *code elements* separated by slashes and enclosed in parentheses.

A code element is built from one or more data elements, separated by plus (+) or minus (−) signs. A data element is either an integer constant, a variable identifier, a procedure identifier, a function identifier, or a location counter reference. A location counter reference is written as an asterisk (*).

Example:
```
inline (10/$2345/count+1/sort-*+2);
```

Each code element generates one byte or one word (two bytes) of code. The value of the byte or the word is calculated by adding or subtracting the values of the data elements according to the signs that separate them. The value of a variable identifier is the address (or offset) of the variable. The value of a procedure or function identifier is the address (or offset) of the procedure or function. The value of a location counter reference is the address (or offset) of the location counter, i.e. the address at which to generate the next byte of code.

A code element will generate one byte of code if it consists of integer constants only, and if its value is within the 8-bit range (0..255). If the value is outside the 8-bit range, or if the code element refers to variable, procedure, or function identifiers, or if the code element contains a location counter reference, one word of code is generated (least significant byte first).

The ' < ' and ' > ' characters may be used to override the automatic size selection described above. If a code element starts with a ' < ' character, only the least significant byte of the value is coded, even if it is a 16-bit value. If a code element starts with a ' > ' character, a word is always coded, even though the most significant byte is zero.

Example:
```
inline (<$1234/>$44);
```

This **inline** statement generates three bytes of code: $34, $44, $00.

The following example of an inline statement generates machine code that will convert all characters in its string argument to upper case.

```
procedure UpperCase(var Strg: Str); {Str is type String[255]}
{$A+}
begin
   inline ($2A/Strg/          {      LD    HL,(Strg)   }
           $46/               {      LD    B,(HL)      }
           $04/               {      INC   B           }
           $05/               { L1:  DEC   B           }
           $CA/*+20/          {      JP    Z,L2        }
           $23/               {      INC   HL          }
           $7E/               {      LD    A,(HL)      }
           $FE/$61/           {      CP    'a'         }
           $DA/*-9/           {      JP    C,L1        }
           $FE/$7B/           {      CP    'z'+1       }
           $D2/*-14/          {      JP    NC,L1       }
           $D6/$20/           {      SUB   20H         }
           $77/               {      LD    (HL),A      }
           $C3/*-20);         {      JP    L1          }
                              { L2:  EQU   $           }
end;
```

Inline statements may be freely mixed with other statements throughout
the statement part of a block, and **inline** statements may use all CPU
registers. **Note**, however, that the contents of the stack pointer register
(SP) must be the same on exit as on entry.

Interrupt Handling

The TURBO Pascal run time package and the code generated by the compiler are both fully interruptable. Interrupt service routines must preserve all registers used.

If required, interrupt service procedures may be written in Pascal. Such procedures should always be compiled with the **A** compiler directive active (({$A + }), they must not have parameters, and they must themselves insure that all registers used are preserved. This is done by placing an **inline** statement with the necessary PUSH instructions at the very beginning of the procedure, and another **inline** statement with the corresponding POP instructions at the very end of the procedure. The last instruction of the ending **inline** statement should be an EI instruction ($FB) to enable further interrupts. If daisy chained interrupts are used, the **inline** statement may also specify a RETI instruction ($ED, $4D), which will override the RET instruction generated by the compiler.

The general rules for register usage are that integer operations use only the AF, BC, DE, and HL registers, other operations may use IX and IY, and real operations use the alternate registers.

An interrupt service procedure should not employ any I/O operations using the standard procedures and functions of TURBO Pascal, as these routines are not re-entrant. Also note that BDOS calls (and in some instances BIOS calls, depending on the specific CP/M implementation) should not be performed from interrupt handlers, as these routines are not re-entrant.

The programmer may disable and enable interrupts throughout a program using DI and EI instructions generated by **inline** statements.

If mode 0 (IM 0) or mode 1 (IM 1) interrupts are employed, it is the responsibility of the programmer to initialize the restart locations in the base page (note that RST 0 cannot be used, as CP/M uses locations 0 through 7).

If mode 2 (IM 2) interrupts are employed, the programmer should generate an initialized jump table (an array of integers) at an absolute address, and initialize the I register through a **inline** statement at the beginning of the program.

Internal Data Formats

In the following descriptions, the symbol @ denotes the address of the first byte occupied by a variable of the given type. The standard function *Addr* may be used to obtain this value for any variable.

Basic Data Types

The basic data types may be grouped into structures (arrays, records, and disk files), but this structuring will not affect their internal formats.

Scalars

The following scalars are all stored in a single byte: *Integer* subranges with both bounds in the range 0..255, *Booleans, Chars*, and declared scalars with less than 256 possible values. This byte contains the ordinal value of the variable.

The following scalars are all stored in two bytes: *Integers, Integer* subranges with one or both bounds not within the range 0..255, and declared scalars with more than 256 possible values. These bytes contain a 2's complement 16-bit value with the least significant byte stored first.

Reals

Reals occupy 6 bytes, giving a floating point value with a 40-bit mantissa and an 8-bit 2's exponent. The exponent is stored in the first byte and the mantissa in the next five bytes which the least significant byte first:

@	Exponent
@ +1	LSB of mantissa
:	
@ +5	MSB of mantissa

The exponent uses binary format with an offset of $80. Hence, an exponent of $84 indicates that the value of the mantissa is to be multiplied by $2\hat{\ }(\$84-\$80) = 2\hat{\ }4 = 16$. If the exponent is zero, the floating point value is considered to be zero.

The value of the mantissa is obtained by dividing the 40-bit unsigned integer by 2 ^40. The mantissa is always normalized, i.e. the most significant bit (bit 7 of the fifth byte) should be interpreted as a 1. The sign of the mantissa is stored in this bit, a 1 indicating that the number is negative, and a 0 indicating that the number is positive.

Strings

A string occupies the number of bytes corresponding to one plus the maximum length of the string. The first byte contains the current length of the string. The following bytes contain the actual characters, with the first character stored at the lowest address. In the table shown below, **L** denotes the current length of the string, and *Max* denotes the maximum length:

@	Current length (*L*)
@ + 1	First character
@ + 2	Second character
:	
@ + *L*	Last character
@ + *L* + 1	Unused
:	
@ + *Max*	Unused

Sets

An element in a **set** occupies one bit, and as the maximum number of elements in a set is 256, a set variable will never occupy more than 32 bytes (256/8).

If a set contains less than 256 elements, some of the bits are bound to be zero at all times and need therefore not be stored. In terms of memory efficiency, the best way to store a set variable of a given type would then be to "cut off" all insignificant bits, and rotate the remaining bits so that the first element of the set would occupy the first bit of the first byte. Such rotate operations, however, are quite slow, and TURBO therefore employs a compromise: Only bytes which are statically zero (i.e. bytes of which no bits are used) are not stored. This method of compression is very fast and in most cases as memory efficient as the rotation method.

The number of bytes occupied by a set variable is calculated as (*Max* **div** 8) − (*Min* **div** 8) + 1, where *Max* and *Min* are the upper and lower bounds of the base type of that set. The memory address of a specific element *E* is:

MemAddress = @ + (*E* **div** 8) − (*Min* **div** 8)

and the bit address within the byte at MemAddress is:

BitAddress = *E* **mod** 8

where *E* denotes the ordinal value of the element.

File Interface Blocks

The table below shows the format of a FIB in TURBO Pascal-80:

@ + 0	Flags byte.
@ + 1	Character buffer.
@ + 2	Sector buffer pointer (LSB).
@ + 3	Sector buffer pointer (MSB).
@ + 4	Number of records (LSB).
@ + 5	Number of records (MSB).
@ + 6	Record length (LSB).
@ + 7	Record length (MSB).
@ + 8	Current record (LSB).
@ + 9	Current record (MSB).
@ + 10	Unused.
@ + 11	Unused.
@ + 12	First byte of CP/M FCB.
:	
@ + 47	Last byte of CP/M FCB.
@ + 48	First byte of sector buffer.
:	
@ + 175	Last byte of sector buffer.

The format of the flags byte at @ + 0 is:

Bit 0..3	File type.
Bit 4	Read semaphore.
Bit 5	Write semaphore.
Bit 6	Output flag.
Bit 7	Input flag.

File type 0 denotes a disk file, and 1 through 5 denote the TURBO Pascal logical I/O devices (CON:, KBD:, LST:, AUX:, and USR:). For typed files, bit 4 is set if the contents of the sector buffer is undefined, and bit 5 is set if data has been written to the sector buffer. For textfiles, bit 5 is set if the character buffer contains a pre-read character. Bit 6 is set if output is allowed, and bit 7 is set if input is allowed.

The sector buffer pointer stores an offset (0..127) in the sector buffer at @ + 48. For typed and untyped files, the three words from @ + 4 to @ + 9 store the number of records in the file, the record length in bytes, and the current record number. The FIB of an untyped file has no sector buffer, and so the sector buffer pointer is not used.

When a text file is assigned to a logical device, only the flags byte and the character buffer are used.

Pointers

A pointer consists of two bytes containing a 16-bit memory address, and it is stored in memory using byte reversed format, i.e. the least significant byte is stored first. The value **nil** corresponds to a zero word.

Data Structures

Data structures are built from the basic data types using various structuring methods. Three different structuring methods exist: arrays, records, and disk files. The structuring of data does not in any way affect the internal formats of the basic data types.

Arrays

The components with the lowest index values are stored at the lowest memory address. A multi-dimensional array is stored with the rightmost dimension increasing first, e.g. given the array

```
Board: array[1..8,1..8] of Square
```

you have the following memory layout of its components:

lowest address:	Board[1,1]
	Board[1,2]
	:
	Board[1,8]
	Board[2,1]
	Board[2,2]
	:
	:
Highest address:	Board[8,8]

Records

The first field of a record is stored at the lowest memory address. If the record contains no variant parts, the length is given by the sum of the lengths of the individual fields. If a record contains a variant, the total number of bytes occupied by the record is given by the length of the fixed part plus the length of largest of its variant parts. Each variant starts at the same memory address.

Disk Files

Disk files are different from other data structures in that data is not stored in internal memory but in a file on an external device. A disk file is controlled through a file interface block (FIB) as described on page 280. In general there are two different types of disk files: random access files and text files.

Random Access Files

A random access file consists of a sequence of records, all of the same length and same internal format. To optimize file storage capacity, the records of a file are totally contiguous. The first four bytes of the first sector of a file contains the number of records in the file and the length of each record in bytes. The first record of the file is stored starting at the fourth byte.

sector 0, byte 0:	Number of records (LSB)
sector 0, byte 1:	Number of records (MSB)
sector 0, byte 2:	Record length (LSB)
sector 0, byte 3:	Record length (MSB)

Text Files

The basic components of a text file are characters, but a text file is sub-divided into *lines*. Each line consists of any number of characters ended by a CR/LF sequence (ASCII $0D/ $0A). The file is terminated by a Ctrl-Z (ASCII $1A).

Parameters

Parameters are transferred to procedures and functions via the Z-80 stack. Normally, this is of no interest to the programmer, as the machine code generated by TURBO Pascal will automatically PUSH parameters onto the stack before a call, and POP them at the beginning of the sub-program. However, if the programmer wishes to use **external** subpro-grams, these must POP the parameters from the stack themselves.

On entry to an **external** subroutine, the top of the stack always contains the return address (a word). The parameters, if any, are located below the return address, i.e. at higher addresses on the stack. Therefore, to access the parameters, the subroutine must first POP off the return ad-dress, then all the parameters, and finally it must restore the return ad-dress by PUSHing it back onto the stack.

Variable Parameters

With a variable (VAR) parameter, a word is transferred on the stack giv-ing the absolute memory address of the first byte occupied by the actual parameter.

Value Parameters

With value parameters, the data transferred on the stack depends upon the type of the parameter as described in the following sections.

Scalars

Integers, Booleans, Chars and declared scalars are transferred on the stack as a word. If the variable occupies only one byte when it is stored, the most significant byte of the parameter is zero. Normally, a word is POPped off the stack using an instruction like POP HL.

Reals

A real is transferred on the stack using six bytes. If these bytes are POPped using the instruction sequence:

```
POP     HL
POP     DE
POP     BC
```

then L will contain the exponent, H the fifth (least significant) byte of the mantissa, E the fourth byte, D the third byte, C the second byte, and B the first (most significant) byte.

Strings

When a string is at the top of the stack, the byte pointed to by SP contains the length of the string. The bytes at addresses SP + 1 through SP + n (where n is the length of the string) contain the string with the first character stored at the lowest address. The following machine code instructions may be used to POP the string at the top of the stack and store it in *StrBuf*:

```
LD      DE,StrBuf
LD      HL,0
LD      B,H
ADD     HL,SP
LD      C,(HL)
INC     BC
LDIR
LD      SP,HL
```

Sets

A set always occupies 32 bytes on the stack (set compression only applies to the loading and storing of sets). The following machine code instructions may be used to POP the set at the top of the stack and store it in *SetBuf*:

```
LD      DE,SetBuf
LD      HL,0
ADD     HL,SP
LD      BC,32
LDIR
LD      SP,HL
```

This will store the least significant byte of the set at the lowest address in *SetBuf*.

Pointers

A pointer value is transferred on the stack as a word containing the memory address of a dynamic variable. The value NIL corresponds to a zero word.

Arrays and Records

Even when used as value parameters, *Array* and *Record* parameters are not actually PUSHed onto the stack. Instead, a word containing the address of the first byte of the parameter is transferred. It is then the responsibility of the subroutine to POP this word, and use it as the source address in a block copy operation.

Function Results

User written **external** functions must return their results exactly as specified in the following:

Values of scalar types, must be returned in the HL register pair. If the type of the result is expressed in one byte, then it must be returned in L and H must by zero.

Reals must be returned in the BC, DE, and HL register pairs. B, C, D, E, and H must contain the mantissa (most significant byte in B), and L must contain the exponent.

Strings and **sets** must be returned on the top of the stack on the formats described on page 284.

Pointer values must be returned in the HL register pair.

The Heap and The Stacks

As indicated by the memory maps in previous sections, three stack-like structures are maintained during execution of a program: The *heap*, the *CPU stack*, and the *recursion stack*.

The heap is used to store dynamic variables, and is controlled with the standard procedures *New, Mark,* and *Release*. At the beginning of a program, the heap pointer *HeapPtr* is set to the address of the bottom of free memory, i.e the first free byte after the object code.

The CPU stack is used to store intermediate results during evaluation of expressions and to transfer parameters to procedures and functions. An active **for** statement also uses the CPU stack, and occupies one word. At the beginning of a program, the CPU stack pointer *StackPtr* is set to the address of the top of free memory.

The recursion stack is used only by recursive procedures and functions, i.e. procedures and functions compiled with the **A** compiler directive passive (($A-)). On entry to a recursive subprogram it copies its workspace onto the recursion stack, and on exit the entire workspace is restored to its original state. The default initial value of *RecurPtr* at the beginning of a program, is 1K ($400) bytes below the CPU stack pointer.

Because of this technique, variables local to a subprogram must not be used as **var** parameters in recursive calls.

The pre-defined variables:

HeapPtr:	The heap pointer,
RecurPtr:	The recursion stack pointer, and
StackPtr:	The CPU stack pointer

allow the programmer to control the position of the heap and the stacks.

The type of these variables is *Integer*. Notice that *HeapPtr* and *RecurPtr* may be used in the same context as any other *Integer* variable, whereas *StackPtr* may only be used in assignments and expressions.

When these variables are manipulated, always make sure that they point to addresses within free memory, and that:

HeapPtr < *RecurPtr* < *StackPtr*

Failure to adhere to these rules will cause unpredictable, perhaps fatal, results.

Needless to say, assignments to the heap and stack pointers must never occur once the stacks or the heap are in use.

On each call to the procedure *New* and on entering a recursive procedure or function, the system checks for collision between the heap and the recursion stack, i.e. checks if *HeapPtr* is less than *RecurPtr*. If not, a collision has occurred, which results in an execution error.

Note that **no** checks are made at any time to insure that the CPU stack does not overflow into the bottom of the recursion stack. For this to happen, a recursive subroutine must call itself some 300-400 times, which must be considered a rare situation. If, however, a program requires such nesting, the following statement executed at the beginning of the program block will move the recursion stack pointer downwards to create a larger CPU stack:

```
RecurPtr := StackPtr -2 *MaxDepth -512;
```

where *MaxDepth* is the maximum required depth of calls to the recursive subprogram(s). The extra approx. 512 bytes are needed as a margin to make room for parameter transfers and intermediate results during the evaluation of expressions.

Memory Management

Memory Maps

The following diagrams illustrate the contents of memory at different stages of working with the TURBO system. Solid lines indicate fixed boundaries (i.e. determined by amount of memory, size of your CP/M, version of TURBO, etc.), whereas dotted lines indicate boundaries which are determined at run-time (e.g. by the size of the source text, and by possible user manipulation of various pointers, etc.). The sizes of the segments in the diagrams do not necessarily reflect the amounts of memory actually consumed.

Compilation in Memory

During compilation of a program in memory (**M**emory-mode on compiler **O**ptions menu, see page 259), the memory is mapped as follows:

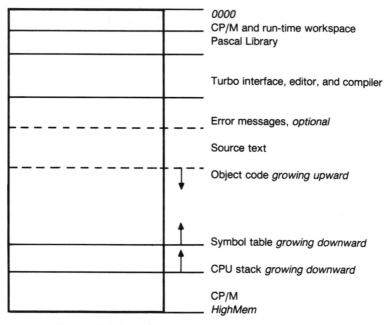

Figure 22-5: Memory map during compilation in memory

If the error message file is not loaded when starting TURBO, the source text starts that much lower in memory. When the compiler is invoked, it generates object code working upwards from the end of the source text. The CPU stack works downwards from the logical top of memory, and the compiler's symbol table works downwards from an address 1K ($400 bytes) below the logical top of memory.

Compilation To Disk

During compilation to a .COM or .CHN file (**C**om-mode or c**H**n-mode on compiler **O**ptions menu, see page 259), the memory looks much as during compilation in memory (see preceding section) *except* that generated object code does not reside in memory but is written to a disk file. Also, the code starts at a higher address (right after the Pascal library instead of after the source text). Compilation of much larger programs is thus possible in this mode.

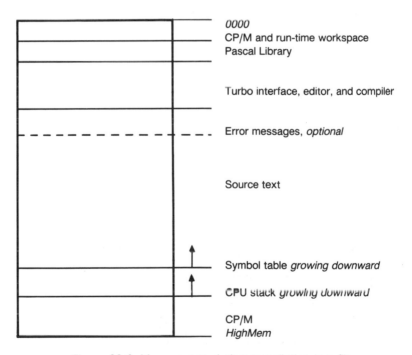

0000
CP/M and run-time workspace
Pascal Library

Turbo interface, editor, and compiler

Error messages, *optional*

Source text

Symbol table *growing downward*

CPU stack *growing downward*

CP/M
HighMem

Figure 22-6: Memory map during compilation to a file

Execution in Memory

When a program is executed in direct - or memory - mode (i.e. the Memory-mode on compiler Options menu is selected, see page 259), the memory is mapped as follows:

```
0000
CP/M and run-time workspace
Pascal Library

Turbo interface, editor, and compiler

Error messages, optional


Source text


Object code


Default initial value of HeapPtr
Heap growing upward

Recursion stack growing downward
Default initial value of RecurPtr
CPU stack growing downward
Default initial state of StackPtr

Program variables growing downward
CP/M
HighMem
```

Figure 22-7: Memory map during execution in direct mode

When a program is compiled, the end of the object code is known. The heap pointer *HeapPtr* is set to this value by default, and the heap grows from here and upwards in memory towards the recursion stack. The maximum memory size is BDOS minus one (indicated on the compiler Options menu). Program variables are stored from this address and downwards. The end of the variables is the 'top of free memory' which is the initial value of the CPU stack pointer *StackPtr*. The CPU stack grows downwards from here towards the position of the recursion stack pointer *RecurPtr*, $400 bytes lower than *StackPtr*. The recursion stack grows from here downward towards the heap.

Execution of A Program File

When a program file is executed (either by the **R**un command with the **M**emory-mode on the compiler **O**ptions menu selected, by an e**X**ecute command, or directly from CP/M), the memory is mapped as follows:

```
                                    0000
                                    CP/M and run-time workspace
                                    Pascal Library
                                    Default program start address


                                    Object code


  — — — — — — — — — — —     —       Default initial value of HeapPtr
                              ↓     Heap growing upward



                              ↑     Recursion stack growing downward
  — — — — — — — — — — —   — —  —    Default initial value of RecurPtr
                              ↑     CPU stack growing downward
  — — — — — — — — — — —   — —  —    Default initial state of StackPtr


                                    Program variables growing downward
  — — — — — — — — — — — — — —       Default end address
            Loader                  Maximum memory size
                                    CP/M
                                    HighMem
```

Figure 22-8: Memory map during execution of a program file

This map resembles the previous, except for the absence of the TURBO interface, editor, and compiler (and possible error messages) and of the source text. The *default program start address* (shown on the compiler **O**ptions menu) is the first free byte after the Pascal runtime library. This value may be manipulated with the **S**tart address command of the compiler **O**ptions menu, e.g. to create space for **absolute** variables and/or external procedures between the library and the code. The *maximum memory size* is BDOS minus one, and the default value is determined by the BDOS location on the computer in use.

If programs are to be translated for other systems, care should be taken to avoid collision with the BDOS. The maximum memory may be manipulated with the **E**nd address command of the compiler **O**ptions menu. Notice that the *default end address* setting is approx. 700 to 1000 bytes lower than maximum memory. This is to allow space for the loader which resides just below BDOS when .COM files are **R**un or e**X**ecuted from the TURBO system. This loader restores the TURBO editor, compiler, and possible error messages when the program finishes and thus returns control to the TURBO system.

Chapter 23
TURBO-BCD

TURBO-BCD is a special version of TURBO Pascal which is not included in the standard TURBO Pascal package. It employs binary coded decimal (BCD) *Real* numbers to obtain higher accuracy, especially needed in programs for business applications.

If you are interested in purchasing TURBO-BCD, please see page 3 for ordering information.

TURBO-BCD will compile and run any program written for standard TURBO or TURBO-87 Pascal; the only difference being in real number processing and real number format.

Files On the TURBO-BCD Distribution Diskette

In addition to the files listed on page 8, the TURBO-BCD distribution diskette contains the file

TURBOBCD.COM

(TURBOBCD.CMD for CP/M-86). This file contains the special TURBO-BCD system. If you want to install it with TINST, you must first temporarily rename it to TURBO.COM (or .CMD).

BCD Range

TURBO-BCD's BCD *Reals* have a range of 1E-63 through 1E + 63 with 18 significant digits.

Form function

Syntax: Form(*St, Var1, Var2,.., VarN*)

The *Form* function provides advanced numeric and string formatting. *St* is a string expression giving an image of the format string, as detailed in the following, and *Var1, Var2,.., VarN* are *Real*, *Integer*, or *String* expressions. The result is a *String* of the same length as *St*.

St is made up of a number of field specifiers, each of which corresponds to one parameter in the parameter list. Blanks and characters other than the ones defined in the following serve to separate fields and will also appear in the formatted result, viz:

```
Form('Total: $#,###.##',1234.56) = 'Total: $1,234.56'
```

The arguments in the argument list use the field specifiers in the order of appearance:

```
Form('Please @@@@@@ us at (###) ### ####','phone',408,438,8400) =
'Please  phone us at (408) 438 8400 '
```

If there are more arguments in the argument list than there are field specifiers in the format string, the arguments in excess are ignored. If there are less arguments than field specifiers, the field specifiers in excess are returned unchanged:

```
Form('###.##',12.34,43.21) = '  12.34'
Form('###.## -##.##',123.4) = '123.40 -##.##'
```

There are two types of field specifiers: **numeric** and **string**.

Numeric Fields

A numeric field is a sequence of one or more of the following characters:

```
#   @   *   $   -   +   ,   .
```

Any other character terminates the numeric field. The number is returned right-justified within the field, decimals are rounded if they exceed the number of decimals specified by the format, and if the number is too large to be returned in the field, all digit positions are filled with asterisks.

A digit position. If the numeric field contains no @ or * characters, unused digits are returned as blanks. If the numeric field contains no sign positions ('-' or ' + ' characters) and the number is negative, a floating minus is returned in front of the number.

Examples:
```
Form('####',34.567)     = '  35'
Form('###.##',12.345')  = ' 12.35'
Form('####.##',-12.3)   = ' -12.30'
Form('###.##',1234.5)   = '***.**'
```

@   A digit position. Unused digits are forced to be returned as zeros instead of blanks. The @ character needs only occur once in the numeric field to activate this effect. The sign of the number will not be returned unless the field contains a sign position ('-' or ' + ' character).

Examples:
```
Form('@##',9)           = '009'
Form('@@@.@@',12.345)   = '012.35'
```

*   A digit position. Unused digits are forced to be returned as asterisks instead of blanks. The * character needs only occur once in the numeric field to activate this effect. The sign of the number will not be returned unless the field contains a sign position ('-' or ' + ' character).

Examples:
```
Form('*##.#',4.567)     = '**4.57'
Form('****',123)        = '*123'
```

$ A digit position. A floating $-sign is returned in front of the number. The '$' character need only occur once in the numeric field to activate this effect.

Examples:
```
Form('$#####.##',123.45)   = '   $123.45'
Form('######.#$',-12.345) = '   -$12.35'
Form('*$####.##',12.34)    = '***$12.34'
```

-   A sign position. If the number is negative, a minus will be returned in that position; if it is positive, a blank is returned.

Examples:
```
Form('-###.##',-1.2)         = '-  1.20'
Form('-###.##',12)           = '  12.00'
Form('*#####.##-',-123.45)  = '***123.45-'
```

+   A sign position. If the number is positive, a plus will be returned in that position; if it is negative, a minus is returned.

Examples:
```
Form('+###.##',-1.2)         = '-  1.20'
Form('+###.##',12)           = '+ 12.00'
Form('*$####.##+',12.34)    = '***$12.34+'
```

,   A decimal comma or a separator comma. The last period or comma in the numeric image is considered the decimal delimiter.

.   A decimal period or a separator period. The last period or comma in the numeric image is considered the decimal delimiter.

Examples:
```
Form('##,###,###.##',12345.6)   = '    12,345.60'
Form('$#.###.###,##',-12345.6) = '   -$12.345,60'
Form('*$,###,###.##+',12345.6) = '***$12,345.60+'
Form('##,###.##',123456.0)       = '**,***.**'
```

String Fields

A string field is a sequence of # or @ characters. If the string parameter is longer than the string field, only the first characters of the string are returned.

\#   If the field contains only # characters, the string will be returned left justified.

@   If one or more '@' characters are present in the field, the string will be returned right justified within the length of the field.

Examples:

```
Form('##########','Pascal') = 'Pascal    '
Form('@#########','Pascal') = '    Pascal'
Form('####','TURBO Pascal') = 'TURB0 '
Form('@@@@','TURBO Pascal') = 'TURB0 '
```

Writing BCD Reals

BCD *Reals* are written on a format slightly different from the standard format, as described below.

R   The decimal representation of the value of *R* is output in a field 25 characters wide, using floating point format. For $R >= 0.0$, the format is:

␣␣#.################E*##

For $R < 0.0$, the format is:

␣-#.################E*##

where ␣ represents a blank, # represents a digit, and * represents either plus or minus.

R:n The decimal representation of the value of *R* is output, right adjusted in a field *n* characters wide, using floating point format. For $R \geq 0.0$:

```
blanks#.digitsE*##
```

For $R < 0.0$:

```
blanks-#.digitsE*##
```

where *blanks* represents zero or more blanks, *digits* represents from 1 to 17 digits, # represents a digit, and * represents either plus or minus.

Formatted Writing

The *Form* standard function can be used as a *write parameter* to produce formatted output:

```
Write(Form('The price is $###,###,###.##',Price));
```

Internal Data Format

The BCD *Real* variable occupies 10 bytes, and consists of a floating point value with an 18 digit binary coded decimal mantissa, a 7-bit 10's exponent, and a 1-bit sign. The exponent and the sign are stored in the first byte and the mantissa in the next nine bytes with the least significant byte first:

```
@+0      Exponent and sign.
@+1      LSB of mantissa.
:
@+9      MSB of mantissa.
```

The most significant bit of the first byte contains the sign. 0 means positive and 1 means negative. The remaining seven bits contain the exponent in binary format with an offset of $3F. Thus, an exponent of $41 indicates that the value of the mantissa is to be multiplied by 10^($41-$3F) = 10^2 = 100. If the first byte is zero, the floating point value is considered to be zero. Starting with the tenth byte, each byte of the mantissa contains two digits in BCD format, with the most significant digit in the upper four bits. The first digit contains the 1/10's, the second contains the 1/100's, etc. The mantissa is always normalized, i.e. the first digit is never 0 unless the entire number is 0.

This 10-byte *Real* is not compatible with TURBO standard or 8087 *Reals*. This, however, should only be a problem if you develop programs in different versions of TURBO which must interchange data. The trick then is simply to provide an interchange-format between the programs in which you transfer *Reals* on ASCII format, for instance.

Notes:

Chapter 24
TURBO-87

TURBO-87

TURBO-87 is a special version of TURBO Pascal which is not included in the standard TURBO Pascal package. It uses the Intel 8087 math-processor for real number arithmetic, providing a significant gain in speed. TURBO-87 does not include the 8087 chip.

If you are interested in purchasing TURBO-87, please see page 3 for ordering information.

TURBO-87 will compile and run any program written for standard TURBO Pascal; the only difference being in real number processing and real number format.

TURBO-87 programs will **not** run on a computer without the 8087-chip installed, whereas the opposite will work.

Files On the TURBO-87 Distribution Diskette

In addition to the files listed on page 8, the TURBO-87 distribution diskette contains the file

TURBO-87.COM

(TURBO-87.CMD for CP/M-86). This file contains the special TURBO-87 system. If you want to install it with TINST, you must first temporarily rename it to TURBO.COM (or .CMD).

Writing 8087 Reals

8087 *Reals* are written on a format slightly different from the standard format, as described below.

R The decimal representation of the value of *R* is output in a field 23 characters wide, using floating point format. For *R* > = 0.0, the format is:

    ␣␣#.##############E*##

For *R* < 0.0, the format is:

    ␣-#.##############E*##

where ␣ represents a blank, # represents a digit, and * represents either plus or minus.

R:n The decimal representation of the value of *R* is output, right adjusted in a field *n* characters wide, using floating point format. For *R* > = 0.0:

    `blanks#.digitsE*##`

For *R* < 0.0:

    `blanks-#.digitsE*##`

where *blanks* represents zero or more blanks, *digits* represents from 1 to 14 digits, # represents a digit, and * represents either plus or minus.

Internal Data Format

The 8087 chip supports a range of data types. The one used by TURBO-87 is the *long real*; its 64-bits yielding 16 digits accuracy and a range of 4.19E-307 to 1.67E + 308.

This 8-byte *Real* is not compatible with TURBO standard or BCD *Reals*. This, however, should only be a problem if you develop programs in different versions of TURBO which must interchange data. The trick then is simply to provide an interchange-format between the programs in which you transfer *Reals* on ASCII format, for instance.

Appendix A
SUMMARY OF STANDARD PROCEDURES AND FUNCTIONS

This appendix lists all standard procedures and functions available in TURBO Pascal and describes their application, syntax, parameters, and type. The following symbols are used to denote elements of various types:

type	any type
string	any string type
file	any file type
scalar	any scalar type
pointer	any pointer type

Where parameter type specification is not present, it means that the procedure or function accepts variable parameters of any type.

Input/Output Procedures and Functions

The following procedures use a non-standard syntax in their parameter lists:

procedure
Read (**var** *F*: **file of** *type*; **var** *V*: *type*);
Read (**var** *F*: text; **var** *I*: Integer);
Read (**var** *F*: text; **var** *R*: Real);
Read (**var** *F*: text; **var** *C*: Char);
Read (**var** *F*: text; **var** *S*: *string*);
Readln (**var** *F*: text);
Write (**var** *F*: **file of** *type*; **var** *V*: *type*);
Write (**var** *F*: text; *I*: Integer);
Write (**var** *F*: text; *R*: Real);
Write (**var** *F*: text; *B*: Boolean);
Write (**var** *F*: text; *C*: Char);
Write (**var** *F*: text; *S*: *string*);
Writeln (**var** *F*: text);

Arithmetic Functions

function
> Abs (I: Integer): Integer;
> Abs (R: Real): Real;
> ArcTan (R: Real): Real;
> Cos (R: Real): Real;
> Exp (R: Real): Real;
> Frac (R: Real): Real;
> Int (R: Real): Real;
> Ln (R: Real): Real;
> Sin (R: Real): Real;
> Sqr (I: Integer): Integer;
> Sqr (R: Real): Real;
> Sqrt (R: Real): Real;

Scalar Functions

function
> Odd (I: Integer): Boolean;
> Pred (X: scalar): scalar;
> Succ (X: scalar): scalar;

Transfer Functions

function
> Chr (I: Integer): Char;
> Ord (X: scalar): Integer;
> Round (R: Real): Integer;
> Trunc (R: Real): Integer;

String Procedures and Functions

The *Str* procedure uses a non-standard syntax for its numeric parameter.

procedure
Delete (var S: string; Pos, Len: Integer);
Insert (S: string; var D: string; Pos: Integer);
Str (I: Integer; var S: string);
Str (R: Real; var S: string);
Val (S: string; var R: Real; var P: Integer);
Val (S: strIng; var I, P: Integer);

function
Concat (S1,S2,...,Sn: string): string;
Copy (S: string; Pos, Len: Integer): string;
Length (S: string): Integer;
Pos (Pattern, Source: string): Integer;

File Handling Routines

procedure
Append (var F: file; Name: String);
Assign (var F: file; Name: string);
BlockRead (var F: file; var Dest: Type; Num: Integer);
BlockWrite (var F: file; var Dest:Type; Num: Integer);
Chain (var F: file);
Close (var F: file);
Erase (var F: file);
Execute (var F: file);
Rename (var F: file; Name: string);
Reset (var F: file);
Rewrite (var F: file);
Seek (var F: file of type; Pos: Integer);

function
Eof (var F: file): Boolean;
Eoln (var F: Text): Boolean;
FilePos (var F: flle of type): Integer;
FilePos (var F: file): Integer;
FileSize (var F: file of type): Integer;
FileSize (var F: file): Integer;
SeekEof (var F: file): Boolean;
SeekEoln (var F: Text): Boolean;

Heap Control Procedures and Functions

procedure
>   Dispose(var P: Pointer);
>   FreeMem(var P: Pointer, I: Integer);
>   GetMem (var P: pointer; I: Integer);
>   Mark (var P: pointer);
>   New (var P: pointer);
>   Release (var P: pointer);

function
>   MaxAvail: Integer;
>   MemAvail: Integer;
>   Ord (P: pointer): Integer;
>   Ptr (I: Integer): Pointer;

Screen Related Procedures and Functions

procedure
>   CrtExit;
>   CrtInit;
>   ClrEol;
>   ClrScr;
>   DelLine;
>   GotoXY (X, Y: Integer);
>   InsLine;
>   LowVideo;
>   NormVideo;

function
>   WhereX: Integer; (IBM PC only)
>   WhereY: Integer; (IBM PC only)

Miscellaneous Procedures and Functions

procedure

      Bdos (Func,Param: Integer); (CP/M only)
      Bios (Func,Param: Integer); (CP/M only)
      ChDir (Path: String);
      Delay (mS: Integer);
      FillChar (var Dest, Length: Integer; Data: Char);
      FillChar (var Dest, Length: Integer; Data: byte);
      Halt;
      GetDir (Drv:integer; var Path: String);
      MkDir (Path: String);
      MsDos (Func: Integer; Param: record); (PC/MS-DOS only)
      Move (var Source,Dest:type; Length: Integer);
      Randomize;
      RmDir (Path: String);

function

      Addr (var Variable): Pointer; (PC/MS-DOS, CP/M-86)
      Addr (var Variable): Integer; (CP/M-80)
      Addr (< function identifier >): Integer; (CP/M-80)
      Addr (< procedure identifier >): Integer;(CP/M-80)
      Bdos (Func, Param: Integer): Byte;
      BdosHL (Func, Param: Integer): Integer;
      Bios (Func, Param: Integer): Byte;
      BiosHL (Func, Param: Integer): Integer;
      Hi (I: Integer): Integer;
      IOresult : Boolean;
      KeyPressed : Boolean;
      Lo (I: Integer): Integer;
      ParamCount : Integer;
      ParamStr (N: Integer): String
      ParamCount: Integer;
      ParamStr (N: Integer): String;
      Random (Range: Integer): Integer;
      Random : Real;
      SizeOf (var Variable): Integer;
      SizeOf (< type identifier >): Integer;
      Swap (I: Integer): Integer;
      UpCase (Ch: Char): Char;

IBM PC Procedures and Functions

The following procedures and functions apply to the IBM PC implementations only.

Basic Graphics, Windows, and Sound

procedure

Draw(X1,Y1,X2,Y2,Color);
GraphBackground(Color:Integer);
GraphColorMode;
GraphMode;
GraphWindow(X1,Y1,X2,Y2:Integer);
HiRes;
HiResColor(Color:Integer);
NoSound;
Palette(Color:Integer);
Plot(X,Y,Color:Integer);
Sound(I: Integer);
TextBackground(Color:Integer);
TextColor(Color:Integer);
TextMode(Color:Integer);
Window(X1,Y1,X2,Y2:Integer);

function

WhereX:Integer;
WhereY:Integer;

constant

BW40:Integer;	= 0
C40:Integer;	= 1
BW80:Integer;	= 2
C80:Integer;	= 3
Black:Integer;	= 0
Blue:Integer;	= 1
Green:Integer;	= 2
Cyan:Integer;	= 3
Red:Integer;	= 4
Magenta:Integer;	= 5
Brown:Integer;	= 6
LightGray:Integer;	= 7
DarkGray:Integer;	= 8
LightBlue:Integer;	= 9
LightGreen:Integer;	= 10

LightCyan:Integer;   = 11
LightRed:Integer;   = 12
LightMagenta:Integer; = 13
Yellow:Integer;   = 14
White:Integer;   = 15
Blink:Integer;   = 16

Extended Graphics

procedure
    Arc(X,Y,Angle,Radius,Color: Integer);
    Circle(X,Y,Radius,Color: Integer);
    ColorTable(C1,C2,C3,C4: Integer);
    FillScreen(Color: Integer);
    FillShape(X,Y,FillColor,BorderColor: Integer);
    FillPattern(X1,Y1,X2,Y2,Color: Integer);
    GetPic(var Buffer: AnyType;X1,Y1,X2,Y2: Integer);
    Pattern(P: array[0..7] of Byte);
    PutPic(var Buffer: AnyType;X,Y: Integer);

function
    GetDotColor(X,Y: Integer): Integer;

Turtlegraphics

procedure
    Back(Dist: Integer);
    ClearScreen;
    Forward(Dist: Integer);
    HideTurtle;
    Home;
    NoWrap;
    PenDown;
    PenUp;
    SetHeading(Angle: Integer);
    SetPenColor(Color: Integer);
    SetPosition(X,Y: Integer);
    ShowTurtle;
    TurnLeft(Angle: Integer);
    TurnRight(Angle: Integer);
    TurtleWindow(X,Y,W,H: Integer);
    Wrap;

function
>Heading: Integer;
>Xcor: Integer;
>Ycor: Integer;
>TurtleThere: Boolean;

constant

North:Integer constant	= 0
East:Integer constant	= 90
South:Integer constant	= 180
West:Integer constant	= 270

Appendix B
SUMMARY OF OPERATORS

The following table summarizes all operators of TURBO Pascal. The operators are grouped in order of descending precedence. Where *Type of operand* is indicated as *Integer, Real*, the result is as follows:

Operand	Result
Integer, Integer	Integer
Real, Real	Real
Real, Integer	Real

Operator	Operation	Type of operand(s)	Type of result
+ unary	sign identity	Integer, Real	as operand
- unary	sign inversion	Integer, Real	as operand
not	negation	Integer, Boolean	as operand
*	multiplication	Integer, Real	Integer, Real
	set intersection	any set type	as operand
/	division	Integer, Real	Real
div	Integer division	Integer	Integer
mod	modulus	Integer	Integer
and	arithmetical **and**	Integer	Integer
	logical **and**	Boolean	Boolean
shl	shift left	Integer	Integer
shr	shift right	Integer	Integer
+	addition	Integer, Real	Integer, Real
	concatenation	string	string
	set union	any set type	as operand
-	subtraction	Integer, Real	Integer, Real
	set difference	any set type	as operand
or	arithmetical **or**	Integer	Integer
	logical **or**	Boolean	Boolean
xor	arithmetical **xor**	Integer	Integer
	logical **xor**	Boolean	Boolean

Operator	Operation	Type of operand(s)	Type of result
=	equality	any scalar type	Boolean
	equality	string	Boolean
	equality	any set type	Boolean
	equality	any pointer type	Boolean
< >	inequality	any scalar type	Boolean
	inequality	string	Boolean
	inequality	any set type	Boolean
	inequality	any pointer type	Boolean
> =	greater or equal	any scalar type	Boolean
	greater or equal	string	Boolean
	set inclusion	any set type	Boolean
< =	less or equal	any scalar type	Boolean
	less or equal	string	Boolean
	set inclusion	any set type	Boolean
>	greater than	any scalar type	Boolean
	greater than	string	Boolean
<	less than	any scalar type	Boolean
	less than	string	Boolean
in	set membership	see below	Boolean

The first operand of the **in** operator may be of any scalar type, and the second operand must be a set of that type.

Appendix C
SUMMARY OF COMPILER DIRECTIVES

A number of features of the TURBO Pascal compiler are controlled through compiler directives. A compiler directive is introduced as a comment with a special syntax which means that whenever a comment is allowed in a program, a compiler directive is also allowed.

A compiler directive consists of an opening bracket immediately followed by a dollar-sign immediately followed by one compiler directive letter or a list of compiler directive letters separated by commas, ultimately terminated by a closing bracket.

Examples:
```
{$I-}
{$I INCLUDE.FIL}
{$B-,R+,V-}
(*$U+*)
```

Notice that no spaces are allowed before or after the dollar-sign. A + sign after a directive indicates that the associated compiler feature is enabled (active), and a minus sign indicates that is disabled (passive).

IMPORTANT NOTICE

All compiler directives have default values. These have been chosen to optimize execution speed and minimize code size. This means that e.g. code generation for recursive procedures (CP/M-80 only) and index checking has been disabled. Check below to make sure that your programs include the required compiler directive settings!

Common Compiler Directives

B - *I/O Mode Selection*

Default: B +

The **B** directive controls input/output mode selection. When active, {$B + }, the CON: device is assigned to the standard files *Input* and *Output*, i.e. the default input/output channel. When passive, {$B-}, the TRM: device is used. **This directive is global to an entire program block** and cannot be re-defined throughout the program. See pages 105 and 108 for further details.

C - *Control C and S*

Default: C +

The **C** directive controls control character interpretation during console I/O. When active, {$C + }, a Ctrl-C entered in response to a *Read* or *Readln* statement will interrupt program execution, and a Ctrl-S will toggle screen output off and on. When passive, {$C-}, control characters are not interpreted. The active state slows screen output somewhat, so if screen output speed is imperative, you should switch off this directive. **This directive is global to an entire program block** and cannot be re-defined throughout the program.

I - *I/O Error Handling*

Default: I +

The **I** directive controls I/O error handling. When active, {$I + }, all I/O operations are checked for errors. When passive, {$I-}, it is the responsibility of the programmer to check I/O errors through the standard function *IOresult*. See page 116 for further details.

I - *Include Files*

The **I** directive succeeded by a file name instructs the compiler to include the file with the specified name in the compilation. Include files are discussed in detail in chapter 17.

R - *Index Range Check*

Default: R-

The **R** directive controls run-time index checks. When active, {$R + }, all array indexing operations are checked to be within the defined bounds, and all assignments to scalar and subrange variables are checked to be within range. When passive, {$R-}, no checks are performed, and index errors may well cause a program to go haywire. It is a good idea to activate this directive while developing a program. Once debugged, execution will be speeded up by setting it passive (the default state).

V - *Var-parameter Type Checking*

Default: V +

The **V** compiler directive controls type checking on strings passed as var-parameters. When active, {$V + }, strict type checking is performed, i.e. the lengths of actual and formal parameters must match. When passive, {$V-}, the compiler allows passing of actual parameters which do not match the length of the formal parameter. See pages 203, 236, and 267 for further details.

U - *User Interrupt*

Default: U-

The **U** directive controls user interrupts. When active, {$U + }, the user may interrupt the program anytime during execution by entering a Ctrl-C. When passive, {$U-}, this has no effect. Activating this directive will significantly slow down execution speed.

PC-DOS and MS-DOS Compiler Directives

The following directives are unique to the PC/MS-DOS implementations:

G - *Input File Buffer*

Default: G0

The **G** (get) directive enables I/O re-direction by defining the standard *Input* file buffer. When the buffer size is zero (default), the *Input* file refers to the *CON:* or *TRM:* device. When non-zero (e.g. {$G256}), it refers to the MS-DOS standard input handle.

The **D** compiler directive applies to such non-zero-buffer input and output files. The **G** compiler directive must be placed before the declaration part.

P - *Output File Buffer*

Default: P0

The **P** (put) directive enables I/O re-direction by defining the standard *Output* file buffer. When the buffer size is zero (default), the *Output* file refers to the *CON:* or *TRM:* device. When non-zero (e.g. {$G512}), it refers to the MS-DOS standard output handle.

The **D** compiler directive applies to such non-zero-buffer input and output files. The **P** compiler directive must be placed before the declaration part.

D - *Device Checking*

Default: D +

When a text file is opened by *Reset*, *Rewrite* or *Append*, TURBO Pascal asks MS-DOS for the status of the file. If MS-DOS reports that the file is a device, TURBO Pascal disables the buffering that normally occurs on text files, and all I/O operations on the file are done on a character by character basis.

The **D** directive may be used to disable this check. The default state {$D + }, and in this state, device checks are made. In the {$D-} state, no checks are made and all device I/O operations are buffered. In this case, a call to the standard procedure *Flush* will ensure that the characters you have written to a file have actually been sent to it.

F - *Number of Open Files*

Default: F16

The **F** directive controls the number of files that may be open simultaneously. The default setting is {$F16}, which means that up to 16 files may be open at any one time. This directive is global to a program and must be placed before the declaration part. The **F** compiler directive does not limit the number of files that may be declared in a program; it only sets a limit to the number of files that may be open at the same time.

Note that even if the F compiler directive has been used to allocate sufficient file space, you may still experience a 'too many open files' error condition if the operating system runs out of file buffers. If that happens, you should supply a higher value for the *files* = *xx* parameter in the CONFIG.SYS file. The default value is usually 8. For further detail, please refer to your MS-DOS documentation.

PC-DOS, MS-DOS, and CP/M-86 Compiler Directive

The following directive is unique to the 16-bit implementations:

K - *Stack Checking*

Default: K +

The **K** directive controls the generation of stack check code. When active, {$K + }, a check is made to insure that space is available for local variables on the stack before each call to a subprogram. When passive, {$K-}, no checks are made.

CP/M-80 Compiler Directives

The following directives are unique to the 8-bit implementation:

A - *Absolute Code*

Default: A +

The **A** directive controls generation of absolute, i.e. non-recursive, code. When active, {$A + }, absolute code is generated. When passive, {$A-}, the compiler generates code which allows recursive calls. This code requires more memory and executes slower.

W - *Nesting of With Statements*

Default: W2

The **W** directive controls the level of nesting of *With* statements, i.e. the number of records which may be 'opened' within one block. The **W** must be immediately followed by a digit between 1 and 9. For further details, please refer to page 81.

X - *Array Optimization*

Default: X +

The **X** directive controls array optimization. When active, {$X + }, code generation for arrays is optimized for maximum speed. When passive, {$X-}, the compiler minimizes the code size instead. This is discussed further on page 75.

Appendix D
TURBO VS. STANDARD PASCAL

The TURBO Pascal language follows the Standard Pascal defined by Jensen & Wirth in their **User Manual and Report**, with only minor differences introduced for the sheer purpose of efficiency. These differences are described in the following. Notice that the *extensions* offered by TURBO Pascal are not discussed.

Dynamic Variables

The procedure *New* will not accept variant record specifications. This restriction, however, is easily circumvented by using the standard procedure *GetMem*.

Recursion

CP/M-80 version only: Because of the way local variables are handled during recursion, a variable local to a subprogram must not be passed as a **var**-parameter in recursive calls.

Get and Put

The standard procedures *Get* and *Put* are not implemented. Instead, the *Read* and *Write* procedures have been extended to handle all I/O needs. The reason for this is threefold: Firstly, *Read* and *Write* give much faster I/O; secondly, variable space overhead is reduced, as file buffer variables are not required, and thirdly, the *Read* and *Write* procedures are far more versatile and easier to understand that *Get* and *Put*.

Goto Statements

A **goto** statement must not leave the current block.

Page Procedure

The standard procedure *Page* is not implemented, as the CP/M operating system does not define a form-feed character.

Packed Variables

The reserved word **packed** has no effect in TURBO Pascal, but it is still allowed. This is because packing occurs automatically whenever possible. For the same reason, standard procedures *Pack* and *Unpack* are not implemented.

Procedural Parameters

Procedures and functions cannot be passed as parameters.

Appendix E
COMPILER ERROR MESSAGES

The following is a listing of error messages you may get from the compiler. When encountering an error, the compiler will always print the error number on the screen. Explanatory texts will only be issued if you have included error messages (answer **Y** to the first question when you start TURBO).

Many error messages are totally self-explanatory, but some need a little elaboration as provided in the following.

01   ';' expected
02   ':' expected
03   ',' expected
04   '(' expected
05   ')' expected
06   ' = ' expected
07   ': = ' expected
08   '[' expected
09   ']' expected
10   '.' expected
11   '..' expected
12   BEGIN expected
13   DO expected
14   END expected
15   OF expected
16   PROCEDURE or FUNCTION expected
17   THEN expected
18   TO or DOWNTO expected
20   Boolean expression expected
21   File variable expected
22   Integer constant expected
23   Integer expression expected
24   Integer variable expected
25   Integer or real constant expected
26   Integer or real expression expected
27   Integer or real variable expected
28   Pointer variable expected
29   Record variable expected

30   Simple type expected
Simple types are all scalar types, except real.
31   Simple expression expected
32   String constant expected
33   String expression expected
34   String variable expected
35   Textfile expected
36   Type identifier expected
37   Untyped file expected
40   Undefined label
A statement references an undefined label.
41   Unknown identifier or syntax error
Unknown label, constant, type, variable, or field identifier, or syntax error in statement.
42   Undefined pointer type in preceding type definitions
A preceding pointer type definition contains a reference to an unknown type identifier.
43   Duplicate identifier or label
This identifier or label has already been used within the current block.
44   Type mismatch
1) Incompatible types of the variable and the expression in an assignment statement **2)** Incompatible types of the actual and the formal parameter in a call to a subprogram. **3)** Expression type incompatible with index type in array assignment. **4)** Types of operands in an expression are not compatible.
45   Constant out of range
46   Constant and CASE selector type does not match
47   Operand type(s) does not match operator
Example: 'A' div '2'
48   Invalid result type
Valid types are all scalar types, string types, and pointer types.
49   Invalid string length
The length of a string must be in the range 1..255.
50   String constant length does not match type
51   Invalid subrange base type
Valid base types are all scalar types, except real.
52   Lower bound > upper bound
The ordinal value of the upper bound must be greater than or equal to the ordinal value of the lower bound.
53   Reserved word
These may not be used as identifiers.
54   Illegal assignment

55 **String constant exceeds line**
String constants must not span lines.

56 **Error in integer constant**
An *Integer* constant does not conform to the syntax described in page 43, or it is not within the *Integer* range -32768..32767. Whole *Real* numbers should be followed by a decimal point and a zero, e.g. 123456789.0.

57 **Error in real constant**
The syntax of *Real* constants is defined on page 43.

58 **Illegal character in identifier**

60 **Constants are not allowed here**

61 **Files and pointers are not allowed here**

62 **Structured variables are not allowed here**

63 **Textfiles are not allowed here**

64 **Textfiles and untyped files are not allowed here**

65 **Untyped files are not allowed here**

66 **I/O not allowed here**
Variables of this type cannot be input or output.

67 **Files must be VAR parameters**

68 **File components may not be files**
file of file constructs are not allowed.

69 **Invalid ordering of fields**

70 **Set base type out of range**
The base type of a set must be a scalar with no more than 256 possible values or a subrange with bounds in the range 0..255.

71 **Invalid GOTO**
A GOTO cannot reference a label within a FOR loop from outside that FOR loop.

72 **Label not within current block**
A GOTO statement cannot reference a label outside the current block.

73 **Undefined FORWARD procedure(s)**
A subprogram has been **forward** declared, but the body never occurred.

74 **INLINE error**

75 **Illegal use of ABSOLUTE**
1) Only one identifier may appear before the colon in an **absolute** variable declaration. **2)** The **absolute** clause may not be used in a record.

76 **Overlays can not be forwarded**
The FORWARD specification cannot not be used in connection with overlays.

77 **Overlays not allowed in direct mode**
Overlays can only be used from programs compiled to a file.

90 File not found
The specified include file does not exist.

91 Unexpected end of source
Your program cannot end the way it does. The program probably has more **begin**s than **end**s.

92 Unable to create overlay file

93 Invalid compiler directive

97 Too many nested WITHs
Use the W compiler directive to increase the maximum number of nested WITH statements. Default is 2. (CP/M-80 only).

98 Memory overflow
You are trying to allocate more storage for variables than is available.

99 Compiler overflow
There is not enough memory to compile the program. This error may occur even if free memory seems to exist; it is, however, used by the stack and the symbol table during compilation. Break your source text into smaller segments and use include files.

Appendix F.
RUN-TIME ERROR MESSAGES

Fatal errors at run-time result in a program halt and the display of the message:

```
Run-time error NN, PC=addr
    Program aborted
```

where *NN* is the run-time error number, and *addr* is the address in the program code where the error occurred. The following contains explanations of all run-time error numbers. Notice that the numbers are hexadecimal!

01   **Floating point overflow.**

02   **Division by zero attempted.**

03   **Sqrt argument error.**
     The argument passed to the Sqrt function was negative.

04   **Ln argument error.**
     The argument passed to the Ln function was zero or negative.

10   **String length error.**
     1) A string concatenation resulted in a string of more than 255 characters. **2)** Only strings of length 1 can be converted to a character.

11   **Invalid string index.**
     Index expression is not within 1..255 with *Copy, Delete* or *Insert* procedure calls.

90   **Index out of range.**
     The index expression of an array subscript was out of range.

91   **Scalar or subrange out of range.**
     The value assigned to a scalar or a subrange variable was out of range.

92   **Out of integer range.**
     The real value passed to *Trunc* or *Round* was not within the *Integer* range $-32768..32767$.

F0   **Overlay file not found.**

FF   **Heap/stack collision.**
     A call was made to the standard procedure *New* or to a recursive subprogram, and there is insufficient free memory between the heap pointer (HeapPtr) and the recursion stack pointer (RecurPtr).

Notes:

Appendix G
I/O ERROR MESSAGES

An error in an input or output operation at run-time results in in I/O error. If I/O checking is active (**I** compiler directive active), an I/O error causes the program to halt and the following error message is displayed:

```
I/O error NN, PC=addr
Program aborted
```

Where *NN* is the I/O error number, and *addr* is the address in the program code where the error occurred.

If I/O error checking is passive (({$I-}), an I/O error will not cause the program to halt. Instead, all further I/O is suspended until the result of the I/O operation has been examined with the standard function *IOresult*. If I/O is attempted before *IOresult* is called after en error, a new error occurs, possibly hanging the program.

The following contains explanations of all run-time error numbers. Notice that the numbers are hexadecimal!

01 **File does not exist.**
The file name used with *Reset, Erase, Rename, Execute,* or *Chain* does not specify an existing file.

02 **File not open for input.**
1) You are trying to read (with *Read* or *Readln*) from a file without a previous *Reset* or *Rewrite.* **2)** You are trying to read from a text file which was prepared with *Rewrite* (and thus is empty). **3)** You are trying to read from the logical device LST:, which is an output-only device.

03 **File not open for output.**
1) You are trying to write (with *Write* or *Writeln*) to a file without a previous *Reset* or *Rewrite.* **2)** You are trying to read from a text file which was prepared with *Reset.* **3)** You are trying to read from the logical device KBD:, which is an input-only device.

04   File not open.
> You are trying to access (with *BlockRead* or *BlockWrite*) a file without a previous *Reset* or *Rewrite*.

10   Error in numeric format.
> The string read from a text file into a numeric variable does not conform to the proper numeric format (see page 43).

20   Operation not allowed on a logical device.
> You are trying to *Erase, Rename, Execute,* or *Chain* a file assigned to a logical device.

21   Not allowed in direct mode.
> Programs cannot be *Execute*d or *Chain*ed from a program running in direct mode (i.e. a program activated with a **R**un command while the **M**emory compiler option is set).

22   Assign to std files not allowed.

90   Record length mismatch.
> The record length of a file variable does not match the file you are trying to associate it with.

91   Seek beyond end-of-file.

99   Unexpected end-of-file.
> **1)** Physical end-of-file encountered before EOF-character (Ctrl-Z) when reading from a text file. **2)** An attempt was made to read beyond end-of-file on a defined file. **3)** A *Read* or *BlockRead* is unable to read the next sector of a defined file. Something may be wrong with the file, or (in the case of *BlockRead*) you may be trying to read past physical EOF.

F0   Disk write error.
> Disk full while attempting to expand a file. This may occur with the output operations *Write, WriteLn, BlockWrite,* and *Flush,* but also *Read, ReadLn,* and *Close* may cause this error, as they cause the write buffer to be flushed.

F1   Directory is full.
> You are trying to *Rewrite* a file, and there is no more room in the disk directory.

F2   File size overflow.
> You are trying to *Write* a record beyond 65535 to a defined file.

F3   Too many open files.

FF   File disappeared.
> An attempt was made to *Close* a file which was no longer present in the disk directory, e.g. because of an unexpected disk change.

Appendix H
TRANSLATING ERROR MESSAGES

The compiler error messages are collected in the file *TURBO.MSG*. These messages are in English but may easily be translated into any other language as described in the following.

The first 24 lines of this file define a number of text constants for subsequent inclusion in the error message lines; a technique which drastically reduces the disk and memory requirements of the error messages. Each constant is identified by a control character, denoted by a ^ character in the following listing. The value of each constant is anything that follows on the same line. All characters are significant, also leading and trailing blanks.

The remaining lines each contain one error message, starting with the error number and immediately followed by the message text. The message text may consist of any characters and may include previously defined constant identifiers (control characters). Appendix E lists the resulting messages in full.

When you translate the error messages, the relation between constants and error messages will probably be quite different from the English version listed here. Start therefore with writing each error message in full, disregarding the use of constants. You may use these error messages, but they will require excessive space. When all messages are translated, you should find as many common denominators as possible. Then define these as constants at the top of the file and include only the constant identifiers in subsequent message texts. You may define as few or as many constants as you need, the restriction being only the number of control characters.

As a good example of the use of constants, consider errors 25, 26, and 27. These are defined exclusively by constant identifiers, 15 in total, but would require 101 characters if written in clear text.

The TURBO editor may be used to edit the *TURBOMSG.OVR* file. Control characters are entered with the Ctrl-P prefix, i.e. to enter a Ctrl-A (^A) into the file, hold down the < CONTROL > key and press first P, then A. Control characters appear dim on the screen (if it has any video attributes).

Notice that the TURBO editor deletes all trailing blanks. The original message therefore does not use trailing blanks in any messages.

Error Message File Listing

```
^A are not allowed
^B can not be
^C constant
^D does not
^E expression
^F identifier
^G file
^H here
^KInteger
^LFile
^NIllegal
^O or
^PUndefined
^Q match
^R real
^SString
^TTextfile
^U out of range
^V variable
^W overflow
^X expected
^Y type
^[Invalid
^] pointer
01';'^X
02':'^X
03',' ^X
04'('^X
05')'^X
06'='^X
07':='^X
08'['^X
09']'^X
10'.'^X
11'..'^X
12BEGIN^X
13DO^X
14END^X
```

```
150F^X
17THEN^X
18TO^O DOWNTO^X
20Boolean^E^X
21^L^V^X
22^K^C^X
23^K^E^X
24^K^V^X
25^K^O^R^C^X
26^K^O^R^E^X
27^K^O^R^V^X
28Pointer^V^X
29Record^V^X
30Simple^Y^X
31Simple^E^X
32^S^C^X
33^S^E^X
34^S^V^X
35^T^X
36Type^F^X
37Untyped^G^X
40^P label
41Unknown^F^O syntax error
42^P^]^Y in preceding^Y definitions
43Duplicate^F^O label
44Type mismatch
45^C^U
46^C and CASE selector^Y^D^Q
47Operand^Y(s)^D^Q operator
48^[ result^Y
49^[ ^S length
50^S^C length^D^Q^Y
51^[ subrange base^Y
52Lower bound > upper bound
53Reserved word
54^N assignment
55^S^C exceeds line
56Error in integer^C
57Error in^R^C
58^N character in^F
60^Cs^A^H
61^Ls and^]s^A^H
62Structured^Vs^A^H
63^Ts^A^H
```

```
64^Ts and untyped^Gs^A^H
65Untyped^Gs^A^H
66I/0^A
67^Ls must be^V parameters
68^L components^B^Gs
69^[^Ordering of fields
70Set base^Y^U
71^[ GOTO
72Label not within current block
73^P FORWARD procedure(s)
74INLINE error
75^N use of ABSOLUTE
90^L not found
91Unexpected end of source
97Too many nested WITH's
98Memory^W
99Compiler^W
```

Appendix I
TURBO SYNTAX

The syntax of the TURBO Pascal language is presented here using the formalism known as the *Backus-Naur Form*. The following symbols are meta-symbols belonging to the BNF formalism, and not symbols of the TURBO Pascal language:

:: =   Means "is defined as".
| Means "or".
{ }   Enclose items which may be repeated zero or more times.

All other symbols are part of the language. Each syntactic construct is printed in *italics*, e.g.: *block* and *case-element*. reserved words are printed in **boldface**, e.g.: **array** and **for**.

actual-parameter :: = *expression* | *variable*
adding-operator :: = + | - | **or** | **xor**
array-constant :: = (*structured-constant* { , *structured-constant* })
array-type :: = **array** [*index-type* { , *index-type* }] **of** *component-type*
array-variable :: = *variable*
assignment-statement :: = *variable* : = *expression* |
                 function-identifier :: = *expression*
base-type :: = *simple-type*
block :: = *declaration-part statement-part*
case-element :: = *case-list* : *statement*
case-label :: = *constant*
case-label-list :: = *case-label* { , *case-label* }
case-list :: = *case-list-element* { , *case-list-element*}
case-list-element :: = *constant* | *constant* .. *constant*
case-statement :: = **case** *expression* **of** *case-element* { ; *case-element* } **end** |
           case *expression* **of** *case-element* { ;*case-element* }
           otherwise *statement* { ; *statement* } **end**
complemented-factor :: = *signed-factor* | **not** *signed-factor*
component-type :: = *type*
component-variable :: = *indexed-variable* | *field-designator*
compound-statement :: = **begin** *statement* { ; *statement* } **end**
conditional-statement :: = *if-statement* | *case-statement*

constant :: = *unsigned-number* l *sign unsigned-number* l *constant-identifier*
l *sign constant-identifier* l *string*
constant-definition-part :: = **const** *constant-definition*
{ ; *constant-definition* } ;
constant-definition :: = *untyped-constant-definition* l
typed-constant-definition
constant-identifier :: = *identifier*
control-character :: = # *unsigned-integer* l ˆ *character*
control-variable :: = *variable-identifier*
declaration-part :: = { *declaration-section* }
declaration-section :: = *label-declaration-part* l *constant-definition-part* l
type-definition-part l *variable-declaration-part* l
procedure-and-function-declaration-part
digit :: = 0 l 1 l 2 l 3 l 4 l 5 l 6 l 7 l 8 l 9
digit-sequence :: = *digit* { *digit* }
empty :: =
empty-statement :: = *empty*
entire-variable :: = *variable-identifier* l *typed-constant-identifier*
expression :: = *simple-expression* { *relational-operator simple-expression* }
factor :: = *variable* l *unsigned-constant* l (*expression*) l
function-designator l *set*
field-designator :: = *record-variable* . *field-identifier*
field-identifier :: = *identifier*
field-list :: = *fixed-part* l *fixed-part* ; *variant-part* l *variant-part*
file-identifier :: = *identifier*
file-identifier-list :: = *empty* l (*file-identifier* { , *file-identifier* }
file-type :: = **file of** *type*
final-value :: = *expression*
fixed-part :: = *record-section* { ; *record-section* }
for-list :: = *initial-value* **to** *final-value* l *initial-value* **downto** *final-value*
for-statement :: = **for** *control-variable* : = *for-list* **do** *statement*
formal-parameter-section :: = *parameter-group* l **var** *parameter-group*
function-declaration :: = *function-heading block* ;
function-designator :: = *function-identifier* l *function-identifier*
(*actual-parameter* { , *actual-parameter* })
function-heading :: = **function** *identifier* : *result-type* ; l
function *identifier* (*formal-parameter-section*
{ , *formal-parameter-section* }) : *result-type* ;
function-identifier :: = *identifier*
goto-statement :: = **goto** *label*
hexdigit :: = *digit* l A l B l C l D l E l F
hexdigit-sequence :: = *hexdigit* { *hexdigit* }
identifier :: = letter { *letter-or-digit* }
identifier-list :: = *identifier* { , *identifier* }

if-statement :: = **if** *expression* **then** *statement* { **else** *statement* }
index-type :: = *simple-type*
indexed-variable :: = *array-variable* [*expression* { , *expression* }]
initial-value :: = *expression*
inline-list-element :: = *unsigned-integer* I *constant-identifier* I
                        variable-identifier I *location-counter-reference*
inline-statement :: = **inline** *inline-list-element* { , *inline-list-element* }
label :: = *letter-or-digit* { *letter-or-digit* }
label-declaration-part :: = **label** *label* { , *label* } ;
letter :: = A I B I C I D I E I F I G I H I I I J I K I L I M I
            N I O I P I Q I R I S I T I U I V I W I X I Y I Z I
            a I b I c I d I e I f I g I h I i I j I k I l I m I
            n I o I p I q I r I s I t I u I v I w I x I y I z I _
letter-or-digit :: = *letter* I *digit*
location-counter-reference :: = * I * *sign* *constant*
multiplying-operator :: = * I / I **div** I **mod** I **and** I **shl** I **shr**
parameter-group :: = *identifier-list* : *type-identifier*
pointer-type :: = ˆ *type-identifier*
pointer-variable :: = *variable*
procedure-and-function-declaration-part :: =
                                    { *procedure-or-function-declaration* }
procedure-declaration :: = *procedure-heading* *block* ;
procedure-heading :: = **procedure** *identifier* ; I **procedure** *identifier*
                    (*formal-parameter-section*
                    { , *formal-parameter-section* }) ;
procedure-or-function-declaration :: = *procedure-declaration* I
                                    function-declaration
procedure-statement :: = *procedure-identifier* I *procedure-identifier*
                    (*actual-parameter* { , *actual-parameter* })
program-heading :: = *empty* I **program** *program-identifier*
                    file-identifier-list
program :: = *program-heading* *block* .
program-identifier :: = *identifier*
record-constant :: = (*record-constant-element*
                    { ; *record-constant-element* })
record-constant-element :: = *field-identifier* : *structured-constant*
record-section :: = *empty* I *field-identifier* { , *field-identifier* } : *type*
record-type :: = **record** *field-list* **end**
record-variable :: = *variable*
record-variable-list :: = *record-variable* { , *record-variable* }
referenced-variable :: = *pointer-variable* ˆ
relational-operator :: = = I < > I < = I > = I < I > I **in**
repeat-statement :: = **repeat** *statement* { ; *statement* } **until** *expression*
repetitive-statement :: = *while-statement* I *repeat-statement* I *for-statement*

result-type :: = *type-identifier*
scalar-type :: = (*identifier* { , *identifier* })
scale-factor :: = *digit-sequence* I *sign digit-sequence*
set :: = [{ *set-element* }]
set-constant :: = [{ *set-constant-element* }]
set-constant-element :: = *constant* I *constant .. constant*
set-element :: = *expression* I *expression .. expression*
set-type :: = **set of** *base-type*
sign :: = + I -
signed-factor :: = *factor* I *sign factor*
simple-expression :: = *term* { *adding-operator term* }
simple-statement :: = *assignment-statement* I *procedure-statement* I
                goto-statement I *inline-statement* I *empty-statement*
simple-type :: = *scalar-type* I *subrange-type* I *type-identifier*
statement :: = *simple-statement* I *structured-statement*
statement-part :: = *compound-statement*
string :: = { *string-element* }
string-element :: = *text-string* I *control-character*
string-type :: = **string** [*constant*]
structured-constant :: = *constant* I *array-constant* I *record-constant* I
                set-constant
structured-constant-definition :: = *identifier* : *type* = *structured-constant*
structured-statement :: = *compound-statement* I *conditional-statement* I
                repetitive-statement I *with-statement*
structured-type :: = *unpacked-structured-type* I
            packed *unpacked-structured-type*
subrange-type :: = *constant .. constant*
tag-field :: = *empty* I *field-identifier* :
term :: = *complemented-factor* { *multiplying-operator complemented-factor* }
text-string :: = ' { *character* } '
type-definition :: = *identifier* = *type*
type-definition-part :: = **type** *type-definition* { ; *type-definition* } ;
type-identifier :: = *identifier*
type :: = *simple-type* I *structured-type* I *pointer-type*
typed-constant-identifier :: = *identifier*
unpacked-structured-type :: = *string-type* I *array-type* I *record-type* I
                set-type I *file-type*
unsigned-constant :: = *unsigned-number* I *string* I *constant-identifier* I **nil**
unsigned-integer :: = *digit-sequence* I $ *hexdigit-sequence*
unsigned-number :: = *unsigned-integer* I *unsigned-real*
unsigned-real :: = *digit-sequence . digit-sequence* I
            digit-sequence . digit-sequence E *scale-factor* I
            digit-sequence E *scale-factor*
untyped-constant-definition :: = *identifier* = *constant*

variable :: = *entire-variable* I *component-variable* I *referenced-variable*
variable-declaration :: = *identifier-list* : *type* I
                          identifier-list : *type* **absolute** *constant*
variable-declaration-part :: = **var** *variable-declaration*
                             { ; *variable-declaration* } ;
variable-identifier :: = *identifier*
variant :: = *empty* I *case-label* list : (*field-list*)
variant-part :: = **case** *tag-field type-identifier* **of** *variant* { ; *variant* }
while-statement :: = **while** *expression* **do** *statement*
with-statement :: = **with** *record-variable-list* **do** *statement*

Notes:

Appendix J
ASCII TABLE

DEC	HEX	CHAR		DEC	HEX	CHAR	DEC	HEX	CHAR	DEC	HEX	CHAR
0	00	^@	NUL	32	20	SPC	64	40	@	96	60	'
1	01	^A	SOH	33	21	!	65	41	A	97	61	a
2	02	^B	STX	34	22	"	66	42	B	98	62	b
3	03	^C	ETX	35	23	#	67	43	C	99	63	c
4	04	^D	EOT	36	24	$	68	44	D	100	64	d
5	05	^E	ENQ	37	25	%	69	45	E	101	65	e
6	06	^F	ACK	38	26	&	70	46	F	102	66	f
7	07	^G	BEL	39	27	'	71	47	G	103	67	g
8	08	^H	BS	40	28	(	72	48	H	104	68	h
9	09	^I	HT	41	29	)	73	49	I	105	69	i
10	0A	^J	LF	42	2A	*	74	4A	J	106	6A	j
11	0B	^K	VT	43	2B	+	75	4B	K	107	6B	k
12	0C	^L	FF	44	2C	,	76	4C	L	108	6C	l
13	0D	^M	CR	45	2D	-	77	4D	M	109	6D	m
14	0E	^N	SO	46	2E	.	78	4E	N	110	6E	n
15	0F	^O	SI	47	2F	/	79	4F	O	111	6F	o
16	10	^P	DLE	48	30	0	80	50	P	112	70	p
17	11	^Q	DC1	49	31	1	81	51	Q	113	71	q
18	12	^R	DC2	50	32	2	82	52	R	114	72	r
19	13	^S	DC3	51	33	3	83	53	S	115	73	s
20	14	^T	DC4	52	34	4	84	54	T	116	74	t
21	15	^U	NAK	53	35	5	85	55	U	117	75	u
22	16	^V	SYN	54	36	6	86	56	V	118	76	v
23	17	^W	ETB	55	37	7	87	57	W	119	77	w
24	18	^X	CAN	56	38	8	88	58	X	120	78	x
25	19	^Y	EM	57	39	9	89	59	Y	121	79	y
26	1A	^Z	SUB	58	3A	:	90	5A	Z	122	7A	z
27	1B	^[	ESC	59	3B	;	91	5B	[	123	7B	{
28	1C	^\	FS	60	3C	<	92	5C	\	124	7C	|
29	1D	^]	GS	61	3D	=	93	5D	]	125	7D	}
30	1E	^^	RS	62	3E	>	94	5E	^	126	7E	
31	1F	^_	US	63	3F	?	95	5F	_	127	7F	DEL

Notes:

Appendix K
KEYBOARD RETURN CODES

This appendix lists the codes returned from all combinations of keys on the entire IBM PC keyboard, as they are seen by TURBO Pascal. Actually, function keys and 'Alt-ed' keys generate 'extended scan codes', but these are turned into 'escape sequences' by TURBO.

To read the escape sequences, you let your read routine check for ESC, and if detected see if there is another character in the keyboard buffer. If there is, an escape code was received, so you read the next character and set a flag to signal that what you got is not a normal character, but the second part of an 'escape sequence'

```
if KeyPressed then
begin
  Read(Kbd,Ch)                      { ch is char      }
  if (ch = #27) and KeyPressed then { one more char? }
  begin
    Read(Kbd,Ch)
    FuncKey := True;                { FuncKey is boolean }
  end
end;
```

The following table lists the return codes as decimal ASCII values. Normal keys only return a single code; extended codes return an ESC (27) followed by one more character.

Key	Unshifted	Shift	Ctrl	Alt
F1	27 59	27 84	27 94	27 104
F2	27 60	27 85	27 95	27 105
F3	27 61	27 86	27 96	27 106
F4	27 62	27 87	27 97	27 107
F5	27 63	27 88	27 98	27 108
F6	27 64	27 89	27 99	27 109
F7	27 65	27 90	27 100	27 110
F8	27 66	27 91	27 101	27 111
F9	27 67	27 92	27 102	27 112
F10	27 68	27 93	27 103	27 113

KEYBOARD RETURN CODES

Key	Unshifted	Shift	Ctrl	Alt
LArr	27 75	52	27 115	27 178
RArr	27 77	54	27 116	27 180
UArr	27 72	56	27 160	27 175
DArr	27 80	50	27 164	27 183
Home	27 71	55		27 174
End	27 79	49	27 117	27 182
PgUp	27 73	57	27 132	27 176
PgDn	27 81	51	27 118	27 184
Ins	27 82	48	27 165	27 185
Del	27 83	46	27 166	27 186
Esc	27	27	27	
BackSp	8	8	127	
Tab	9	27 15		
RETURN	13	13	10	
A	97	65	1	27 30
B	98	66	2	27 48
C	99	67	3	27 46
D	100	68	4	27 32
E	101	69	5	27 18
F	102	70	6	27 33
G	103	71	7	27 34
H	104	72	8	27 35
I	105	73	7	27 23
J	106	74	10	27 36
K	107	75	11	27 37
L	108	76	12	27 38
M	109	77	13	27 50
N	110	78	14	27 49
O	111	79	15	27 24
P	112	80	16	27 25
Q	113	81	17	27 16
R	114	82	18	27 19
S	115	83	19	27 31
T	116	84	20	27 20
U	117	85	21	27 22
V	118	86	22	27 47
W	119	87	23	27 17
X	120	88	24	27 45
Y	121	89	25	27 21
Z	122	90	26	27 44

Key	Unshifted	Shift	Ctrl	Alt
[	91	123	27	
\	92	124	28	
]	93	125	29	
'	96	126		
0	48	41		27 129
1	49	33		27 120
2	50	64	27 3	27 121
3	51	35		27 122
4	52	36		27 123
5	53	37		27 124
6	54	94	30	27 125
7	55	38		27 126
8	56	42		27 127
9	57	40		27 128
*	42		27 114	
+	43	43		
–	45	95	31	27 130
=	61	43		27 131
,	44	60		
/	47	63		
;	59	58		

Table K-1: Keyboard Return Codes

Notes:

Appendix L
INSTALLATION

Terminal Installation

Before you use TURBO Pascal, it must be installed to your particular terminal, i.e. provided with information regarding control characters required for certain functions. This installation is easily performed using the program *TINST* which is described in this chapter.

After having made a work-copy, please store your distribution diskette safely away and work only on the copy.

Now start the installation by typing *TINST* at your terminal. Select Screen installation from the main menu. Depending on your version of TURBO Pascal, the installation proceeds as described in the following two sections.

IBM PC Display Selection

If you use TURBO Pascal without installation, the default screen set-up will be used. You may override this default by selecting another screen mode from this menu:

```
Choose one of the following displays:

0) Default display mode
1) Monochrome display
2) Color display 80x25
3) Color display 40x25
4) b/w   display 80x25
5) b/w   display 40x25

Which display (enter no. or ^X to exit) ■
```

Figure L-1: IBM PC Screen Installation Menu

Each time TURBO Pascal runs, the selected mode will be used, and you will return to the default mode on exit.

Non-IBM PC Installation

A menu listing a number of popular terminals will appear, inviting you to choose one by entering its number:

```
Choose one of the following terminals:

   1) ADDS 20/25/30          15) Lear-Siegler ADM-31
   2) ADDS 40/60             16) Liberty
   3) ADDS Viewpoint-1A      17) Morrow MDT-20
   4) ADM 3A                 18) Otrona Attache
   5) Ampex D80              19) Qume
   6) ANSI                   20) Soroc IQ-120
   7) Apple/graphics         21) Soroc new models
   8) Hazeltine 1500         22) Teletext 3000
   9) Hazeltine Esprit       23) Televideo 912/920/925
  10) IBM PC CCP/M b/w       24) Visual 200
  11) IBM PC CCP/M color     25) Wyse WY-100/200/300
  12) Kaypro 10              26) Zenith
  13) Kaypro II and 4        27) None of the above
  14) Lear-Siegler ADM-20    28) Delete a definition

Which terminal? (Enter no. or ^X to exit):
```

Figure L-2: Terminal Installation Menu

If your terminal is mentioned, just enter the corresponding number, and the installation is complete. Before installation is actually performed, you are asked the question:

```
Do you want to modify the definition before installation?
```

This allows you to modify one or more of the values being installed as described in the following. If you do not want to modify the terminal definition, just type **N**, and the installation completes by asking you the operating frequency of your CPU (see last item in this appendix).

If your terminal is **not** on the menu, however, you must define the required values yourself. The values can most probably be found in the manual supplied with your terminal.

Enter the number corresponding to **None of the above** and answer the questions one by one as they appear on the screen.

In the following, each command you may install is described in detail. Your terminal may not support all the commands that can be installed. If so, just pass the command not needed by typing RETURN in response to the prompt. If *Delete line*, *Insert line*, or *Erase to end of line* is not installed, these functions will be emulated in software, slowing screen performance somewhat.

Commands may be entered either simply by pressing the appropriate keys or by entering the decimal or hexadecimal ASCII value of the command. If a command requires the two characters 'ESCAPE' and ' = ', may:

either: press first the **Esc** key, then the = . The entry will be echoed with appropriate labels, i.e. <ESC> =.

or: enter the decimal or hexadecimal values separated by spaces. Hexadecimal values must be preceded by a dollar-sign. Enter e.g. 27 61 or $1B 61 or $1B $3D which are all equivalent.

The two methods cannot be mixed, i.e. once you have entered a non-numeric character, the rest of that command must be defined in that mode, and vise versa.

A hyphen entered as the very first character is used to delete a command, and echoes the text *Nothing*.

Terminal type:

Enter the name of the terminal you are about to install. When you complete *TINST* , the values will be stored, and the terminal name will appear on the initial list of terminals. If you later need to reinstall TURBO Pascal to this terminal, you can do that by choosing it from the list.

Send an initialization string to the terminal?
If you want to initialize your terminal when TURBO Pascal starts (e.g. to download commands to programmable function keys), you answer **Y** for yes to this question. If not, just hit RETURN.

Send a reset string to the terminal?
Define a string to be sent to the terminal when TURBO Pascal terminates. The description of the initialization command above applies here.

CURSOR LEAD-IN command:
Cursor Lead-in is a special sequence of characters which tells your terminal that the following characters are an address on the screen on which the cursor should be placed.

When you define this command, you are asked the following supplementary questions:

CURSOR POSITIONING COMMAND to send between line and column:
Some terminals need a command between the two numbers defining the row- and column cursor address.

CURSOR POSITIONING COMMAND to send after line and column:
Some terminals need a command after the two numbers defining the row- and column cursor address.

Column first?
Most terminals require the address on the format: first ROW, then COLUMN. If this is the case on your terminal, answer **N**. If your terminal wants COLUMN first, then ROW, then answer **Y**.

OFFSET to add to LINE
Enter the number to add to the LINE (ROW) address.

OFFSET to add to COLUMN
Enter the number to add to the COLUMN address.

Binary address?
Most terminals need the cursor address sent on binary form. If that is true for your terminal, enter **Y**. If your terminal expects the cursor address as ASCII digits, enter **N**. If so, you are asked the supplementary question:

2 or 3 ASCII digits?
> Enter the number of digits in the cursor address for your terminal.

CLEAR SCREEN command:
> Enter the command that will clear the entire contents of your screen, both foreground and background, if applicable.

Does CLEAR SCREEN also HOME cursor?
> This is normally the case; if it is not so on your terminal, enter **N**, and define the cursor HOME command.

DELETE LINE command:
> Enter the command that deletes the entire line at the cursor position.

INSERT LINE command:
> Enter the command that inserts a line at the cursor position.

ERASE TO END OF LINE command:
> Enter the command that erases the line at the cursor position from the cursor position through the right end of the line.

START OF 'LOW VIDEO' command:
> If your terminal supports different video intensities, then define the command that initiates the **dim** video here. If this command is defined, the following question is asked:

START OF 'NORMAL VIDEO' command:
> Define the command that sets the screen to show characters in 'normal' video.

Number of rows (lines) on your screen:
> Enter the number of horizontal lines on your screen.

Number of columns on your screen:
> Enter the number of vertical column positions on your screen.

Delay after CURSOR ADDRESS (0-255 ms):
Delay after CLEAR, DELETE, and INSERT (0-255 ms):
Delay after ERASE TO END OF LINE and HIGHLIGHT On/Off (0-255 ms):
> Enter the delay in milliseconds required after the functions specified. RETURN means 0 (no delay).

Is this definition correct?
If you have made any errors in the definitions, enter **N**. You will then return to the terminal selection menu. The installation data you have just entered will be included in the installation data file and appear on the terminal selection menu, but installation will **not** be performed. When you enter **Y** in response to this question, you are asked:

Operating frequency of your microprocessor in MHz (for delays):
As the delays specified earlier are depending on the operating frequency of your CPU, you must define this value.

The installation is finished, installation data is written to TURBO Pascal, and you return to the outer menu (see section 12). Installation data is also saved in the installation data file and the new terminal will appear on the terminal selection list when you run *TINST* in future.

Editing Command Installation

The built-in editor responds to a number of commands which are used to move the cursor around on the screen, delete and insert text, move text etc. Each of these functions may be activated by either of two commands: a primary command and a secondary command. The secondary commands are installed by Borland and comply with the 'standard' set by *WordStar*. The primary commands are un-defined for most systems, and using the installation program, they may easily be defined to fit your taste or your keyboard. IBM PC systems are supplied with the arrows and dedicated function keys installed as primary commands as described in chapter 19.

When you hit **C** for Command installation, the first command appears:

```
CURSOR MOVEMENTS:

1:  Character left    Nothing -> ■
```

This means that no primary command has been installed to move the cursor one character left. If you want to install a primary command (in **addition** to the secondary *WordStar*-like Ctrl-S, which is not shown here), you may enter the desired command following the -> prompt in either of two ways:

1) Simply press the key you want to use. It could be a function key (for example a left-arrow-key, if you have it) or any other key or sequence of keys that you choose (max. 4). The installation program responds with a mnemonic of each character it receives. If you have a left-arrow-key that transmits an < ESCAPE > character followed by a lower case **a**, and you press this key in the situation above, your screen will look like this:

```
CURSOR MOVEMENTS:

1:   Character left     Nothing -> <ESC> a ■
```

2) Instead of pressing the actual key you want to use, you may enter the ASCII value(s) of the character(s) in the command. The values of multiple characters are entered separated by spaces. Decimal values are just entered: 27; hexadecimal values are prefixed by a dollar-sign: $1B. This may be useful to install commands which are not presently available on your keyboard, for example if you want to install the values of a new terminal while still using the old one. This facility has just been provided for very few and rare instances, because there is really no idea in defining a command that cannot be generated by pressing a key. But it's there for those who wish to use it.

In both cases terminate your input by pressing < RETURN > .Notice that the two methods cannot be mixed within one command. If you have started defining a command sequence by pressing keys, you must define all characters in that command by pressing keys and vise versa.

You may enter a - (minus) to remove a command from the list, or a **B** to back through the list one item at a time.

The editor accepts a total of 45 commands, and they may all be installed to your specification. If you make an error in the installation, like defining the same command for two different purposes, an self-explanatory error message is issued, and you must correct the error before terminating the installation. A primary command, however, may conflict with one of the *WordStar*-like secondary commands; that will just render the secondary command inaccessible.

The following table lists the secondary commands, and allows you to mark any primary commands installed by yourself:

```
CURSOR MOVEMENTS:
 1:  Character left       Ctrl-S           _____
 2:     Alternative       Ctrl-H           _____
 3:  Character right      Ctrl-D           _____
 4:  Word left            Ctrl-A           _____
 5:  Word right           Ctrl-F           _____
 6:  Line up              Ctrl-E           _____
 7:  Line down            Ctrl-X           _____
 8:  Scroll up            Ctrl-W           _____
 9:  Scroll down          Ctrl-Z           _____
10:  Page up              Ctrl-R           _____
11:  Page down            Ctrl-C           _____
12:  To left on line      Ctrl-Q Ctrl-S    _____
13:  To right on line     Ctrl-Q Ctrl-D    _____
14:  To top of page       Ctrl-Q Ctrl-E    _____
15:  To bottom of page    Ctrl-Q Ctrl-X    _____
16:  To top of file       Ctrl-Q Ctrl-R    _____
17:  To end of file       Ctrl-Q Ctrl-C    _____
18:  To beginning of block   Ctrl-Q Ctrl-B _____
19:  To end of block         Ctrl-Q Ctrl-B _____
20:  To last cursor position Ctrl-Q Ctrl-P _____
```

INSERT & DELETE:

```
21:   Insert mode on/off          Ctrl-V         _____
22:   Insert line                 Ctrl-N         _____
23:   Delete line                 Ctrl-Y         _____
24:   Delete to end of line       Ctrl-Q Ctrl-Y  _____
25:   Delete right word           Ctrl-T         _____
26:   Delete character under cursor Ctrl-G       _____
27:   Delete left character       <DEL>          _____
28:     Alternative:              Nothing        _____
```

BLOCK COMMANDS:

```
29:   Mark block begin      Ctrl-K Ctrl-B     _____
30:   Mark block end        Ctrl-K Ctrl-K     _____
31:   Mark single word      Ctrl-K Ctrl-T     _____
32:   Hide/display block    Ctrk-K Ctrl-H     _____
33:   Copy block            Ctrl-K Ctrl-C     _____
34:   Move block            Ctrl-K Ctrl-V     _____
35:   Delete block          Ctrl-K Ctrl-Y     _____
36:   Read block from disk  Ctrl-K Ctrl-R     _____
37:   Write block to disk   Ctrl-K Ctrl-W     _____
```

MISC. EDITING COMMANDS:

```
38:   End edit                  Ctrl-K Ctrl-D   _____
39:   Tab                       Ctrl-I          _____
40:   Auto tab on/off           Ctrl-Q Ctrl-I   _____
41:   Restore line              Ctrl-Q Ctrl-L   _____
42:   Find                      Ctrl-Q Ctrl-F   _____
43:   Find & replace            Ctrl-Q Ctrl-A   _____
44:   Repeat last find          Ctrl-L          _____
45:   Control character prefix  Ctrl-P          _____
```

Table L-1: Secondary Editing Commands

Items 2 and 28 let you define alternative commands to *Character Left* and *Delete left Character* commands. Normally <BS> is the alternative to Ctrl-S, and there is no defined alternative to <DEL>. You may install primary commands to suit your keyboard, for example to use the <BS> as an alternative to <DEL> if the <BS> key is more conveniently located. Of course, the two alternative commands must be unambiguous like all other commands.

Notes:

Appendix M
CP/M PRIMER

How to use TURBO on a CP/M system

When you turn on your computer, it reads the first couple of tracks on your CP/M diskette and loads a copy of the CP/M operating system into memory. Each time you re-boot your computer, CP/M also creates a list of the disk space available for each disk drive. Whenever you try to save a file to the disk, CP/M checks to make sure that the diskettes have not been changed. If you have changed the diskette in Drive A without re-booting, for example, CP/M will generate the following error message when a disk-write is attempted:

```
BDOS ERROR ON A:   R/O
```

Control will return to the operating system and your work was NOT saved! This can make copying diskette a little confusing for the beginner. If you are new to CP/M, follow these instructions:

Copying Your TURBO Disk

To make a working copy of your TURBO MASTER DISK, do the following:

1. Make a blank diskette and put a copy of CP/M on it (see your CP/M manual for details). This will be is your TURBO **work disk**.

2. Place this disk in Drive A:. Place a CP/M diskette with a copy of PIP.COM in Drive B (PIP.COM is CP/M's file copy program that should be on your CP/M diskette. See your CP/M manual for details).

3. Re-boot the computer. Type B:PIP and then press < RETURN >

4. Remove the diskette from Drive B: and insert your TURBO MASTER DISK.

5. Now type: A:=B:*.*[V] and then press < RETURN >

You have instructed PIP it to copy all the files from the diskette in Drive B: onto the diskette in Drive A:. Consult your CP/M manual if any errors occur.

The last few lines on your screen should look like this:

```
A> B:PIP

*A:=B:*.*[V]

COPYING -
FIRSTFILE
:
:
LASTFILE
*
```

6.   Press < RETURN > , and the PIP program will end.

Using Your TURBO Disk

Store your TURBO MASTER DISK in a safe place. To use TURBO PASCAL, place your new TURBO **work disk** in drive A: and re-boot the system. Unless your TURBO came pre-installed for your computer and terminal, you should install TURBO (see 12). When done, type

TURBO

and TURBO Pascal will start.

If you have trouble copying your diskette, please consult your CP/M user manual or contact your hardware vendor for CP/M support.

Appendix N
HELP!!!

This appendix lists a number of the most commonly asked questions and their answers. If you don't find the answer to *your* question here, you can either call Borland's technical support staff, or you can access CompuServe's Consumer Information 24 hours a day and 'talk' to the Borland Special Interest Group. See insert in the front of this manual for details.

Q: How do I use the system?
A: Please read the manual, specifically chapter 1 . If you must get started immediately do the following:
   1) Boot up your operating system
   2) If you have a computer other than an IBM PC, run Tinst to install Turbo for your equipment.
   3) Run Turbo
   4) Start programming!

Q: I am having trouble installing my terminal!
A: If your terminal is not one that is on the installation menu you must create your own. All terminals come with a manual containing information on codes that control video I/O. You must answer the questions in the installation program according to the information in your hardware manual. The terminology we use is the closest we could find to a standard. Note: most terminals do not require an initialization string or reset string. These are usually used to access enhanced features of a particular terminal; for example on some terminals you can send an initialization string to make the keypad act as a cursor pad. You can put up to 13 characters into the initialization or reset strings.

Q: I am having disk problems. How do I copy my disks?
A: Most disk problems do not mean you have a defective disk. Specifically, if you are on a CP/M-80 system you may want to look up the brief CP/M primer on page 355 . If you can get a directory of your distribution disk, then chances are that it is a good disk.

To make a backup copy of Turbo you should use a file-by-file copy program like *COPY* for PC/MS-DOS or *PIP* for CP/M-80/86. The reason is that for those of you who have quad density disk drives, you may have trouble using a DISKCOPY type program. These programs are expecting the exact same format for the Source diskette as well as the Destination diskette.

Q: Do I need an 8087 chip to use Turbo-87?
A: Yes, if you want to compile programs for the 8087 chip, that chip must be in your machine. The standard TURBO compiler, however, is included on the Turbo-87 disk, so you can have it both ways!

Q: Do I need any special equipment to use TURBO-BCD?
A: No, but the BCD reals package works on 16 bit implementations of Turbo only.

Q: Do I need Turbo to run programs I developed in Turbo?
A: No, Turbo can make .COM or .CMD files.

Q: How do I make .COM or .CMD files?
A: Type O from the main menu for Compiler Options and then select "C" for .COM or .CMD file.

Q: What are the limits on the compiler as far as code and data?
A: The compiler can handle up to 64K of code, 64K of data, 64K of stack and unlimited heap. The object code, however, cannot exceed 64K.

Q: What are the limits of the editor as far as space?
A: The editor can edit as much as 64K at a time. If this is not enough, you can split your source into more than one file using the *$I* compiler directive. This is explained in chapter 17.

Q: What do I do when I get error 99 (Compiler overflow)?
A: You can do two things: break your code into smaller segments and use the *$I* compiler directive (explained in chapter 17) or compile to a .COM or .CMD file.

Q: What do I do if my object code is going to be larger than 64K?
A: Either use the chain facility or use overlays.

Q: How do I read from the keyboard without having to hit return (duplicate BASIC's INKEY$ function)?
A: Like this: `read(Kbd,Ch)` where *Ch:Char*.

Q: How do I get output to go to the printer?
A: Try: `Writeln(Lst, ...)`.

Q: How can I get a listing of my source code to my printer?
A: You can use the following program. If you wish to have a listing that underlines or highlights reserved words, puts in page breaks, and lists all Include files, there is one included free (including source) on the Turbo Tutor diskette.

```
program TextFileDemo;

var
  TextFile : Text;
  Scratch  : String[128];

begin
  Write('File to print: ');              { Get file name      }
  Readln(Scratch);
  Assign(TextFile, Scratch);             { Open the file      }
  {$I-}
  Reset(TextFile);
  {$I+}
  if IOresult <> 0 then
    Writeln('Cannot find ', Scratch)     { File not found     }
  else                                   { Print the file.. }
  begin
    while not Eof(TextFile) do
    begin
      Readln(TextFile, Scratch);         { Read a line        }
      Writeln(Lst, Scratch)              { Print a line       }
    end; { while }
    Writeln(Lst)                         { Flush printer buffer }
  end { else }
end.
```

Q: How do I get output to and input from COM1:?
A: Try: writeln(AUX, ...) after setting up the port using MODE from MSDOS or an equivalent ASSIGN type program from CP/M. To read try read(AUX, ...). You must remember that there is no buffer set up automatically when reading from AUX.

Q: How do I read a function key?

A: Function keys generate 'extended scan codes' which are turned into 'escape sequences' by TURBO, that is, **two** characters are sent from the keyboard: first an Esc (decimal ASCII value 27), then some other character. You'll find a table of all values on page 341.

To read these extended codes, you check for ESC and if detected see if there is another character in the keyboard buffer. If there is, a function key was pressed, so you read the next character and set a flag to signal that what you got is not a normal character, but the second part of an 'escape sequence'

```
if KeyPressed then
begin
  Read(Kbd,Ch)                          {ch is char}
  if (ch = #27) and KeyPressed then {one more char?}
  begin
    Read(Kbd,Ch)
    FuncKey := True;              {FuncKey is boolean}
  end
end;
```

Q: I am having trouble with file handling. What is the correct order of instructions to open a file?

A: The correct manner to handle files is as follows:

To create a new file:

```
Assign(FileVar,'NameOf.Fil');
Rewrite(FileVar);
:
:
Close(FileVar);
```

To open an existing file:

```
Assign(fileVar,'NameOf.Fil');
Reset(FileVar);
:
:
Close(FileVar);
```

Q: Why do my recursive procedures not work?
A: Set the A compiler directive off:{$A-}(CP/M-80 only)

Q: How can I use EOF and EOLN without a file variable as a parameter?
A: Turn off buffered input:{$B-}

Q: How do I find out if a file exists on the disk?
A: Use {$I-} and {I+}. The following function returns *True* if the file name passed as a parameter exists, otherwise it returns *False*:

```
type
 Name=string[66];
 :
 :
function Exist(FileName: Name): Boolean;
Var
  Fil: file;
begin
  Assign(Fil, FileName);
  {$I-}
  Reset(Fil);
  {$I+}
  Exist := (IOresult = 0)
end;
```

Q: How do I disable CTRL-C?
A: Set compiler directive: {$C-}.

Q: I get a Type Mismatch error when passing a string to a function or procedure as a parameter.
A: Turn off type checking of variable parameters: {$V-}.

Q: I get file not found error on my include file when I compile my program - even though the file is in the directory.
A: When using the include compiler directive *{$I filename.ext}* there must be a space separating the filename from the terminating brace, if the extension is not three letters long: {$ISample.F }. Otherwise the brace will be interpreted as part of the file name.

Q: Why does my program behave differently when I run it several times in a row?
A: If you are running programs in Memory mode and use typed constants as initialized variables, these constants will only be initialized right after a compilation, not each time you Run the program as they reside in the code segment. With .COM files, this problem does not exist, but if you still experience different results when using arrays and sets, turn on range checking {$R + }.

Q: I don't get the results I think I should when using *Reals* and *Integers* in the same expression.

A: When assigning an Integer expression to a Real variable, the expression is converted to Real. However, the expression itself is calculated as an integer, and you should therefore be aware of possible integer overflow in the expression. This can lead to surprising results. Take for instance:

```
RealVar := 40 * 1000;
```

First, the compiler multiplies integers 40 and 1000, resulting in 40,000 which gives integer overflow. It will actually come out to -25536 as Integers wrap around. Now it will be assigned to the RealVar as -25536. To prevent this, use either:

```
RealVar := 40.0 * 1000;
```
or
```
RealVar := 1.0 * IntVar1 * IntVar2;
```

to ensure that the expression is calculated as a Real.

Q: How do I get a disk directory from my TURBO program?

A: Sample procedures for accessing the directory are included in the TURBO Tutor package (see how to order the TURBO Tutor on page 3).

Q: My program works well with TURBO 2.0, but now it keeps getting I/O Error F3 (or TURBO Access error 243)

A: TURBO 3.0 uses DOS file handles. When booting your computer, you should have a CONFIG.SYS file in the root directory of your boot drive. Place the statement:

```
FILES=16
```

in this file and re-boot your system. For more information about file handles, please refer to your DOS reference manual.

NOTE: If you distribute your programs, you should include similar instructions in the documentation that you provide.

Appendix O.
SUBJECT INDEX

Borland
Software

 **BORLAND**
INTERNATIONAL   4585 Scotts Valley Drive Scotts Valley, CA 95066

Available at better dealers nationwide.
To order by Credit Card call (800) 255-8008, CA (800) 742-1133

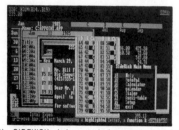
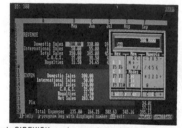

SideKick, the Macintosh Office Manager, brings information management, desktop organization and telecommunications to your Macintosh. Instantly, while running any other program.

A full-screen editor/mini-word processor lets you jot down notes and create or edit files. Your files can also be used by your favorite word processing program like MacWrite™ or MicroSoft® Word .

A complete telecommunication program sends or receives information from any on-line network or electronic bulletin board while using any of your favorite application programs. A modem is required to use this feature.

A full-featured financial and scientific calculator sends a paper-tape output to your screen or printer and comes complete with function keys for financial modeling purposes.

A print spooler prints *any* text file while you run other programs.

A versatile calendar lets you view your appointments for a day, a week or an entire month. You can easily print out your schedule for quick reference.

A convenient "Things-to-Do" file reminds you of important tasks.

A convenient alarm system alerts you to daily engagements.

A phone log keeps a complete record of all your telephone activities. It even computes the cost of every call. Area code hook-up provides instant access to the state, region and time zone for all area codes.

An expense account file records your business and travel expenses.

A credit card file keeps track of your credit card balances and credit limits.

A report generator prints-out your mailing list labels, phone directory and weekly calendar in convenient sizes.

A convenient analog clock with a sweeping second-hand can be displayed anywhere on your screen.

On-line help is available for all of the powerful SIDEKICK features.

Best of all, everything runs concurrently.

SIDEKICK, the software Macintosh owners have been waiting for.

SideKick, Macintosh's Office Manager is available now for $84.95 (not copy-protected).

Minimum System Configuration: SIDEKICK is available now for your Macintosh microcomputer in a format that is not copy-protected. Your computer must have at least 128K RAM and one disk drive. Two disk drives are recommended if you wish to use other application programs. A Hayes-compatible modem is required for the telecommunications function. To use SIDEKICK'S autodialing capability you need the Borland phone-link interface.

BORLAND
INTERNATIONAL

INCREASE YOUR PRODUCTIVITY
BY 50% OR YOUR MONEY BACK

SuperKey turns 1,000 keystrokes into 1!

Yes, SuperKey can *record* lengthy keystroke sequences and play them back at the touch of a single key. Instantly. Like Magic.

Say, for example, you want to add a column of figures in 1-2-3. Without SuperKey you'd have to type seven keystrokes just to get started. ["shift-@-s-u-m-shift-("]. With SuperKey you can turn those 7 keystrokes into 1.

SuperKey keeps your 'confidential' files...CONFIDENTIAL!

Time after time you've experienced it: anyone can walk up to your PC, and read your confidential files (tax returns, business plans, customer lists, personal letters...).

With SuperKey you can encrypt any file, even while running another program. As long as you keep the password secret, only YOU can decode your file. SuperKey implements the U.S. government Data Encryption Standard (DES).

SuperKey helps protect your capital investment.

SuperKey, at your convenience, will make your screen go blank after a predetermined time of screen/keyboard inactivity. You've paid hard-earned money for your PC. SuperKey will protect your monitor's precious phosphor...and your investment.

SuperKey protects your work from intruders while you take a break.

Now you can lock your keyboard at any time. Prevent anyone from changing hours of work. Type in your secret password and everything comes back to life...just as you left it.

SUPERKEY is now available for an unbelievable $69.95 (not copy-protected).

Minimum System Configuration: SUPERKEY is compatible with your IBM PC, XT, AT, PCjr. and 100% compatible microcomputers. Your computer must have at least 128K RAM, one disk drive and PC-DOS 2.0 or greater.

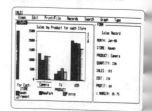
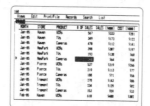

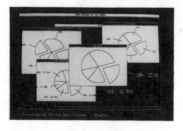 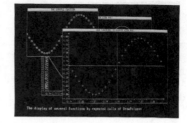

TURBO PASCAL
EDITOR TOOLBOX™

It's All You Need To Build Your Own Text Editor Or Word Processor.

Build your own lightning-fast editor and incorporate it into your Turbo Pascal programs. Turbo Editor Toolbox™ gives you easy-to-install modules. Now you can integrate a fast and powerful editor into your own programs. You get the source code, the manual and the know how.

Create your own word processor. We provide all the editing routines. You plug in the features you want. You could build a WordStar®-like editor with pull-down menus like Microsoft's® Word, and make it work as fast as WordPerfect™.

To demonstrate the tremendous power of Turbo Editor Toolbox, we give you the source code for two sample editors:

Simple Editor A complete editor ready to include in your programs. With windows, block commands, and memory-mapped screen routines.

MicroStar™ A full-blown text editor with a complete pull-down menu user interface, plus a lot more. Modify MicroStar's pull-down menu system and include it in your Turbo Pascal programs.

The Turbo Editor Toolbox gives you all the standard features you would expect to find in any word processor:

- Word wrap
- UNDO last change
- Auto indent
- Find and Find/Replace with options
- Set left and right margin
- Block mark, move and copy.
- Tab, insert and overstrike modes, centering, etc.

MicroStar's pull-down menus.

And Turbo Editor Toolbox has features that word processors selling for several hundred dollars can't begin to match. Just to name a few:

☑ **RAM-based editor.** You can edit very large files and yet editing is lightning fast.

☑ **Memory-mapped screen routines.** Instant paging, scrolling and text display.

☑ **Keyboard installation.** Change control keys from WordStar-like commands to any that you prefer.

☑ **Multiple windows.** See and edit up to eight documents—or up to eight parts of the same document—all at the same time.

☑ **Multi-Tasking.** Automatically save your text. Plug in a digital clock . . . an appointment alarm—see how it's done with MicroStar's "background" printing.

Best of all, **source code is included for everything in the Editor Toolbox.** Use any of the Turbo Editor Toolbox's features in your programs. And pay no royalties.

Minimum system configuration: The Turbo Editor Toolbox requires an IBM PC, XT, AT, 3270, PCjr or true compatible with a minimum 192K RAM, running PC-DOS (MS-DOS) 2.0 or greater. You must be using Turbo Pascal 3.0 for IBM and compatibles.

BORLAND
INTERNATIONAL

Suggested Retail Price $69.95 (not copy-protected)

Turbo Pascal is a registered trademark and Turbo Editor Toolbox and MicroStar are trademarks of Borland International, Inc. WordStar is a registered trademark of MicroPro International Corp. Microsoft and MS-DOS are registered trademarks of Microsoft Corp. WordPerfect is a trademark of Satellite Software International. IBM, IBM PC, XT, AT, PCjr. and PC-DOS are registered trademarks of International Business Machine Corp.

TURBO PASCAL GAMEWORKS

Secrets And Strategies Of The Masters Are Revealed For The First Time

Explore the world of state-of-the-art computer games with Turbo GameWorks™. Using easy-to-understand examples, Turbo GameWorks teaches you techniques to quickly create your own computer games using Turbo Pascal®. Or, for instant excitement, play the three great computer games we've included on disk—compiled and ready-to-run.

TURBO CHESS

Test your chess-playing skills against your computer challenger. With Turbo GameWorks, you're on your way to becoming a master chess player. Explore the complete Turbo Pascal source code and discover the secrets of Turbo Chess.

"What impressed me the most was the fact that with this program you can become a computer chess analyst. You can add new variations to the program at any time and make the program play stronger and stronger chess. There's no limit to the fun and enjoyment of playing Turbo GameWorks' Chess, and most important of all, with this chess program there's no limit to how it can help you improve your game."

—*George Koltanowski, Dean of American Chess, former President of the United Chess Federation and syndicated chess columnist.*

TURBO BRIDGE

Now play the world's most popular card game—Bridge. Play one-on-one with your computer or against up to three other opponents. With Turbo Pascal source code, you can even program your own bidding or scoring conventions.

"There has never been a bridge program written which plays at the expert level, and the ambitious user will enjoy tackling that challenge, with the format already structured in the program. And for the inexperienced player, the bridge program provides an easy-to-follow format that allows the user to start right out playing. The user can "play bridge" against real competition without having to gather three other people."

—*Kit Woolsey, writer and author of several articles and books and twice champion of the Blue Ribbon Pairs.*

TURBO GO-MOKU

Prepare for battle when you challenge your computer to a game of Go-Moku—the exciting strategy game also know as "Pente"™. In this battle of wits, you and the computer take turns placing X's and O's on a grid of 19X19 squares until five pieces are lined up in a row. Vary the game if you like using the source code available on your disk.

Minimum system configuration: IBM PC, XT, AT, Portable, 3270, PCjr, and true compatibles with 192K system memory, running PC-DOS (MS-DOS) 2.0 or later. To edit and compile the Turbo Pascal source code, you must be using Turbo Pascal 3.0 for IBM PC and compatibles.

Suggested Retail Price: $69.95 (not copy-protected)

BORLAND
INTERNATIONAL

Turbo Pascal is a registered trademark and Turbo GameWorks is a trademark of Borland International, Inc. Pente is a registered trademark of Parker Brothers. IBM PC, XT, AT, PCjr and PC-DOS are registered trademarks of International Business Machines Corporation. MS-DOS is a trademark of Microsoft Corporation.

How To Buy Borland Software

BORLAND

I N T E R N A T I O N A L

NOT COPY-PROTECTE

To Order By Credit Card, Call (800) 255-8008

60 DAY MONEY-BACK GUARANTEE

In California call (800) 742-113

Notes:

Notes:

Notes:

Notes:

Notes:

Notes: